Smart Edge Computing

The editors would like to dedicate this book to their parents, life partners, children, students, scholars, friends and colleagues

International Perspectives in Decision Analytics and Operations Research Set

coordinated by
Prasenjit Chatterjee

Volume 2

Smart Edge Computing

An Operation Research Perspective

Edited by

Rajdeep Chakraborty
Anupam Ghosh
Jyotsna Kumar Mandal
Tanupriya Choudhury
Prasenjit Chatterjee

WILEY

First published 2024 in Great Britain and the United States by ISTE Ltd and John Wiley & Sons, Inc.

ISTE Ltd
27-37 St George's Road
London SW19 4EU
UK

www.iste.co.uk

John Wiley & Sons, Inc.
111 River Street
Hoboken, NJ 07030
USA

www.wiley.com

Any opinions, findings, and conclusions or recommendations expressed in this material are those of the author(s), contributor(s) or editor(s) and do not necessarily reflect the views of ISTE Group.

Library of Congress Control Number: 2023944978

British Library Cataloguing-in-Publication Data
A CIP record for this book is available from the British Library
ISBN 978-1-78630-863-4

Contents

Chapter 6. A Smart Payment Transaction Procedure by Smart Edge Computing   113

Animesh UPADHYAYA, Koushik MUKHOPADHYAY, Amejul ISLAM,
Shaon Kalyan MODAK and Debdutta PAL

Chapter 10. A Study of Ultra-lightweight Ciphers and Security Protocol for Edge Computing.
Debasmita PAUL, Aheli ACHARYA and Debajyoti GUHA

Chapter 11. A Study on Security Protocols, Threats and Probable Solutions for Internet of Things Using Blockchain.
Debajyoti GUHA

Preface

Smart edge computing, from an operations research perspective, is a cutting-edge paradigm that integrates computational intelligence, data analytics and network technologies to optimize and enhance the efficiency of edge devices and networks. In this context, operations research plays a crucial role in addressing complex challenges related to resource allocation, task scheduling and decision-making at the edge of the network. By leveraging mathematical models, algorithms and optimization techniques, operations research enables the efficient distribution of computational tasks and data processing among edge devices, minimizing latency, conserving energy and ensuring seamless real-time data processing. Moreover, this approach empowers the deployment of artificial intelligence and machine learning algorithms at the edge, enabling intelligent devices to make autonomous decisions and adapt to dynamic environments. Smart edge computing, underpinned by operations research principles, is poised to revolutionize industries by unlocking the full potential of the Internet of Things (IoT), enhancing mobile computing and fostering the development of smart cities and autonomous systems with unprecedented efficiency and agility. This book is organized into 11 chapters, which are summarized as follows.

Chapter 1 discusses the domain of operational research and its various techniques used for complex problem-solving and decision-making. It also explores mathematical models and cutting-edge approaches for quantitative research, yielding both theoretically sound and practically applicable insights. The main objective of this chapter is to introduce the use of operations research methods in scientific decision-making, design, analysis and management, providing a practical guide to their applications in the context of edge computing.

Chapter 2 provides an overview of edge computing, its functions and applications in various fields, including automated vehicle management, logistics and smart cities.

Chapter 3 discusses how edge computing promotes education and information science, providing a conceptual overview and communication between different layers in digital education using diagrams. It enhances system reliability and scalability. Edge computing is a technology that leverages the massive data generated by IoT devices through distributed computing. It reduces data traffic by sending only relevant data across the network. In healthcare, edge computing combined with the IoT has led to significant digital advancements, enabling remote patient monitoring and various medical applications.

Chapter 4 provides a systematic review of edge computing's reputation in healthcare and its potential to address challenges and open up new opportunities for researchers. Edge computing, along with deep learning, is considered the future of digital products and can have a significant impact on society by solving tasks efficiently.

Chapter 5 applies queueing models to edge computing and analyzes the performance of edge-cloud computing. Performance analysis shows that increasing the number of edge servers reduces waiting time and resource utilization.

Chapter 6 discusses the promising field of smart edge computing and its potential dependency on IoT devices for computationally intensive tasks. It highlights the importance of blockchain-based technologies, especially for tracking and managing transactions. Ethereum's value proposition for decentralized applications is explored, with a focus on smart contracts and their various applications.

Chapter 7 explores the application of operational research and statistical learning in the analysis of cancer progression. It introduces an invariant shape descriptor methodology using geodesic and z-transformations of carcinoma images.

Chapter 8 discusses the burden of chronic diseases, focusing on Alzheimer's disease (AD) as a challenging neurodegenerative disease. The use of AI (Artificial Intelligence) and NLP (Natural Language Processing) is explored to analyze public perceptions of AD through social media. Concerns about unreliable medical records and data security are highlighted, and the potential of blockchain-based methods for data control is suggested.

Chapter 9 discusses the significance of the IoT in various industries and its role in automation for the Industrial IoT. It focuses on assessing the clinical correlation between histological changes in the pre-cancerous tissues of subjects with oral submucous fibrosis and the normal control group using histochemical analysis.

Chapter 10 discusses the importance of security protocols for Internet information transmission, and explores the concepts of lightweight and ultra-lightweight protocols.

Chapter 11 discusses the importance of security in the IoT environment and the need to address security issues at different levels. It highlights the use of lightweight cryptography algorithms to secure IoT devices in various applications.

Dr. Rajdeep CHAKRABORTY
October 2023

Acknowledgments

The editors wish to express their warm thanks and deep appreciation to those who provided input, support, constructive suggestions and comments, and assisted in the editing and proofreading of this book.

This book would not have been possible without the valuable scholarly contributions of authors across the globe.

The editors would like to thank their family members and friends for their endless support and motivation.

They are very grateful to all the members who contributed to the editorial and review process of this book.

Mere words cannot express the editors' deep gratitude to the entire ISTE publishing team for keeping faith and showing the right path to accomplish this very timely book.

Finally, the editors take this opportunity to thank all the readers and expect that this book will continue to inspire and guide them in their future endeavors.

The editors

Introduction to Operations Research Methodologies

The domain of operational research involves various techniques applied for complex problem-solving and arriving at decisions. Operations research methodologies are applied by organizations to solve real-life problems, as they assist in managing all operations efficiently. Hence, operations research has emerged as a scientific method for problem-solving by engaging quantitative information for enhanced decision-making methodologies of operations research including probability, statistics, simulation and optimization. This study provides an introduction to the use of methods from operations research in scientific decision-making, design, analysis and management. It also includes a guide to using these approaches. The objective of this project was to produce a text that is both comprehensible and practical. An in-depth investigation into the mathematical models and the tried-and-true and cutting-edge approaches to problem-solving that lie at the foundation of today's software tools for quantitative research and deliberation has yielded insights that are both theoretically sound and practically applicable. While probability and statistics enable us to arrive at predictable solutions applicable in risk scenarios by applying mathematical algorithms, simulation allows the construction of models for solution testing before applying them. Optimization allows us to achieve optimum results within a given condition. Arriving at suitable solutions using operations research follows several steps by way of problem identification, construction of the mathematical model, deriving solutions from the model constructed, testing of the model, establishing control over solutions and finally arriving at the solution to implement them. The scope of this chapter will explore all such methodologies in detail and evaluate concepts that can be reliably applied in cases of smart edge computing.

1.1. Introduction

The use of quantitative techniques for the purpose of assisting analysts and decision-makers in the process of creating, assessing and improving the performance

Chapter written by Trishit BANERJEE and Arup DASGUPTA.

or operation of various types of systems is what is known as "*operations research*". It does not matter whether the systems studied are monetary, scientific or industrial in nature; all of them can be examined within the rigorous framework of the scientific method (Gupta et al. 2021). When used logically, the analytical techniques from many different disciplines that make up operations research can aid decision-makers in problem-solving and maintaining optimal control over the workings of systems and organizations. If a system is poorly defined or understood, operations researchers can use their methods to better understand its behavior and, perhaps more importantly, identify which parts are within their control. Quantitative decision problems, especially those involving the management of scarce resources, are the primary focus of operations research, an applied discipline that focuses on optimization. Industrial companies, banks, hospitals, transit systems, power plants and governments all face such challenges in their daily operations. Operations research analysts create and use mathematical and statistical models to help analyze and solve complex decision-making problems. They are problem formulators and solvers, just like engineers. Mathematical modeling, analysis and prediction of outcomes under many scenarios are central to their work. Techniques for mathematical optimization, probability and statistical approaches, experimentation and computational modeling can be used in the investigation.

Furthermore, systems whose behavior is already well known can be optimized with the use of operations research techniques. After all, the purpose of using mathematical, computational, and analytical tools and devices is to simply provide information and insight; ultimately, it is the human decision-makers who will use and implement what has been learned through the analysis process in order to achieve the best possible performance of the system (Conboy et al. 2020). The management of businesses can benefit from the use of the analytical approach known as operations research (OR), which is used to solve problems and make decisions. In the field of operations research, issues are first deconstructed into components before being addressed using mathematical analysis in predetermined processes. The procedure of operations research can often be summarized as follows:

– determine the nature of the issue that requires resolution;

– develop a model for the issue at hand that is reflective of the external factors and the world as a whole (Thies et al. 2019);

– apply the model to provide potential solutions for the issue;

– conduct tests of each solution on the model and evaluate how well it works (Kraus et al. 2020);

– put the solution to use so that it can address the real problem.

During World War II, many military strategists came up with the idea that would later become known as operations research. After the war, the methodologies that were developed via their operations research were used to find solutions to issues that arose in the realms of industry, the government and society (Hubbs et al. 2020). In the years leading up to World War II, operations research developed into a distinct academic field. During the 1930s, the primary focus of the expansion of the British military was on the creation of new weapons, gadgets and other forms of support equipment. However, the build-up was of unprecedented magnitude, and it became clear that there was also an urgent need to develop systems that would ensure the most advantageous deployment and management of materials and manpower.

Gonçalves et al. (2020; Hsu et al. 2020) state that the goal of operations research is to optimize system performance such that it functions at its highest level possible given the constraints of the problem. Comparison and elimination of potentially useful solutions are also part of the optimization process. Compared to traditional software and data analytics tools, a better way to make decisions is provided by the field of operations research. Businesses can benefit from enlisting the help of operations research experts when it comes to collecting more comprehensive datasets, weighing all their options, making more accurate predictions and estimating their level of risk.

This chapter is organized into four areas, beginning with an introduction to the areas of operations research in the modern field of computing. Second, the application of operations research in the IIoT (Industrial Internet of Things), smart edge computing and sensor data is discussed. Subsequently, paradigms and procedures are represented. Finally, the chapter concludes with a summary of the applications of operations research.

1.2. Decision-making framework/models for operations research

Operations research is a science that focuses on problem-solving as well as decision-making, and it is widely regarded as a valuable tool for assisting in the resolution of management issues. Making decisions that have a significant impact on many people may be quite challenging. A decision-maker must carefully consider their options after considering several factors that interact with one another (Pokrovsky 2009). Making a choice is sometimes referred to as a cognitive process. This word is used in cognitive psychology to describe the action of thinking and relates to the processing of information. Each decision that is made ultimately leads to a real consequence, which can take the form of a choice or an action.

Decision-making begins with the definition of a problem and concludes with the evaluation of the efficiency of the proposed solutions, whether they are concrete or alternative (Huang et al. 2022).

According to scholars, operations research is closely related to both computer science and analytics due to the computational and statistical aspects that are prevalent in most of both subjects (Božanić et al. 2020). Researchers in operational research who are presented with a new challenge have the responsibility of determining which of these methods is the most applicable, given the characteristics of the system, the objectives for its development and the limitations of both time and processing capacity. The issue of decision-making is of significant practical importance in a wide variety of domains involving human actions. Probabilistic techniques form the basis for most of the decision-making methods that are currently in use, since it is common to have some uncertainty in the parameters of a real-life system. It is possible that our lack of assurance may be communicated via one of these other forms (Pereira et al. 2020).

Erdogan et al. (2019) claimed that OR is the only option for decision-making (DM), it delivers the facts to managers and allows managers to make correct choices; the problems found were broken down into their fundamental components in order to solve the difficulties. It is also known as a programming approach or applied decision-making, and decision-makers use it as a model-building tool. Researchers put it in a nutshell that OR models eventually became the primary driving factor for the operation of computer tools. According to Liao et al. (2022), the processes of knowledge management include three primary activities: generation, transfer and storage of information. They went into technical detail on how operational research is an applied decision-making theory that involves the use of any mathematical, scientific or logical techniques to deal with the challenges faced by the executive who strives for complete rationalism in resolving their choice issues. Following the potential identification and picking options, DM comes to a conclusion about the specific solutions to a problem according to the scenario of demand. This can be done officially or informally. Informal decision-making is not routine; it is somewhat difficult, and it does not involve repetition (Whitley et al. 2016). It is possible that being creative will get you farther in these kinds of selections. Such judgments may not always have criteria, processes and techniques attached to them since the issue at hand may not have precedence. In contrast, formal DM is characterized by its inherent predictability and monotony. In this context, there are often criteria, processes and approaches available to assist decision-makers.

In order to enhance decision-making and provide solutions to a wide variety of challenges faced by businesses and other types of organizations, operations research uses advanced methods of statistical analysis and mathematical modeling. Due to the increasing complexity of the business environment, companies and government agencies are increasingly relying on analysis to guide choices that earlier depended primarily on managerial intuition (Ding et al. 2021). The contemporary difficulties associated with a global economy and the expansion of technology have both contributed to an increase in the complexity of the business environment. Modern day companies often aim to service a global client base as opposed to a regional or national consumer base and must contend with competitors from across the globe. Operations research can review all the available alternatives that a company is confronted with, project the various outcomes, and analyze the risks that relate to certain selections because it relies on complex mathematical models and cutting-edge software tools (Yoo and Kim 2018). According to the Institute for Operations Research and the Management Sciences, INFORMS for short, a national organization of professionals working in operations research, the result is information that is more comprehensive on which management can base decisions and policies.

The issue of decision-making (DM) is of significant practical importance in a wide variety of domains involving human actions. As noted earlier, models that depict the operation of numerous actual systems or objects make up most DM problems, and they benefit from probabilistic approaches to form the basis of their solutions (Zhao et al. 2019). Therefore, operations research is the mathematically inventive discipline of employing sophisticated analytical approaches to assist commercial organizations in improving the quality of the judgments that they make. Mathematical programming has been successfully used to solve a wide variety of challenges faced by commercial organizations, including the formation of equity portfolios, employee-oriented, customer-oriented, product-oriented and production-oriented challenges (Liu et al. 2022). Today, customers expect high-quality goods and services to be available to them whenever and wherever they need them because of the proliferation of global marketplaces and immediate communication. It is essential for businesses, whether public or private, to provide these goods and services as productively and economically as possible, using all available mathematical tools.

The *Bayesian decision theory* is based on statistical inference, which is the process of using facts or observations to revise or infer again the likelihood that a hypothesis may be correct. Bayesian inference makes use of components of the scientific process, one of which is the gathering of data that is intended to be either consistent or inconsistent with a certain hypothesis (Zhang et al. 2021). It is reasonable to expect that our level of confidence in a theory will shift when new information comes to light. To the extent that evidence supports either a high or low value, such values should be implemented. Since this is the case, proponents of Bayesian inference claim that it may be used to evaluate contradictory theories. According to this school of thought, the hypotheses with the most support should be taken as true, while those with the least evidence should be dismissed as untrue. However, Billings et al. (2022) argued that this approach of drawing conclusions may be susceptible to bias because the user is required to have pre-existing opinions before the collection of any information. With Bayesian inference, we first get a numerical estimate of how confident we are in a hypothesis before any evidence is seen, and then we get another numerical estimate of how confident we are in the hypothesis after we have seen some evidence. During induction in Bayesian inference, degrees of belief, also known as subjective probabilities, are often used. Bayesian inference is not guaranteed to provide a purely deductive method (McNamara and Chen 2021).

The purpose of operations research is to offer a framework for developing models of decision-making issues, discovering the best solutions for a particular measure of quality and applying the solutions to address the problems that are being modeled. Here, we will go through the several stages of the OR process that, starting with a problem, ultimately result in a solution. The issue at hand is a predicament that has arisen inside the company and calls for a solution of some kind (Yazdani et al. 2020). The person or group tasked with deciding how to proceed with implementing the solution is referred to as the decision-maker. The analyst is the person or group that is called upon to provide assistance to the decision-maker throughout the problem-solving process. Companies gather vast volumes of data, but they may not have the time or the knowledge to completely analyze this data, turning them into information that can be used to make choices (Zhao et al. 2021). These companies may feel overwhelmed by the volume of data that they collect. According to the Science of Better website published by INFORMS, operations research uses complex mathematical and statistical tools such as linear programming and regression analysis, to help businesses make the most of the data they have at their disposal. According to Bahramara et al. (2020), operations research analysts can assist in the discovery of alternative paths that result in increased revenues, improved operational efficiency and reduced risk by conducting in-depth analyses of the data.

Cardil et al. (2021) state that the world's population is growing at an alarming rate, and as a direct consequence of this, there is a severe lack of food in many parts of the world. In addition, every nation on the planet is struggling with the issue of how to make the most efficient use of the land available to them in order to cultivate their crops. In addition, the subject of water resource distribution and allocation is also a concern in emerging nations. Developing countries face this issue. Therefore, the operational research approaches provide the facts that are needed to decide the policy, and by analyzing the impacts of the policy, appropriate action may be taken in the right direction (Pei and Pardalos 2022). For the sake of the country's overall economic development, it is very necessary for each government to carry out detailed planning. For a nation to be ready to tackle the current economic crisis, a profit plan may be established by an institution via the use of the operational research technique. By making better use of the resources that are available, it is also possible to raise the income per person. The OR approaches will determine how the replacement and alternative policies are handled.

When it comes to determining where to sell a product and how to move it at the lowest feasible cost, OR techniques can give invaluable guidance to marketing professionals. A product's future demand can be factored into the pricing and stock level decisions. The correct choice of advertising medium can be made in accordance with the cost constraints by making use of the right OR strategy (Zhu et al. 2020). OR methods can be used by personnel management in order to appoint an individual who is highly appropriate and competent at an inexpensive level of remuneration. Additionally, OR techniques can be used to determine the retirement age of staff members. Hence, OR techniques are used to recruit personnel in accordance with the requirements of the company, whether the job is done on a contract or permanent basis, whether it is full time or seasonal (Wang et al. 2018). The OR approach assists the production manager in calculating the size and the appropriate number of things to manufacture. It is useful in arranging the schedule for the machine and ordering the steps. The OR technique provides assistance in selecting an acceptable site for the plant, plant design and other aspects of the facility.

Operations research is an essential factor that must be considered in almost every aspect of the decision-making process. The scope of finance and investment policies includes the analysis of the credit and loan policy, fund flow and cash flow, and the assessment of the dividend, share and bonus policy (Siebert et al. 2020). It also reflects the firm's investment portfolio. The emphasis is on picking the right product at the right time, which means figuring out what it is that needs to be created and when. It places an emphasis on the many channels of public relations, including the possibility of using print and electronic media. In the past, it was also found capable of determining the total number of salespeople that must be assigned to a certain region (Louis and Dunston 2018). In addition, OR can also be used to pick the product mix, which consists of the product, the price, the venue and the promotions. The methodologies of operational research are being used to acquire, restructure and replace the policies to provide the greatest benefits.

1.3. Operations research in IoT, IIoT, edge and smart edge computing, sensor data

The introduction of new and better tools, equipment, gadgets or manufacturing procedures into industrial processes that either boost work efficiency or conserve raw resources or energy contributes to the progression of technology. Today's market is in transition towards a more digital and eco-friendly form. The process of sustainable development is now receiving a lot of attention and focus (Chalapathi et al. 2021). One notion that can assist all elements of sustainability is the idea of zero-defect manufacturing, which has received a lot of attention recently. This is because if we can avoid flaws, we are also able to prevent the waste of resources and energy, as well as the unnecessary expenditures and extra effort that would be required to either eradicate faults or build a new product that does not include any problems (Sodhro et al. 2019). As a result, eliminating errors and ensuring quality output from the start should be the primary objectives.

The term "Internet of Things" is used to describe a global system of interconnected smart devices. The foundation of the Internet of Things (IoT) systems is the utilization of many intelligent devices that can gather, analyze, send and receive data between themselves and other devices. With this fundamental framework in place, any given environment, control system or device can be reliably monitored and controlled with pinpoint accuracy by a distributed network of smart devices. The IoT is expected to have a cumulative annual economic impact of between \$3.9 and \$11.1 trillion in 2025 (Bellavista et al. 2020). This is because it is expected that by 2022, almost 28.5 billion network-connected gadgets will have been activated. So far, most IoT system advancements have targeted the consumer sector. However, IIoT technology has also emerged because of the disruptive nature of this technology's applicability across a broad range of industrial contexts (Sulieman et al. 2022). Sensors, actuators, controllers and machines are only some of the resources that can be linked together and analyzed by these devices, as well as the intelligent control systems that can then optimize the current industrial processes based on the information they have gathered. Faster execution, lower costs and more agile management of the manufacturing setting are all possible outcomes of this optimization.

One of the primary reasons for the explosive growth of IIoT systems in many industries is the dramatic improvements they may bring to efficiency, throughput and response time. Then, there are also the following factors: companies in a wide variety of important sectors throughout the world have been profoundly impacted by the IIoT. This includes the mining sector. There has been a 400% boost in output thanks to the use of RFID tracking technology and wireless access points made possible by IIoT systems in the mining industry's tunnels (Narayanan et al. 2020). Both advancements have been made possible by IIoT systems. In agricultural situations, the proposed IIoT systems can assist farmers with nutrient monitoring as well as automatic watering, both of which would boost crop productivity. It is possible that the medical industry will use the features offered by IIoT technologies (Qiu et al. 2020). Data from patients, ambulances and doctors can be accessed by emergency services via these technologies, facilitating better decision-making and more efficient use of available resources.

The phrase "edge computing" is used to describe a model of computing in which computations are performed at the edges of a network rather than at the hub. Any resource located on a network edge, between data-collecting devices and the cloud data center, is referred to as an "edge resource" in this context. Edge computing is predicted on the premise that computations should take place at the network's periphery, or "edge", where it is closest to the data sources (Crăciunescu et al. 2019). The time it takes for data to get to the network's epicenter is reduced as a result. The fog computing paradigm is like the edge computing paradigm in that both use a distributed computing architecture; however, the main difference between the two is that the fog computing paradigm may be extended all the way to the network's epicenter (Xu et al. 2020). This means that both edge and core resources can be used for computations, and as a result, fog computing can facilitate the development of multi-tiered solutions that can shift the burden of meeting rising service demands away from the network's primary data hub. However, in most fog computing systems, the processing power is concentrated with the LAN resources that are situated at a distance from the network core, but closer to the data sources. This is also apparent in edge computing, where it decreases the latency experienced while sending data to the core (Borsatti et al. 2021). Thus, the fundamental difference between edge computing and fog computing models is the location of the processing power and the intelligence that is stored.

Data may be processed almost entirely at the network's periphery thanks to the edge computing concept. Network nodes that reside between client devices and massive data centers in the cloud are referred to as "edge" nodes. The creation of this technology was motivated by the hypothesis that calculations carried out more locally, in proximity to the end devices, would result in a reduced overall latency in the system. This is because the system no longer needs to transport data between the edge devices and the central cloud servers since the computations have been shifted to more convenient areas on the edge (Chen et al. 2018). Therefore, in edge computing systems, edge devices are both data producers and consumers, since they may request information and services from cloud servers and do computational offloading, caching, storing and processing. This is because edge devices can perform all these functions simultaneously.

We can think of the fog computing paradigm as an extension of the standard cloud computing approach. The term "fog computing" refers to a network architecture in which supplementary processing, data handling and networking capabilities are in proximity to the end devices. This paves the way for quicker data processing and improved network speeds. This development broadens the scope of data management, processing, networking and storage activities beyond merely the centralized cloud servers to the links between end devices and the cloud servers (Hsu et al. 2020). Applications that need low latency, or those that generate a large amount of data that cannot be transferred to cloud servers in real time due to bandwidth constraints, can benefit greatly from fog computing. The evaluated work by Caiza et al. (2020) also mentioned the following technologies in addition to edge computing: artificial intelligence (AI), machine learning (ML), reinforcement learning (RL), deep RL, inverse RL, neural networks (NN), deep NN, convolutional NN, distributed ensemble learning (DEL), dynamic knowledge bases (DKB), emotion interaction (EI), facial recognition (FR), image mining (IM), mobile cloud computing (5G), blockchain (Blockchain), augmented reality (AR), mixed reality (MR), hololens (AR), discrete-event simulation (DES).

A distributed generator, energy storage units, flexible loads and energy conversion gadgets all make up what is known as the "smart energy system", which is an integrated management system. These components work together to create a smart energy system. The integrated energy management platform is responsible for coordinating the interactions of the electrical energy within the power network (Yun and Lee 2021). To implement the core features of the smart energy system, this framework uses a microgrid central controller, a distributed power grid connection interface device and an intelligent control terminal. Depending on requirements, the cloud layer may construct a public cloud, a private cloud or a hybrid cloud. Unregulated distributed power sources like solar panels and wind turbines, regulated distributed power sources such as diesel generators and power conversion devices such as inverters, energy storage devices such as electric vehicle charging piles and batteries, and a wide variety of loads all make up the equipment layer. Items such as laptops, TVs, refrigerators and washers may all be part of a load. Photovoltaic panels and wind generators are examples of dispersed, unregulated sources of energy (Ren et al. 2021). Diesel generators are an example of a controlled, dispersed power source. The edge gateway, the edge platform and the edge services make up the edge layer, which is the most crucial aspect of the architecture. At the edge of the device, near the data source, the edge layer oversees the provision of several services, including computing, storage, application deployment, etc. A key part of any edge computing design is the edge gateway. It oversees the collection and uploading of real-time data on the performance of distributed power generators, loads, power converters and energy storage devices (Zhu et al. 2022). With the help of the edge platform, each edge gateway oversees the control of the dispatchable power devices based on the control instructions derived from the edge-side calculations.

1.4. Paradigms and procedures

Speed, efficiency, cost and accuracy form a natural quartet of metrics to judge optimization algorithms. The complexities described in the previous section make the corresponding optimization problems expensive to solve, and the best objective function is often unknown due to murky underlying mechanisms.

The first step is to quantify the problem suitably (Stork et al. 2020):

– determine a real-valued input vector $x \in R^n$ that adequately describes the state of the underlying system;

– determine the global earth space relevant to the problem: $S = \{x \mid x_{lower} \leq x \leq x_{upper}\}$;

– construct an objective function on this space: $g: S \to R$ from R^n to R.

After these steps are completed, the choice of the optimization algorithm comes into play:

– All a priori information about the function (due to knowledge of the problem) must be incorporated as far as possible. This leads to gray-box optimization (Belhadi et al. 2021).

– In black-box optimization, the evaluated inputs provide the only source of information and the search strategy must balance the two competing goals (Stork et al. 2020):

- efficient exploration to distribute the initial points in the solution space;

- efficient exploitation to generate the next set of candidates (based on the behavior of the objective function at the previous set of points).

Algorithms that are exact with sufficient a priori information may be forced to use heuristics if used in a black-box mode. Splitting the problem into smaller sub-problems can also help to achieve optimality.

Several optimization algorithms belong to the class of metaheuristics (Boussaïd et al. 2013), with a nature-inspired concept (the "meta") applied to the actual heuristics of the computation:

– stochastic tools are used;

– parameter values may be improved using a priori information;

– they can also work in a black-box mode.

Surrogate optimization is used when the original objective function is too expensive (Søndergaard 2003):

– An empirical functional "surrogate" (a substitute function) is created (usually by a data-driven regression model) from a sparse sampling of the solution space in terms of the expensive function.

– This surrogate is then evaluated at a denser sampling of this space.

– A comparison function takes these surrogate values and their distance from the original sparse sample to determine the best candidate point.

– This is called the adaptive point, which is added to the sparse sample with an evaluation of the expensive objective function.

– This is used to update the surrogate, and the process is repeated.

Evolutionary computation can further enhance the effectiveness of this process leading to surrogate-assisted optimization (Jin 2011).

It is interesting to note the relation between the cost and the fidelity in Figure 1.1: as the researcher moves from the real-world model to the surrogate model, the cost and the fidelity both decrease.

An example of the abstraction process that converts a real-world problem to a quantitative format can be seen in the modeling of service requests raised by multiple devices near-simultaneously impacting the cloud computing infrastructure (Figure 1.2) through an interface whose scheduling load can be optimized using a queuing paradigm (Guo et al. 2014).

The model in Figure 1.2 can then be interpreted by a queuing model using stochastic descriptors of real-life dependencies, as shown in Figure 1.3.

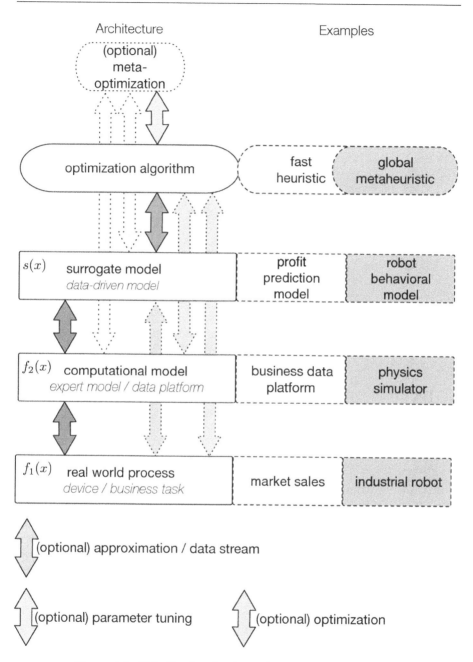

Figure 1.1. *Objective function layers in surrogate optimization (source: Stork et al. 2020). For a color version of this figure, see www.iste.co.uk/chakraborty/smartedge.zip*

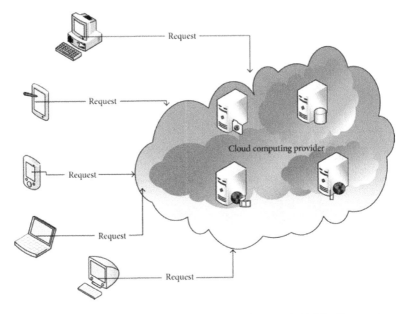

Figure 1.2. *Requests to the cloud (source: Guo et al. 2014). For a color version of this figure, see www.iste.co.uk/chakraborty/smartedge.zip*

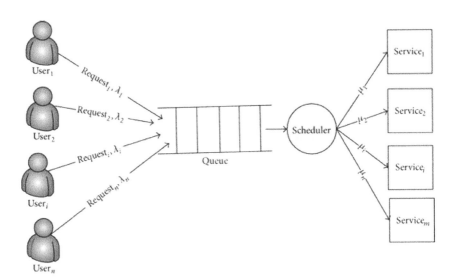

Figure 1.3. *Queuing model for scheduler load optimization (source: Guo et al. 2014)*

The subsequent algorithm optimizes an objective function that is linearly modeled on average time to service, number of customers and server utilization level, using parameters obtained by regression on training datasets (Figure 1.4).

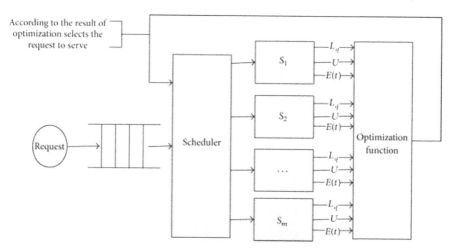

Figure 1.4. *Queuing model for scheduling optimization (source: Guo et al. 2014)*

A different point of view on the optimization of cloud resources for a streaming service is the pertinent use of operations research methodologies. In Ekholm and Englund (2020), time series trajectories of the logarithm of the number of monthly active users of a cloud streaming platform were modeled by a stochastic differential equation in a framework that encourages movement-to-mean and has the additional Brownian motion term. This Ornstein–Uhlenbeck process was then populated by Monte Carlo simulation. A policy for controlling the cost of computational resources while providing adequate services was sought. A multi-stage stochastic programming model was used for optimization. The paradigms and procedures described in this section are tabulated in Table 1.1. Depending on the requirements described above and the nature of the real-world problems, as described in the previous section, a possible algorithm selection guideline can be created (Stork et al. 2020), as shown in Table 1.2.

	Non-Heuristic	Heuristic and Metaheuristic		Surrogate Optimization	Hyperheuristic and Hybrid
1966 Leon		Blind search / Local search	Non-local search		
1984 Archetti	Deterministic methods	Probabilistic methods			
	Covering methods	Random sampling / Random search methods		Stochastic model	
1989 Töm and Žilinskas	Guaranteed accuracy	Direct methods		Indirect methods	
1992 Žilinskas	Covering methods	Random search methods / Clustering methods		Approximating objective function	
1995 Arora	Deterministic	Stochastic			
2001 Jones				Interpolating or Non-Interpolating	
2002 Talbi	Exact	Heuristic and Metaheuristic			Hybrid
2004 Neumaier	Complete and rigorous	Incomplete and Asymptotically Complete			
2004 Zlochin		Instance-Based / Model-Based			
2010 Burke					Hyperheuristic
2011 Jin				Surrogate-Assisted	
2013 Boussaïd		Single-Solution / Population-Based			

Table 1.1. *Global optimization taxonomy history (source: Stork et al. 2020)*

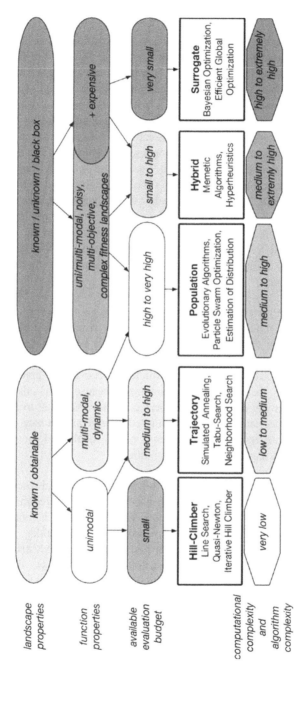

Table 1.2. Criterion of the algorithm selection (source: Stork et al. 2020)

1.5. Conclusion

Quantitative approaches are used for analysis, optimization and decision-making, which represent the three pillars of operations research. During World War II, the principles and techniques that would later become known as operations research started to take form. Since then, these ideas and methods have been used in a broad range of industrial, financial and scientific activities, with positive results. The use of mathematical models to describe real-world systems or processes is fundamental to both the academic study of operations research and its practical application. A model that has been constructed with skill incorporates enough of the details of the real entity that is being modeled so that it can capture the essential characteristics of the entity, but at the same time, the model is simple enough so that it can be studied using standard analytical techniques. In addition, a human analyst's expertise, experience, intuition and sound judgment are essential to developing an accurate model. The computational procedures known as algorithms can be used in the application of mathematical models' underlying structures. The length of time it takes for a computer to apply an algorithm is often used as a metric for evaluating an algorithm's performance.

It is possible for algorithms to run extremely quickly (efficiently), or for their execution to take so much time that the algorithm is almost useless for real problems. This depends on the kind of problem that is being addressed. Exactly what degree of performance may be anticipated from each of the computational approaches that are described should be determined whenever it is practicable to do so. This is something that should be recognized because many algorithms are designed to solve their intended problems perfectly. However, due to imperfect or incomplete models, uncertain data and the limited numerical accuracy of computer hardware, it may be necessary to compromise on the quality of the solutions to obtain answers within a reasonable computing time.

According to the new circumstances, the function of operational research and the methods that it uses justify its role in decision-making in the realm of business and industry, and the availability of computer resources makes it more powerful. OR methods may potentially advance in order to successfully combat the ever-increasing challenges that are plaguing the commercial and industrial landscape and provide useful assistance to the decision-making process. By using it, decision-makers can determine an ideal policy that would be beneficial for the business under a plan about how to go forward to solve the challenges. However, operational research only provides the data necessary to make decisions; it is up to human intelligence to determine how best to use this data in order to make the best possible decisions. In a nutshell, management is where its application lies. However, the success of its implementation is contingent on the mathematical models and computations. The operational research approach can be beneficial in improving control and management, as well as maximizing profit and minimizing loss, among other things. The process of achieving the best possible outcome under a set of constraints is called optimization.

Recent developments in the field of IIoT have led to the observation of significant patterns that point to a meteoric increase in the number of smart devices linked to IIoT networks. However, this increase is beyond the capabilities of conventional cloud computing platforms. As a result, systems based on edge computing and fog computing have emerged as promising frameworks for meeting the increasing automation needs of a variety of industries. The resources of systems built using these paradigms are dispersed over the network's edges, which results in lower latency and more dependability for the services they provide. In this chapter, the building blocks of edge and fog computing through operations research have been laid out and an in-depth look at the advantages these systems have over the more conventional cloud-based ones has been provided. It also analyzes in depth the suggested system architectures for various industrial use cases, detailing multiple applications for both edge and fog computing. In this article, a compelling argument for the widespread adoption of operations research methodologies in these computing paradigms in today's cutting-edge industrial systems is provided. Finally, the most pressing problems with these models are outlined with some promising avenues for further study.

1.6. References

Bahramara, S., Mazza, A., Chicco, G., Shafie-khah, M., Catalão, J. (2020). Comprehensive review on the decision-making frameworks referring to the distribution network operation problem in the presence of distributed energy resources and microgrids. *International Journal of Electrical Power & Energy Systems*, 115, 105466. doi: 10.1016/j.ijepes. 2019.105466 [Accessed 17 October 2022].

Belhadi, A., Kamble, S., Fosso Wamba, S., Queiroz, M. (2021). Building supply-chain resilience: An artificial intelligence-based technique and decision-making framework. *International Journal of Production Research*, 60(14), 4487–4507. doi: 10.1080/00207543. 2021.1950935 [Accessed 17 October 2022].

Bellavista, P., Penna, R., Foschini, L., Scotece, D. (2020). Machine learning for predictive diagnostics at the edge: An IIoT practical example. *ICC 2020 – 2020 IEEE International Conference on Communications (ICC)*. doi: 10.1109/icc40277.2020.9148684 [Accessed 17 October 2022].

Billings, B., Smith, P., Smith, S., Powell, K. (2022). Industrial battery operation and utilization in the presence of electrical load uncertainty using Bayesian decision theory. *Journal of Energy Storage*, 53, 105054. doi: 10.1016/j.est.2022.105054 [Accessed 17 October 2022].

Borsatti, D., Davoli, G., Cerroni, W., Raffaelli, C. (2021). Enabling industrial IoT as a service with multi-access edge computing. *IEEE Communications Magazine*, 59(8), 21–27. doi: 10.1109/mcom.001.2100006 [Accessed 17 October 2022].

Boussaïd, I., Lepagnot, J., Siarry, P. (2013). A survey on optimization metaheuristics. *Information Sciences*, 237, 82–117.

Božanić, D., Tešić, D., Milić, A. (2020). Multicriteria decision making model with z-numbers based on FUCOM and MABAC model. *Decision Making: Applications in Management and Engineering*, 3(2), 19–36. doi: 10.31181/dmame2003019d [Accessed 17 October 2022].

Caiza, G., Saeteros, M., Oñate, W., Garcia, M. (2020). Fog computing at industrial level, architecture, latency, energy, and security: A review. *Heliyon*, 6(4), e03706. doi: 10.1016/j.heliyon.2020.e03706 [Accessed 17 October 2022].

Cardil, A., Monedero, S., Schag, G., de-Miguel, S., Tapia, M., Stoof, C.R., Silva, C.A., Mohan, M., Cardil, A., Ramirez, J. (2021). Fire behavior modeling for operational decision-making. *Current Opinion in Environmental Science & Health*, 23, 100291. doi: 10.1016/j.coesh.2021.100291 [Accessed 17 October 2022].

Chalapathi, G., Chamola, V., Vaish, A., Buyya, R. (2021). Industrial Internet of Things (IIoT) applications of edge and fog computing: A review and future directions. *Fog/Edge Computing for Security, Privacy, and Applications*, 293–325. doi: 10.1007/978-3-030-57328-7_12 [Accessed 17 October 2022].

Chen, B., Wan, J., Celesti, A., Li, D., Abbas, H., Zhang, Q. (2018). Edge computing in IoT-based manufacturing. *IEEE Communications Magazine*, 56(9), 103–109. doi: 10.1109/mcom.2018.1701231 [Accessed 17 October 2022].

Conboy, K., Mikalef, P., Dennehy, D., Krogstie, J. (2020). Using business analytics to enhance dynamic capabilities in operations research: A case analysis and research agenda. *European Journal of Operational Research*, 281(3), 656–672. doi: 10.1016/j.ejor.2019.06.051 [Accessed 17 October 2022].

Crăciunescu, M., Chenaru, O., Dobrescu, R., Florea, G., Mocanu, Ş. (2019). IIoT gateway for edge computing applications. *Service Oriented, Holonic and Multi-agent Manufacturing Systems for Industry of the Future*, 220–231. doi: 10.1007/978-3-030-27477-1_17 [Accessed 17 October 2022].

Ding, Z., Wen, X., Tan, Q., Yang, T., Fang, G., Lei, X., Zhang, Y., Wang, H. (2021). A forecast-driven decision-making model for long-term operation of a hydro-wind-photovoltaic hybrid system. *Applied Energy*, 291, 116820. doi: 10.1016/j.apenergy.2021.116820 [Accessed 17 October 2022].

Ekholm, H. and Englund, D. (2020). Cost optimization in the cloud: An analysis on how to apply an optimization framework to the procurement of cloud contracts at Spotify. *DIVA*, [Online]. Available at: http://urn.kb.se/resolve?urn=urn:nbn:se:liu:diva-168441.

Erdogan, S., Šaparauskas, J., Turskis, Z. (2019). A multi-criteria decision-making model to choose the best option for sustainable construction management. *Sustainability*, 11(8), 2239. doi: 10.3390/su11082239 [Accessed 17 October 2022].

Gonçalves, J., Sameiro Carvalho, M., Cortez, P. (2020). Operations research models and methods for safety stock determination: A review. *Operations Research Perspectives*, 7, 100164. doi: 10.1016/j.orp.2020.100164 [Accessed 17 October 2022].

Guo, L., Yan, T., Zhao, S., Jiang, C. (2014). Dynamic performance optimization for cloud computing using M/M/m queueing system. *Journal of Applied Mathematics*, 1–8.

Hsu, H.-Y., Srivastava, G., Wu, H.-T., Chen, M.-Y. (2020). Remaining useful life prediction based on state assessment using edge computing on deep learning. *Computer Communications*, 160, 91–100. doi: 10.1016/j.comcom.2020.05.035.

Huang, X., Xu, B., Zhong, P., Yao, H., Yue, H., Zhu, F., Lu, Q., Sun, Y., Mo, R., Li, Z., Liu, W. (2022). Robust multi-objective reservoir operation and risk decision-making model for real-time flood control coping with forecast uncertainty. *Journal of Hydrology*, 605, 127334. doi: 10.1016/j.jhydrol.2021.127334 [Accessed 17 October 2022].

Hubbs, C., Li, C., Sahinidis, N., Grossmann, I., Wassick, J. (2020). A deep reinforcement learning approach for chemical production scheduling. *Computers & Chemical Engineering*, 141, 106982. doi: 10.1016/j.compchemeng.2020.106982.

Jin, Y. (2011). Surrogate-assisted evolutionary computation: Recent advances and future challenges. *Swarm and Evolutionary Computation*, 1(2), 61–70.

Kraus, M., Feuerriegel, S., Oztekin, A. (2020). Deep learning in business analytics and operations research: Models, applications and managerial implications. *European Journal of Operational Research*, 281(3), 628–641. doi: 10.1016/j.ejor.2019.09.018 [Accessed 17 October 2022].

Liao, S., Liu, H., Liu, B., Zhao, H., Wang, M. (2022). An information gap decision theory-based decision-making model for complementary operation of hydro-wind-solar system considering wind and solar output uncertainties. *Journal of Cleaner Production*, 348, 131382. doi: 10.1016/j.jclepro.2022.131382 [Accessed 17 October 2022].

Liu, B., Zhou, J., Xu, Y., Lai, X., Shi, Y., Li, M. (2022). An optimization decision-making framework for the optimal operation strategy of pumped storage hydropower system under extreme conditions. *Renewable Energy*, 182, 254–273. doi: 10.1016/j.renene.2021.09.080 [Accessed 17 October 2022].

Louis, J. and Dunston, P. (2018). Integrating IoT into operational workflows for real-time and automated decision-making in repetitive construction operations. *Automation in Construction*, 94, 317–327. doi: 10.1016/j.autcon.2018.07.005 [Accessed 17 October 2022].

McNamara, T. and Chen, X. (2021). Bayesian decision theory and navigation. *Psychonomic Bulletin & Review*, 29(3), 721–752. doi: 10.3758/s13423-021-01988-9 [Accessed 17 October 2022].

Narayanan, A., Sena, A.S., Gutierrez-Rojas, D., Melgarejo, D.C., Hussain, H.M., Ullah, M., Bayhan, S., Nardelli, P.H. (2020). Key advances in pervasive edge computing for industrial internet of things in 5G and beyond. *IEEE Access*, 8, 206734–206754. doi: 10.1109/access.2020.3037717 [Accessed 17 October 2022].

Pei, J. and Pardalos, P. (2022). Scalable optimization and decision-making in operations research. *Annals of Operations Research*, 316(1), 1–4. doi: 10.1007/s10479-022-04895-x [Accessed 17 October 2022].

Pereira, D., Oliveira, J., Carravilla, M. (2020). Tactical sales and operations planning: A holistic framework and a literature review of decision-making models. *International Journal of Production Economics*, 228, 107695. doi: 10.1016/j.ijpe.2020.107695 [Accessed 17 October 2022].

Pokrovsky, O. (2009). Operational research approach to decision making. *NATO Science for Peace and Security Series B: Physics and Biophysics*, 235–258. doi: 10.1007/978-1-4020-9253-4_12 [Accessed 17 October 2022].

Qiu, T., Chi, J., Zhou, X., Ning, Z., Atiquzzaman, M., Wu, D. (2020). Edge computing in industrial internet of things: Architecture, advances and challenges. *IEEE Communications Surveys & Tutorials*, 22(4), 2462–2488. doi: 10.1109/comst.2020.3009103 [Accessed 17 October 2022].

Ren, S., Kim, J., Cho, W., Soeng, S., Kong, S., Lee, K. (2021). Big data platform for intelligence industrial IoT sensor monitoring system based on edge computing and AI. *2021 International Conference on Artificial Intelligence in Information and Communication (ICAIIC)*. doi: 10.1109/icaiic51459.2021.9415189 [Accessed 17 October 2022].

Siebert, J., Kunz, R., Rolf, P. (2020). Effects of proactive decision making on life satisfaction. *European Journal of Operational Research*, 280(3), 1171–1187. doi: 10.1016/j.ejor.2019.08.011 [Accessed 17 October 2022].

Sodhro, A., Pirbhulal, S., de Albuquerque, V. (2019). Artificial intelligence-driven mechanism for edge computing-based industrial applications. *IEEE Transactions on Industrial Informatics*, 15(7), 4235–4243. doi: 10.1109/tii.2019.2902878 [Accessed 17 October 2022].

Søndergaard, J. (2003). Optimization using surrogate models – by the space mapping technique. *Technical University of Denmark (DTU)* [Online]. Available at: https://orbit.dtu.dk/en/publications/optimization-using-surrogate-models-by-the-space-mapping-techniqu.

Stork, J., Eiben, A., Bartz-Beielstein, T. (2020). A new taxonomy of global optimization algorithms. *Natural Computing*, 21(2), 219–242.

Sulieman, N., Ricciardi Celsi, L., Li, W., Zomaya, A., Villari, M. (2022). Edge-oriented computing: A survey on research and use cases. *Energies*, 15(2), 452. doi: 10.3390/en15020452 [Accessed 17 October 2022].

Thies, C., Kieckhäfer, K., Spengler, T., Sodhi, M. (2019). Operations research for sustainability assessment of products: A review. *European Journal of Operational Research*, 274(1), 1–21. doi: 10.1016/j.ejor.2018.04.039 [Accessed 17 October 2022].

Wang, Y., Yu, Z., Shen, L. (2018). Study on the decision-making and coordination of an e-commerce supply chain with manufacturer fairness concerns. *International Journal of Production Research*, 57(9), 2788–2808. doi: 10.1080/00207543.2018.1500043 [Accessed 17 October 2022].

Whitley, L., Chicano, F., Goldman, B. (2016). Gray box optimization for Mk landscapes (NK landscapes and MAX-kSAT). *Evolutionary Computation*, 24(3), 491–519.

Xu, X., Zeng, Z., Yang, S., Shao, H. (2020). A novel blockchain framework for industrial IoT edge computing. *Sensors*, 20(7), 2061. doi: 10.3390/s20072061 [Accessed 17 October 2022].

Yazdani, M., Chatterjee, P., Pamucar, D., Chakraborty, S. (2020). Development of an integrated decision-making model for location selection of logistics centers in the Spanish autonomous communities. *Expert Systems with Applications*, 148, 113208. doi: 10.1016/j.eswa.2020.113208 [Accessed 17 October 2022].

Yoo, S. and Kim, B. (2018). A decision-making model for adopting a cloud computing system. *Sustainability*, 10(8), 2952. doi: 10.3390/su10082952 [Accessed 17 October 2022].

Yun, D. and Lee, W. (2021). Intelligent dynamic real-time spectrum resource management for industrial IoT in edge computing. *Sensors*, 21(23), 7902. doi: 10.3390/s21237902 [Accessed 17 October 2022].

Zhang, Z., Qian, K., Schuller, B., Wollherr, D. (2021). An online robot collision detection and identification scheme by supervised learning and Bayesian decision theory. *IEEE Transactions on Automation Science and Engineering*, 18(3), 1144–1156. doi: 10.1109/tase.2020.2997094 [Accessed 17 October 2022].

Zhao, Z., Yang, J., Yang, W., Hu, J., Chen, M. (2019). A coordinated optimization framework for flexible operation of pumped storage hydropower system: Nonlinear modeling, strategy optimization and decision making. *Energy Conversion and Management*, 194, 75–93. doi: 10.1016/j.enconman.2019.04.068 [Accessed 17 October 2022].

Zhao, Y., Yu, Y., Shakeel, P., Montenegro-Marin, C. (2021). Research on operational research-based financial model based on e-commerce platform. *Information Systems and e-Business Management*. doi: 10.1007/s10257-021-00509-4 [Accessed 17 October 2022].

Zhu, F., Zhong, P., Sun, Y., Xu, B., Ma, Y., Liu, W., Zhang, D., Dawa, J. (2020). A coordinated optimization framework for long-term complementary operation of a large-scale hydro-photovoltaic hybrid system: Nonlinear modelling, multi-objective optimization, and robust decision-making. *Energy Conversion and Management*, 226, 113543. doi: 10.1016/j.enconman.2020.113543 [Accessed 17 October 2022].

Zhu, S., Ota, K., Dong, M. (2022). Green AI for IIoT: Energy efficient intelligent edge computing for industrial internet of things. *IEEE Transactions on Green Communications and Networking*, 6(1), 79–88. doi: 10.1109/tgcn.2021.3100622 [Accessed 17 October 2022].

Edge Computing: The Foundation, Emergence and Growing Applications

Edge computing is an important concept and technology within information technology, which is close to cloud computing in some contexts. It has the potential of getting close to the end device or simply to end-users. It is the computational processing of sensor data and normally stays away from the centralized system or nodes. This kind of computing is close to the logical edge of the network and also particular individual data source. Edge computing is sometimes considered to be similar to fog computing. Edge computing is referred to as a distributed IT network architecture which uses mobile computing and practically data produced locally. In this computing mechanism, instead of forwarding data from the data centers (which are cloud enables) to the decentralized system for confirming real-time processing, it offers without latency while reducing bandwidth and also storage requirements. Since edge computing works with distributed information technology (IT), it therefore offers benefits on data sovereignty, autonomy and effective data security. Although effective, implementing edge computing requires security, connectivity, management and physical maintenance. This chapter offers a comprehensive overview on the foundation and basics of edge computing, emphasizing its benefits and functions. It also briefly highlights different field-specific applications of edge computing such as automated vehicle management, logistic management, smart cities etc.

2.1. Introduction

Edge computing believes in distributed information systems of architecture, and here clients' data are basically processed in the periphery of a network. Traditional computing lies in virtual data flood, and here data models are restricted on centralized systems. However, the obstacle of bandwidth limitations, latency issues and an unpredictable network can be solved with edge computing architecture (Paul et al. 2015; Krestinskaya et al. 2019). In this type of computing platform, some of

Chapter written by P.K. Paul.

the services and portions are allowed out of the central data center, which also brings them closer to the source data. In edge computing, after generating data, data are not normally transferred to the central data system and center; rather, operations are worked or performed in the place itself where data are being generated. However, in the edge computing real-time data results, required actionable answers are normally provided to the center for review. Thus, edge computing is reshaping IT and business computing. Take a comprehensive look at what edge computing is, how it works, the influence of the cloud, edge use cases, tradeoffs and implementation considerations. With the edge computing, the cloud is normally considered to become more available to the end-user, and it also performs similar operations such as fog computing. The characteristics of edge computing are diverse (see Figure 2.1).

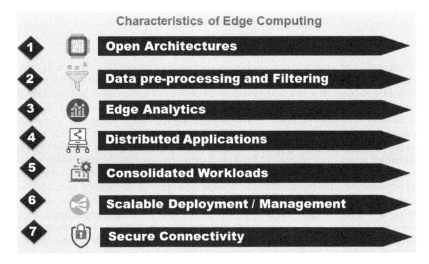

Figure 2.1. *Basic characteristics of edge computing. For a color version of this figure, see www.iste.co.uk/chakraborty/smartedge.zip*

According to the experts, there are many similarities between edge computing and fog computing; however, the reality is that fog computing depends on end devices and IoT-focused systems, while edge computing is based on distributed models and is also managed by operators and can be extended (Satyanarayanan 2017; Hassan et al. 2018). Due to the benefits of edge computing, it is considered to be a synonym for mobile edge computing and also multiaccess edge computing. In 1990s, Akamai introduced web traffic solutions by the content delivery network, and this technology basically involved network nodes storing static cached media information at locations which are much closer to the end-users. This concept was later moved and computational capabilities were also fixed.

2.2. Objective of the work

The present work is conceptual in nature and deals with the following core objectives and agenda (but is not limited to):

– to learn about the basics of edge computing including its foundation and development root;

– to know about the function and feature of edge computing with special reference to the contemporary scenario;

– to collect information about various edge devices with fundamental specifications in a brief manner;

– to know about the basic and emerging applications and utilizations of the edge computing in the current context;

– the future of edge computing in a concise manner with future potential is another important aim of the study.

2.3. Methods adopted

This chapter, entitled "Edge Computing: The Foundation, Emergence and Growing Applications", is an interdisciplinary work, and deals with the basics and an overview of edge computing, with a focus on its basic structure, characteristics and functions, and hence a review of literature that is deemed worthy of doing this work. Various primary and secondary sources are used to carry out the work. The data collected from different sources are therefore analyzed and reported in this work.

2.4. Edge computing and edge cloud: basics

In edge computing, resources of the edge server are basically stored using the Internet and here mobile devices, sensors and various other latest technologies are used. To describe edge computing hardware, some of the similar terminologies are used such as cloudlets, fog, small data centers, etc. (Mach and Becvar 2017; Deng et al. 2020). According to most experts, edge computing is basically responsible for enabling technologies that allow computation in the edge of the network. As far as edge computing is concerned, downstream data are considered for cloud-related services, whereas upstream data are considered on behalf of Internet of Things services. It is worthy to note that, in the edge of the Internet, just one hop is basically associated with the end devices. It is suitable for the low latency offload facilities and infrastructure and supports various emerging applications, which include autonomous car, digital healthcare, augmented reality and public safety. Edge computing is dedicated to aggregating and analyzing data, i.e. sensor data. Cloud computing models are used in a basic three-tier edge computing model.

Although edge computing and edge cloud always refer to the same context, there are technical differences in both cases. Edge computing is about the physical infrastructure and circled within devices and supports various allied devices and applications. Edge cloud is the virtualization of infrastructure; therefore, it works in remote systems and has flexibility and scalability, and furthermore has the ability to manage end-user activity and load balancing (Yu et al. 2017; Chen and Ran 2019). Edge cloud also helps to test as well as deploy new applications and thus it offers great solutions for the enterprise. Edge cloud is able to perform functions with virtualization roadmaps.

Figure 2.2. *Ample benefits are possible from edge computing. For a color version of this figure, see www.iste.co.uk/chakraborty/smartedge.zip*

As far as *functions* are concerned, edge computing is suitable for different works and activities. Edge computing works upstream, which is device-to-the-cloud-based and another one is cloud-to-device-based, which is downstream. Furthermore, in edge computing, the end-user acts as a data producer and not just a data consumer. With edge computing, user-centric services become possible using the performance of computing offloading, data storage as well as processing, distributing services, cloud-based facilities, etc. Edge computing therefore offers tremendous benefits, as shown in Figure 2.2.

2.5. Edge computing and edge devices

Edge computing is supported by the **edge device** that provides all kinds of services through the Internet and networks such as routers, switches, multiplexers, MAN and WAN. Furthermore, edge devices also provide connections to the carriers and also to the service provider networks. Edge devices are connected or backed by the edge concentrator that is dedicated to a carrier as well as service provider networks. Edge devices are types of routers dedicated to providing authenticated, faster and efficient services as well as core networks, and here PPPoA and PPPoE are considered worthy. Edge devices offer quality of services (QoS), OSPF (Open shortest path first), multiprotocol label switching (MPLS) for the purpose of reliability and also scalability. It is worthy to mention that edge devices are suitable in translating one type of network protocol to another one such as Ethernet type of LAN or xDSL equipment is positively useful in an ATM backbone. Here, ATM networks basically send data to the cell and are also worthy in the virtual circuit connection (Tran et al. 2017; Xiao et al. 2019).

2.6. Edge computing: working fashions, buying and deploying and 5G

Edge computing supports low latency applications, and 5G is here considered to be worthy with reduced latency, and this is considered as growth full applications in a wide range of areas such as augmented reality, virtual reality, autonomous cars, industry 4.0, Internet of Things (IoT), etc. There is a need to achieve latency below 10 milliseconds, although there are challenges to implementing all of the services using 4G and therefore 5G is considered to be worthy and necessary.

Edge computing is architected with complex systems though the basic concept is client devices that connect with a nearest edge module for a healthy and intelligent processing as well as smooth operations. There are a lot of devices such as laptop, notebook and even a smartphone that can be connected in a workplace for a superb edge computing operations. Even CCTV cameras, microwaves and similar devices can be connected to edge computing. Therefore, in the organizational context, edge computing is supported by edge devices that are autonomous mobile robots. As far as the healthcare segment is concerned, remote-based surgical operations can be possible with edge computing. Here, edge devices are worthy of developing edge computing infrastructure (Mao et al. 2017). Edge network is supported by edge network devices that are important in deploying services for the support in the edge network. The edge system can be purchased and deployed in a variety of ways; first, setting the requirement and selecting the edge devices are considered as worthy, and here hardware such as Dell, IBM and other reputed vendors in this field can be chosen. Building an edge system requires high-end expertise, and therefore it is important to consider its architecture accordingly. The availability of fully customized edge deployment is considered to be important in the proper implementation and growth. Many organizations offer hardware, software and networking services using an edge system, and IoT-based services can also be incorporated accordingly (Corcoran and Datta 2016; Yang et al. 2019). Such services are easy and hassle-free to install for heavily managed services and so on.

2.7. Functions and features of edge computing

Edge computing is applicable to different areas and fields due to its role and functionalities, and some of them are listed below.

2.7.1. *Privacy and security*

With the help of the Internet, data can travel from one place to another in the distributed nodes in edge computing. Therefore, special encryption mechanisms are used in the independent cloud environment. Being a resource-constrained device, edge nodes can have limited choice methods in terms of security. It also requires a top-down infrastructure and a decentralized model, both of which are trustworthy. The storage and processing of data has become smooth in edge computing, and the privacy of data becomes possible effectively.

2.7.2. *Scalability*

Edge computing also has issues related to the scalability, but it solves heterogeneous problems of devices having different performances and also energy constraints.

2.7.3. *Reliability*

In terms of reliability, edge computing is considered to be important and valuable for various purposes, including being important in the event of a single node failure and in an unreachable mode. Furthermore, edge computing also provides actions for recovering failure and incident management. In order to maintain reliability, each device must maintain a network topology for finding the errors and recovery process (Sonmez et al. 2018; Wang et al. 2019). The edge devices are so reliable that we can still benefit from the voice assistant service available to local users even in the event of Internet outages.

2.7.4. Speed

One of the important functions of edge computing is to offer speed to the users and all stakeholders with its analytical computational resources. A properly designed edge computing system is well designed and traditionally cloud-based. Therefore, it works with a short response time, which significantly reduces the timing. Therefore, edge computing is helpful for cloud- and IoT-based autonomous cars, health and telemedicine, facial recognition, etc.

2.7.5. Efficiency

Edge computing significantly offers efficiency at different levels as it is supported by the analytical resources including artificial intelligence tools, etc. It offers operational efficiency and various advantages to the client devices. As a result, it offers time management, external server management, etc. Edge computing offers significant efficiency in voice recognition and bandwidth management (Corcoran and Datta 2016; Sodhro et al. 2019). In the edge computing system, data centers are considered to be important and are closer to the systems for the data management. In this computing mechanism, edge devices are used for controlling data and data flow management, minimizing bandwidth need, sensor data and its management.

2.7.6. Latency and bandwidth

Edge computing is featured with the benefits of latency, and data between two places are transferred easily without any kind of delay. Therefore, it is designed to eliminate latency in physical distances between two points including help with network congestion. The rate of data transformation is called bandwidth, and here the amount of data can be transferred and further managed based on the situation. As this kind of computing allows different devices to a smaller as well as efficient network by adding data servers, therefore data management can be effective with a healthy bandwidth (Paul and Dangwal 2014; Shi et al. 2016; Deng et al. 2020).

2.7.7. *Reduction in congestion*

Due to the benefits of the managing congestion in edge computing, it is always reduced. As in a single day, billions of devices can cause significant congestion and therefore in a local storage edge computing can be effective and able to execute network failure management.

Due to the observation of edge computing, it has been studied and found that there are many similarities with edge computing and other similar computing platforms and some of them are shown in Table 2.1.

Early computing	In this computing, only single or isolated computers are used.
Personal computing	Data is basically used in individual computers or personal storage.
Cloud computing	In this computing system, data centers are used in data storage and other activities via the Internet.
Edge computing	In edge computing, data can be considered for the users and are kept close to the users.

Table 2.1. *Different types of computing in contrast to edge computing*

2.8. Edge computing: applications and examples

Edge computing provides edge application services responsible for reducing data volume, also providing low latency as well as deducting transmission costs. For different real-time applications, edge computing is considered as valuable and important (Shi and Dustdar 2016; Ahmed and Rehmani 2017; Satyanarayanan 2017). There are numerous and emerging applications of edge computing, and some of the most important ones are mentioned here (see also Figure 2.3):

– connected cars;

– autonomous cars;

– vehicle management;

– smart cities and towns;

– intelligent home appliances;

– Industry 4.0;

– fleet management;

– predictive maintenance;

– voice assistance;

– intelligent and smart healthcare;

– AI for virtual assistant.

Edge computing provides services in association and support from other electronic devices such as IoT, cloud computing, Big Data Analytics, etc. A combination of such technologies helps us to improve the performance, security and productivity of the organizations and institutions.

2.8.1. *Self-managed and automated cars/vehicles*

The advancement in information and communication technology leads to the development of self-automated cars, and in this regard, autonomous vehicles play a vital role in replacing humans (Liang et al. 2017; Ranaweera et al. 2021). Such a system has to work in real time, and the data transformation between the vehicles' sensor and the backend datacenters must hardly take a hundred milliseconds. However, such a timing gap may also even be critical in some contexts. According to vehicle manufacturer Toyota, the amount of data transferred between cars and the cloud system may reach an average of 10 exabytes per month by 2025.

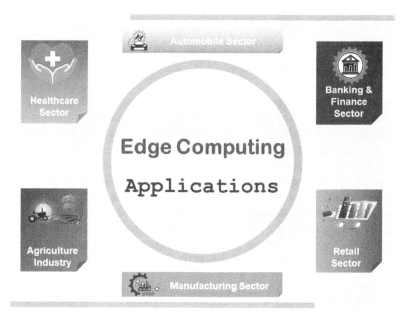

Figure 2.3. *Emerging and most used areas of edge systems. For a color version of this figure, see www.iste.co.uk/chakraborty/smartedge.zip*

Therefore, a proper and effective network management plays a leading role in advancing the systems. The 5G system and artificial intelligence play a leading role in supporting autonomous cars. Since the 5th generation is helpful in deploying computing capabilities, designing a logical network is also considered valuable. Greater data aggregation and processing can be possible while maintaining data communication and vehicles. Similar to the 5G in autonomous cars supported by edge computing, another valuable technique is AI and robotics for healthy, intelligent and sophisticated decision-making in a real-time context.

2.8.2. *Fleet management*

Edge computing is helpful in managing logistic services and vehicle management using proper and sophisticated technologies. IoT and cloud-supported edge systems can be effective in fleet management operations and services. For better decisions of the drivers such as vehicle-to-vehicle communication, edge system is considered valuable. Location management is also an important feature; modern transport system and here edge systems are valuable. Since autonomous cars have emerged significantly for real-time computation, data analysis and decision-making, edge computing is considered to be valuable. The computational capabilities are important in fleet vehicle management, traffic and transportation, car parking management and so on. For an effective vehicle-to-vehicle communication, AI-based and edge-supported systems are valuable in many contexts.

2.8.3. *Predictive maintenance*

Edge computing is applicable to the manufacturing industry due to the requirement and need of the hour. The combination of the edge computing with the IoT changes the entire arena of the manufacturing and industrial sector. The automated machines empower the automated industry and also increase the advanced systems towards sophisticated automations and systems. In the healthcare and medical sectors, edge computing also helps in predictive maintenance by providing real-time data management and analysis. The data is analyzed and reported in the automated mechanism. Predictive maintenance in healthcare is required to detect anomalies, offer corrective measures, etc. Therefore, the edge system enables low maintenance costs, including an improvement in operational effectiveness, etc. (Corcoran and Datta 2016; Porambage et al. 2018; Cao et al. 2020).

2.8.4. *Voice assisting systems*

Edge computing empowers different kinds of voice assistance systems. In this segment, various companies and organizations are putting efforts in using edge computing, among which the main ones include Amazon Echo, Google Home, etc. The growing voice assisting system requires edge computing including AI and Intelligent system's support. In particular, AI is required for a low-latency response and also for sophisticated and effective interactions with the consumer or end-users. Sensitive personal information is sometimes considered to be important due to data security and privacy, and in this regard edge computing is considered valuable and reliable. To protect the challenges and issues, edge computing takes the help of AI for the advanced and intelligent voice assisting system. Amazon Echo devices are considered as an important example in this regard.

2.8.5. *Smart cities and town planning*

As regards the advancement in the information system, it depends on edge computing in many ways, and hence this emerging edge computing is perfectly applicable in the fields of smart cities and urban planning. Since edge computing helps in perfect working conditions in a real-time context, it also helps in better public administration and governance of the city and town. Autonomous vehicles are on the rise everywhere day by day, and here along with edge computing, another important beneficial object technology is the IoT. As a whole, edge-based systems help in advancing lifestyle, different city-related features and aspects, urban development, etc. According to the data from the UN report on promoting urbanization by 2050, approximately 68% of the world's population will achieve urbanization, starting from 30% in 1950. Therefore, the use of technologies in developing smart cities is necessary. Emerging technologies include the IoT, robotics and AI, machine learning, and very recent edge computing (Ahmed et al. 2017; Cao et al. 2020). Therefore, in the collection of real-time data, emerging technologies are important for the development of smart traffic management system, parking space management, digital systems and sustainability, efficient and important energy grids, etc. (Zhou et al. 2019).

2.8.6. *Manufacturing and core sector*

As regards the manufacturing sector, edge computing is important in enhancing manufacturing equipment, real-time data collection and management, technology savvy manufacturing world in performing well with support from intelligent system and edge computing. Gearing of speed and reduction of the costs are empowered by edge computing in many ways. In order to organize and modernize operations effectively, the manufacturing industry performs well with proper information technology systems for more and advanced transparency, efficiency and timely data analysis. In reducing plant emissions, a richer customer experience is created, where edge computing is valuable. Using the predictive analytics with support from the automation powered by other edge systems, the manufacturing section can gear up with other issues and concerns. Edge computing enables manufacturing systems, advanced factory floor management, supply chain process, defect detection, fatigue detection and latency reduction. Furthermore, as a whole, edge computing is important in the following processes (Mach and Becvar 2017; Mao et al. 2017; Wang et al. 2020):

– sophisticated condition-based monitoring;

– healthy predictive maintenance;

– manufacturing as a service;

– using augmented and virtual reality systems in manufacturing systems;

– developing precision monitoring, etc.

2.8.7. *Healthcare and medical segment*

Edge computing is an important gift to the healthcare and the entire clinical sector including healthcare management and monitoring. Edge-connected IoT devices are able to collect a huge amount of data from the patient or in short PDHD (Patient Generated Health Data). Healthcare suppliers are getting essential data from the patient particularly from fragmented databases. Today, the healthcare sector is booming, and therefore it is required to manage a large amount of unpredictable datasets. Since daily data consumption increases with bandwidth costs, edge computing helps to provide data processing, analytics as well as storage in the hospital, medical units and across the healthcare sector. Regarding immediate healthcare-related decision-making, finding a suitable strategy, allowing and spreading workloads and allied activities, edge systems are valuable and important. The main reasons for using edge computing in healthcare systems are decision-making, cost-effectiveness, speed, timeliness, security and advanced technologies. According to the experts, edge computing is useful in healthcare and applicable to various smallest areas to broadest areas, namely:

– at hospital and healthcare units;

– at mobile vans and cars;

– operation theaters and rooms;

– clinical and diagnostics units.

The expert believes that, despite the fact that the recent applications of edge are not so enriched, in the coming years there will be different potentialities in healthcare such as remote patient monitoring, remote and quick healthcare equipment manufacturing. By 2024, it is also expected that 60% of healthcare organizations will adopt AI-based IT Infrastructure, and edge computing can play an important role here. It is also expected that by 2025, about 60% of providers will move to the concept of full deployment using edge-supported AR/VR technologies (Hu et al. 2015; Krestinskaya et al. 2019; Sittón-Candanedo et al. 2019).

2.8.8. *Edge computing and augmented reality*

In response to edge computing applications in augmented reality devices, it is an important trend and future trend too. Edge systems supported by the cloud help in the better processing of the visual information as well as digital components of augmented reality. Adopting edge computing in the AI-based virtual assistant is also an important concept and would be trendy in the coming days due to its importance in improving the performance and data processing systems. In edge-based augmented reality data processing, speed becomes important with sophisticated bandwidth and latency. AI enables AR supported by edge systems and also ensures and increases the lifespan of the augmented reality systems (Pan and McElhannon 2017; Chen and Ran 2019).

Overall, therefore, edge computing is applicable to different areas of IT and computing and modern devices such as (Yu et al. 2017; Premsankar et al. 2018; Deng et al. 2020):

– in monitoring of the security systems with sophisticated performance;

– in effective IoT system designing, connection and performances with other smart device connectivities;

– in advancing self-driving cars with real-time data processing, edge computing is important and emerging;

– in monitoring of the medical and healthcare equipment, edge-based systems are crucial with real-time data management for cloud services;

– in designing, developing and creating better performing video conferencing systems, edge computing has greater potentiality. Edge computing supports bandwidth and advances in the management of video conferencing;

– in cloud gaming, edge computing is important as it reduces latency.

2.9. Drawbacks, obstacles and issues in edge computing

Although edge computing offers different kinds of benefits and advantages, it also has some disadvantages and obstacles:

– Implementation cost is important in designing and developing edge computing systems as the entire infrastructure is complicated and costly. It is urgent to review the existing scope and goal regarding the project which includes infrastructure, technologies and applications, human resources, etc.

– In many contexts in edge computing systems, data can be lost as it is able to process only a subset of data. Therefore, in advanced stages, there is a high chance of losing crucial data and information. According to experts, edge-based systems are having problems related to security risks at the local level. Although edge adopts cloud-based systems, it, at the same time, opens the back doors for the critical information security issues.

– Security is a crucial and growing issue in edge computing systems, and because these systems use distributed architectures, proper security may be compromised. As edge follows the data of external networks, it also holds reasons for various hazards.

– Geographic disparities are considered as important drawbacks in edge computing implementation as in many regions and organizations there are localized issues and problems of technical infrastructure and skilled human resources. According to the experts, unpopulated, remote and technologically poor areas may be deprived of the benefits of edge computing and allied systems (Ahmed and Rehmani 2017; Hassan et al. 2018).

– In terms of financial issues and aspects, edge computing may face the problem of implementation and ongoing projects. Since edge computing needs proper funding, it therefore may be considered as a big obstacle (Paul and Dangwal 2014; Liu et al. 2019).

– Availability of skilled manpower can be considered as an important obstacle in implementing and designing edge computing. IT professionals working in edge systems need a higher level of technical skills and knowledge. And this may be considered as an important obstacle in the implementation of edge-based systems.

– A non-supportive built-in authentication including capabilities of the security concern is considered as crucial drawbacks in edge computing systems. It results in different suspected broaches.

Some of the issues and challenges are shown in Figure 2.5. It is worth noting that organizations and the IT Infrastructure team can make efforts to solve such challenges.

2.10. Edge computing, cloud computing and Internet of Things: some concerns

Edge computing is similar to the IoT in some contexts. Since IoT is dedicated to the collection of data from the physical devices or simply the data source, when transferring data from one place to another place, IoT takes the help of edge computing and systems. Today, the data collected by IoT systems are processed and further analyzed with edge-supported systems. Edge computing requires a local source of processing and storage for the IoT devices and for different reasons, namely:

– edge computing helps in reducing latency within the devices supported by IoT and also core central IT networks;

– supported by edge, the IoT-based systems offer faster response including helping for a healthy and sophisticated operational efficiency;

– edge computing-supported IoT system offers improved network bandwidth and therefore justified in modern IT-enabled work place;

– in situations where Internet connectivity is lost, including poor network connectivity and infrastructure, edge computing-supported IoT goes with active operations;

– with edge-supported systems, local data processing and aggregation including rapid decision-making become easy, effective and advanced.

Furthermore, IoT-based systems supported by edge computing are important for proper data management. Here, cloud or centralized data centers help in processing locally. Here, traditional cloud computing also performs the activities as transferring data through the network and this ultimately helps in solving computing problems in a centralized way with the solutions in computing. However, it is noteworthy that the emergence of edge computing and similar platforms does not mean the replacement of the existing cloud computing systems (Paul et al. 2015). Both the concepts complement each other for better digital transformation of the industries and organizations. Many experts claim that edge computing is simply the extension of the cloud computing; however, they are connected as per the architecture (see

Figure 2.4). Here, greater benefits include reducing latency and bringing services to the end-users. The edge network also helps with load balancing. There are many concepts and requirements where both are important, for example some Internet services require data to be returned to the cloud and similar systems for processing after processing at the edge. Regarding in-depth analysis of data mining and sharing, cloud and edge are vice versa important. However, the basic differences between the cloud computing and edge computing are also important to note. In *cloud computing*, a large amount of data can be processed in conduction of in-depth analysis and it also plays a valuable role (Paul et al. 2012; Paul and Dangwal 2014). Cloud-based systems also help in non-real-time data processing including business supporting systems and decision-making and in other concerns. As far as *edge computing* is concerned, it is emphasized on local data that is in-device data and is therefore important in better role-playing in small scale and also in real-time intelligence analysis. Here, real-time data are important and require distributed services and systems. And at this very moment, edge computing needs sharing the pressure of cloud and also takes charge of tasks and this falls under the scope of edge.

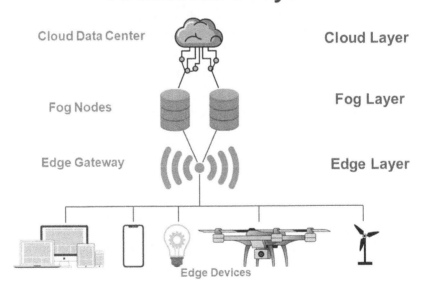

Figure 2.4. *Depicted simple edge to cloud architecture layers. For a color version of this figure, see www.iste.co.uk/chakraborty/smartedge.zip*

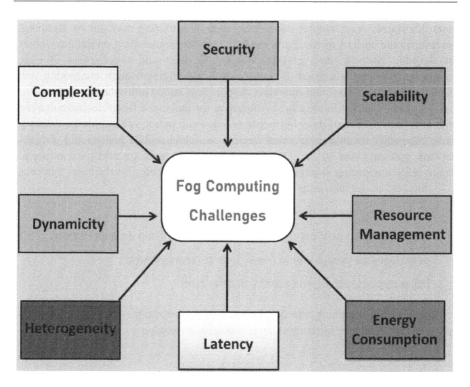

Figure 2.5. *Some of the challenges of edge computing and similar systems*

2.11. Future and emergence of edge computing

Most of the market predicting organizations are satisfied with the recent growth and development of the edge computing, and it is expected to reach higher in coming years. With the ongoing research in AI and 5G connectivity systems, IoT, cloud computing, and Big Data management and analytics, edge computing is expected to grow more rapidly, even more so than expected or predicted. According to scientists, the entire world's data may reach 61–175 zettabytes by 2025, and they also reveal that about 10% data of such category would be from the outside of the organization. This amount is even predicted to increase up to 75%. The growing IoT devices are also producing massive amount of data, and here, the concern is of the bandwidth. Although network technology has improved radically, it is a fact that data centers cannot guarantee the acceptance rate and response time. Here is the role of cloud-enabled systems and emerging edge computing systems that consume data from the cloud while empowering organizations towards decentralized data storage, including leveraging physical proximity to end-users. We all use the Internet for different purposes. For example, for entertainment purposes, we use various online video platforms. Any Internet issues here such as buffering may not be alarming, however in the case of medical and medicine purposes, including operations, this is an alarming concern. And in this context, the uses and introduction of edge computing can be considered as worthy deal and strategy. Such computing will ensure data connectivity, real-time data support, less bandwidth-related issues and so on. Designing a server in the edge is important for quick and better decision-making and reducing volumes of data. Furthermore, edge computing is no doubt an amazing move altogether for managing smart devices including mobile phones and gadgets, network gateways and so on. Therefore, the organizations are really expecting to deploy edge computing systems in the existing infrastructure for different purposes as highlighted in the following:

– in moving services to the edge;

– for providing content caching and data management and decision-making;

– persistent data storage and IoT-based system management;

– better response timing and healthy transfer rates.

Therefore, in designing and development of sophisticated, smart, real-time and advanced IT systems, edge computing is crucial and necessary.

2.12. Conclusion

Edge computing is an emerging information science and technology practice, which is dedicated to bringing and exploring new age data management for centralized systems. It is growing in different sectors such as manufacturing, medical and healthcare, virtual and augmented reality, smart cities and voice assisting systems. Edge computing is also useful for healthy data services, emerging and smart application push, wide scope of technologies, etc. Edge computing needs to be integrated with cloud computing, Big Data systems and analytics, and the IoT for better results and decision-making. IoT-supported devices are booming in the market, and in this regard, fundamentally, a huge amount of data is generated, and here, the concern for edge-based systems is important for designing and developing healthy and intelligent information infrastructures. Initially, only the developed countries were concerned about edge computing implementations, but now different developing countries and many research institutions and universities are concerned about implementation and the further development of edge computing. If different challenges and problems can be addressed with the right steps, then the edge-based systems would undoubtedly be a valuable deal.

2.13. Acknowledgment

The author wishes to convey his sincere thanks to the members of Information Designing at Informatics Research Group, Department of Computer and Information Science, Raiganj University, West Bengal, India.

2.14. References

Ahmed, E. and Rehmani, M.H. (2017). Mobile edge computing: Opportunities, solutions, and challenges. *Future Generation Computer Systems*, 70, 59–63.

Ahmed, E., Ahmed, A., Yaqoob, I., Shuja, J., Gani, A., Imran, M., Shoaib, M. (2017). Bringing computation closer toward the user network: Is edge computing the solution? *IEEE Communications Magazine*, 55(11), 138–144.

Cao, K., Liu, Y., Meng, G., Sun, Q. (2020). An overview on edge computing research. *IEEE Access*, 8, 85714–85728.

Chen, J. and Ran, X. (2019). Deep learning with edge computing: A review. *Proceedings of the IEEE*, 107(8), 1655–1674.

Corcoran, P., and Datta, S.K. (2016). Mobile-edge computing and the internet of things for consumers: Extending cloud computing and services to the edge of the network. *IEEE Consumer Electronics Magazine*, 5(4), 73–74.

Deng, S., Zhao, H., Fang, W., Yin, J., Dustdar, S., Zomaya, A.Y. (2020). Edge intelligence: The confluence of edge computing and artificial intelligence. *IEEE Internet of Things Journal*, 7(8), 7457–7469.

Hassan, N., Gillani, S., Ahmed, E., Yaqoob, I., Imran, M. (2018). The role of edge computing in internet of things. *IEEE Communications Magazine*, 56(11), 110–115.

Hu, Y.C., Patel, M., Sabella, D., Sprecher, N., Young, V. (2015). Mobile edge computing – A key technology towards 5G. *ETSI White Paper*, 11(11), 1–16.

Krestinskaya, O., James, A.P., Chua. L.O. (2019). Neuromemristive circuits for edge computing: A review. *IEEE Transactions on Neural Networks and Learning Systems*, 31(1), 4–23.

Liang, B., Wong, V.W.S., Schober, R., Ng, D.W.K., Wang, L.C. (2017). Mobile edge computing. *Key Technologies for 5G Wireless Systems*, 16(3), 1397–1411.

Liu, F., Li, G., Tang, Y., Cai, Z., Zhang, X., Zhou, T. (2019). A survey on edge computing systems and tools. *Proceedings of the IEEE*, 107(8), 1537–1562.

Mach, P. and Becvar, Z. (2017). Mobile edge computing: A survey on architecture and computation offloading. *IEEE Communications Surveys & Tutorials*, 19(3), 1628–1656.

Mao, Y., You, C., Zhang, J., Huang, K., Letaief, K.B. (2017). A survey on mobile edge computing: The communication perspective. *IEEE Communications Surveys & Tutorials*, 19(4), 2322–2358.

Pan, J. and McElhannon, J. (2017). Future edge cloud and edge computing for internet of things applications. *IEEE Internet of Things Journal*, 5(1), 439–449.

Paul, P.K. and Dangwal, K.L. (2014). Cloud based educational systems and its challenges and opportunities and issues. *Turkish Online Journal of Distance Education*, 15(1), 89–98.

Paul, P.K., Karn, B., Chaterjee, D. (2012). Cloud computing: Issues and challenges emphasizing its application in information networks & its sub systems in the perspective of developing countries. *International Journal of Information Dissemination and Technology*, 2(1), 31–33.

Paul, P.K., Karn, B., Rajesh, R. (2015). Cloud computing and its deployment model: A short review. *International Journal of Applied Science and Engineering*, 3(1), 29.

Porambage, P., Okwuibe, J., Liyanage, M., Ylianttila, M., Taleb, T. (2018). Survey on multi-access edge computing for internet of things realization. *IEEE Communications Surveys & Tutorials*, 20(4), 2961–2991.

Premsankar, G., Di Francesco, M., Taleb, T. (2018). Edge computing for the Internet of Things: A case study. *IEEE Internet of Things Journal*, 5(2), 1275–1284.

Ranaweera, P., Jurcut, A.D., Liyanage, M. (2021). Survey on multi-access edge computing security and privacy. *IEEE Communications Surveys & Tutorials*, 23(2), 1078–1124.

Satyanarayanan, M. (2017). The emergence of edge computing. *Computer*, 50(1), 30–39.

Shi, W. and Dustdar, S. (2016). The promise of edge computing. *Computer*, 49(5), 78–81.

Shi, W., Cao, J., Zhang, Q., Li, Y., Xu, L. (2016). Edge computing: Vision and challenges. *IEEE Internet of Things Journal*, 3(5), 637–646.

Sittón-Candanedo, I., Alonso, R.S., Corchado, J.M., Rodríguez-González, S., Casado-Vara, R. (2019). A review of edge computing reference architectures and a new global edge proposal. *Future Generation Computer Systems*, 99, 278–294.

Sodhro, A.H., Pirbhulal, S., De Albuquerque, V.H.C. (2019). Artificial intelligence-driven mechanism for edge computing-based industrial applications. *IEEE Transactions on Industrial Informatics*, 15(7), 4235–4243.

Sonmez, C., Ozgovde, A., Ersoy, C. (2018). Edgecloudsim: An environment for performance evaluation of edge computing systems. *Transactions on Emerging Telecommunications Technologies*, 29(11), e3493.

Sun, X. and Ansari, N. (2016). EdgeIoT: Mobile edge computing for the Internet of Things. *IEEE Communications Magazine*, 54(12), 22–29.

Tran, T.X., Hajisami, A., Pandey, P., Pompili, D. (2017). Collaborative mobile edge computing in 5G networks: New paradigms, scenarios, and challenges. *IEEE Communications Magazine*, 55(4), 54–61.

Wang, S., Zhao, Y., Xu, J., Yuan, J., Hsu, C.H. (2019). Edge server placement in mobile edge computing. *Journal of Parallel and Distributed Computing*, 127, 160–168.

Wang, X., Han, Y., Leung, V.C., Niyato, D., Yan, X. Chen, X. (2020). Convergence of edge computing and deep learning: A comprehensive survey. *IEEE Communications Surveys & Tutorials*, 22(2), 869–904.

Xiao, Y., Jia, Y., Liu, C., Cheng, X., Yu, J., Lv, W. (2019). Edge computing security: State of the art and challenges. *Proceedings of the IEEE*, 107(8), 1608–1631.

Yang, R., Yu, F.R., Si, P., Yang, Z., Zhang, Y. (2019). Integrated blockchain and edge computing systems: A survey, some research issues and challenges. *IEEE Communications Surveys & Tutorials*, 21(2), 1508–1532.

Yu, W., Liang, F., He, X., Hatcher, W.G., Lu, C., Lin, J., Yang, X. (2017). A survey on the edge computing for the Internet of Things. *IEEE Access*, 6, 6900–6919.

Zhou, Z., Li, X., Chen, E., Zeng, L., Luo, K., Zhang, J. (2019). Edge intelligence: Paving the last mile of artificial intelligence with edge computing. *Proceedings of the IEEE*, 107(8), 1738–1762.

Utilization of Edge Computing in Digital Education: A Conceptual Overview

Education in digital mode is one of the important parts of teaching–learning methods. Various modern technologies tried to implement the digital education. Edge computing technologies are one of the emerging technologies which help to implement digital education. In cloud computing, it is very difficult to manage huge amounts of data to process and store. Edge computing technologies actually reduce the overhead of the cloud. Real-time data processing generates more accurate results. Edge computing uses local data, so useless data do not need to be sent to the cloud, which actually reduces cloud storage and makes the network congestion free. Education and information science is also an important field of study. This chapter also discusses how edge computing advances education and information science. It also discusses the conceptual overview of edge computing in digital education and classifies the concept into different layers to easily maintain and understand the concept diagrammatically. The concept of communication between different layers of edge computing in digital education with proposed conceptual figures is provided to understand the concept of communication between different components. Edge computing actually helps improve system performance, which provides good system reliability and scalability.

3.1. Introduction

Modernization of education is an important part of education. It is necessary to use the digital technologies for the expansion of education. Different emerging technologies have been used to implement digital education. Cloud computing, fog computing, edge computing, Big Data management, etc. have been used in digital education. It is necessary to virtualize the digital education to make the system efficient and cost-effective. Cloud computing technologies are used to reduce the

Chapter written by Ritam CHATTERJEE.

cost and to enhance the reliability in digital education. It is noteworthy that the whole system is network dependent. Therefore, to reduce network dependency and improve processing speed, it is necessary to implement edge computing in digital education. The edge server will process the request locally and may take the decision temporarily. When any threshold value occurs, only it will update the cloud server. Al Noor et al. (2010) proposed an architecture of cloud computing for the education system in Bangladesh and the impact on the current education system. Alabbadi (2011) worked on cloud computing for education and learning as a service (ELaaS). Chandra and Borah (2012) worked on the cost–benefit analysis of cloud computing in education. Chandra and Malaya (2012) mentioned the role of cloud computing in education. Fernández-Caramés and Fraga-Lamas (2019) have written reviews on blockchain, IoT, fog and edge computing-enabled smart campuses and universities towards the next generation teaching, learning and context-aware applications for higher education. Khan et al. (2019) made a survey on edge computing. Koch et al. (2016) tried to optimize resource costs of cloud computing for education. Kurelović et al. (2013) showed cloud computing in education and student needs. Liang et al. (2017) worked on mobile edge computing. Liu et al. (2019) highlighted the opportunities and challenges of edge computing for autonomous driving. Paul and Dangwal (2014) worked on cloud-based educational systems and its challenges and opportunities and issues. Paul et al. (2017) showed a fundamental overview on Indian higher education with slant to information technology. Sacco et al. (2020) worked on edge computing for remote pathology consultations and computations. Satyanarayanan (2017) worked on the emergence of edge computing. Stankovski et al. (2021) highlighted the challenges of edge computing in mechatronics education. Sultan (2010) worked on cloud computing for education. Sun et al. (2020) made a comprehensive survey on the convergence of recommender systems and edge computing. Xu et al. (2019) provided a computation offloading method for edge computing with vehicle-to-everything. Yadav (2014) worked on the role of cloud computing in education.

3.2. Objectives

Edge computing is very important in education. This chapter is conceptual and theoretical in nature and deals with the following:

– to give the concept of digital education and to provide an overview of emerging technologies used in digital education;

– to understand the concept of edge computing, education and information science and discuss how edge computing promotes education and information science;

– to discuss the conceptual overview of edge computing in digital education with diagram and to get the concept of communication between different layers of edge computing in digital education with diagram;

– to discuss stakeholders of edge computing in digital education and discuss the advantages and challenges of edge computing in digital education.

3.3. Methodology used

This chapter is a theoretical work and is interdisciplinary in nature. Various primary and secondary sources from different areas and subjects such as IoT, cloud computing, fog computing, edge computing and e-learning are used to complete this work. The concept of this chapter is unique in nature.

3.4. Digital education

Digital education is a technology-based educational framework. Various modern technologies and digital devices have been used to assist in teaching–learning process. It may be through the use of the Internet or perhaps without use of the Internet. It may use some digital tools. Online learning, blended learning, virtual education, ICT-based education, etc. are the parts of digital education. After the incorporation of digital technologies in education, the teaching–learning will become more students centric. The area of education will be expanded. The time, cost and geographic boundary will be reduced. Education can reach a much larger number of people. Digital education is also a field of study (Paul 2021), and many universities have offered it as an educational program (Paul et al. 2018).

3.4.1. *Emerging technologies in digital education*

Modern technologies give a new dimension to the teaching–learning process. Various emerging technologies have been used in digital education. The technologies are cloud computing, fog computing, edge computing, Big Data management, artificial intelligence, machine learning, deep learning IoT, information technology, information and communication technology, etc.

3.5. Education and information science

Education is an interdisciplinary field of study which deals with the overall development of a person. From knowledge acquiring to knowledge processing, from psychological development to knowledge transmission, everything is considered under education. Education is the combination of different subjects such as philosophy, psychology, history, sociology, economics, political science and international relations. Education is also a discipline that deals with different processes of teaching and learning. Education is the process of learning the cultural values, social values and moral values.

Information science is an interdisciplinary field of study that deals with information activity, ranging from data collection to data selection, from organization of data to dissemination of data. It is much wider than computer science, computer application, information technology, information and communication technology, etc. It is the combination of different subjects such as computer, multimedia, networking, managements, cognitive science and NLP (Paul et al. 2012a).

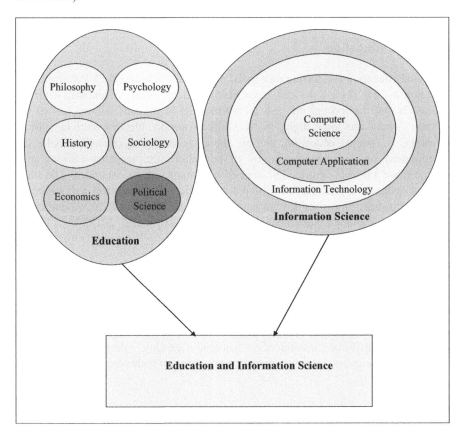

Figure 3.1. *Concept of education and information science. For a color version of this figure, see www.iste.co.uk/chakraborty/smartedge.zip*

Education and information science is the result of merging the education with the information science. It helps to enhance the field of education with the utilization of different technologies. Various emerging technologies and different data processing technologies provide a new dimension to the education (Paul and Aithal 2018). It helps to modernize education system using different technologies. It is a very necessary step to enhance the quality and the mode of education.

3.6. Edge computing

Edge computing is a distributed computing framework, which is used to process the data near to the source of the data. It is a data architecture rather than a specific technology. It is very useful to increase the data access speed and to reduce the network latency time. It works on heterogeneous data; thus, it is more scalable.

It is a network topology where the instant data is processed and stored on the edge nodes. If it is required, then only it sends the data for the cloud computation. It reduces the data sending rate to the cloud and reduces the overhead of the cloud (Khan et al. 2019). It works as an intermediate data storage, which reduces the volume of the data stored in cloud data server. It helps in real-time data computation; thus, it provides a more accurate result. Since it is a distributed technology architecture, it also processes the client data as close as the originating of the data. The cloud computation deals with Big Data management, whereas the edge computing works on real-time instant data. It reduces the network dependency and improves the bandwidth utilization. It is more reliable, more efficient and faster than cloud computing.

Edge computing is used in many different areas such as healthcare, retail, manufacturing, construction, transportation, agriculture, energy sector, gaming, etc. Edge computing is also used in digital education.

3.6.1. *Edge computing promotes education and information science*

Edge computing plays a vital role in promoting education and information science. It has been implemented in various fields of education. Various technologies help to achieve the technological feasibility of education and information science (Paul et al. 2012b). With reference to education and information science, the edge computing concept is used in *online-based classes*.

Edge computing processes the request closer to the connected sensors and devices. Therefore, the propagation delay is reduced. There is no need to transfer all of the data to the server, so it provides a quick response. Thus, it helps to achieve less buffering when streaming during online classes. By placing the cloud in edge environment, the institutions try to reduce the cost of storing data in separate cloud server. Well-connected campuses reduces data traveling costs and increase the bandwidth utilization. Edge computing enhances the *efficiency* of the whole system. It helps to create stronger learning outcomes after applying edge computing in education and information science.

It will help create a different type of learning experience that will help both teachers and students (Sousa et al. 2019). Time-conscious and time-sensitive features of edge computing help us to get instant feedback from both teachers and students. The use of the Internet of Things (IoT) will help us to get more accurate data.

Virtual reality and *augmented reality* are other important aspects of edge computing in education and information science. It is a collection of technologies that create a visual landscape for the student that offers a special viewing experience. The student can view the real objects in the virtual space. It will help to enhance the interactive learning and the problem solving skills of the learners. Edge computing improves the virtual reality and augmented reality concept in education more realistic and mode adaptive for the learning experience.

Various emerging technologies are used in digital education. The edge computing concept is also used in digital education. Using a *smart lesson plan* is another advantage of the concept. Smart lesson plans provide a better educational management. They help us to search for any content quickly and efficiently. Edge computing provides the layer-wise protection so the whole system is more secure. The institutions use different external storage systems to maintain the data of the students, which create external cyber vulnerabilities. In edge computing, the data are maintained locally, minimizing the risk. Therefore, it provides a more *secure* system.

Since the data is processed locally and sending the data to the cloud server is reduced, the overhead of the network is reduced. The distance between the edge nodes is very small, so edge computing supports *flexible* network requirements at peak hours, which could lead to better *connectivity* and better *network management* with real-time data.

3.6.2. *Conceptual overview of edge computing in education*

To improve the performance of digital education, it is necessary to implement edge technologies beside the cloud computing technology. Edge computing concept is divided into three layers, i.e. cloud computing layer, edge computing layers and terminal or device layer. The layers are extended from edge to core, as terminal/device layer (bottom) to cloud computing layers (top), respectively.

In this concept, the main stakeholders are students and teachers who belong to the bottom layer of the diagram. They belong to the leaf node of the diagram. The stakeholders access the edge computing layer using different technologies. Various edge devices such as laptop, PC and smartphone are used by stakeholders to interact with the system. Different IoT devices and blockchain technologies are used in terminal/device layer.

Edge computing layer is the middle layer of this concept. It is the main part of the diagram. It is used to reduce the overhead cloud computing system. Instead of sending all of the data to cloud, the data is processed locally and the resources are managed efficiently. It reduces the network latency time and the volume of the data sending to the cloud. Since the data is processed near the origin of the data source, the processing speed is increased and a more reliable system is provided.

Edges are the node point formed using edge servers and edge networks. The edge nodes get the real-time data and are processed locally. It always analyzes the data. If a threshold value occurs, then only this sends the data to the cloud server. Data optimization is the next phase of data processing. In this phase, the data is caching, buffering and optimized. Resource management is one of the parts of this concept. Edge notes are now ready for machine-to-machine communication.

Fog is the intermediate point between edge computing and cloud computing. It is a network architecture that performs substantial amount of computation, storage and communication. It reduces the overhead of the cloud computing layer.

Cloud computing layer is the top layer of this concept. Cloud computing provides the virtualization of the whole system. Processed and valuable data is contained in this layer. In high-performing infrastructure for data analysis, machine learning has built a reliable and high-performance cloud service for digital education. Cloud data center plays a vital role in storing huge amount of data to give high-performance output.

The edges are mainly responsible for the task performed by the stakeholders and deal with the calculation of the total result of the processing performed by the edges. On the contrary, the core parts are mainly responsible for the subtasks and deal with the processing of the records.

3.6.3. Conceptual diagram of edge computing in education

Figure 3.2 shows the conceptual diagram of edge computing in education.

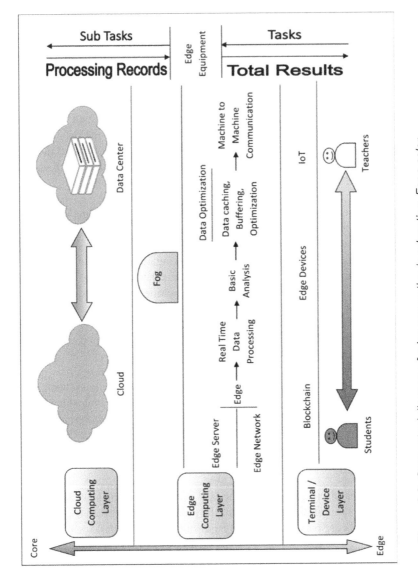

Figure 3.2. *Conceptual diagram of edge computing in education. For a color version of this figure, see www.iste.co.uk/chakraborty/smartedge.zip*

3.6.4. *Concept of communication between different layers of edge computing in education*

Communication between different layers of edge computing in education is a concept that shows diagrammatically the communication between different components of the edge computing concept in education. It has three main components of the system, i.e. student/teacher, edge and cloud. Here, student/teacher represents the end-user who is the view label user of the system. Edge represents the edge computing layer, and cloud represents the cloud computing layer.

In this concept, the student/teacher component will not be able to directly communicate with the cloud computing layer. First, they need to communicate with the edge computing layer and, after the necessary processing of the data by the edge computing layer, only the edge computing layer communicates with the cloud computing layer when needed.

The student/teacher component will request for different services to the edge nodes, which will then send the user interface to the end-user. The student/teacher component sends the request for user authentication to the edge component. The edge component does not have the facility to store critical information, so it sends the request for user authentication to the cloud component. After proper verification, the cloud acknowledges user authentication to the edge component. After that, the edges will reply to the student/teacher for proper authentication.

If any resource is required by the student/teacher component, then it requests the resource allocation of the edge component. The edge computing layer has the power to manage the resources. It will analyze which node needs the resources more according to the priority basis. After processing the current data, the edge component allocates the resources to the student/teacher component.

If there is a requirement of exchanges resources between two leaf nodes, then the leaf node will generate a resource exchange request to the edge component. The edge computing layer will analyze the real-time local data and take the decision about the resource exchange. It allocates the resources to the leaf node. Thus, it helps in better resource management.

If a critical situation occurs, then the edge nodes will send the situation message to the edge component. The edge component will process the message and take steps for the proper situation handling. The edge will not involve the cloud component, so the cloud server network will be overhead free.

3.6.5. *Diagram of communication between different layers of edge computing in education*

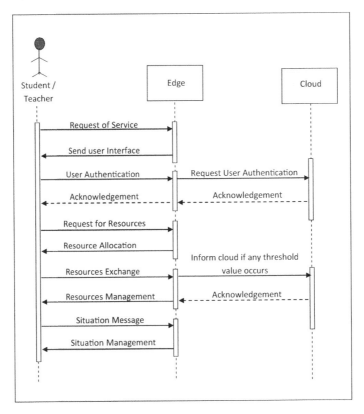

Figure 3.3. *Communication between different layers of edge computing in education*

3.6.6. *Stakeholder of edge computing in digital education*

The edge computing concept in digital education has various stakeholders. Stakeholders play a very important role in the concept of edge computing in digital education. The stakeholders are shown in Figure 3.4.

3.6.7. *Advantages of edge computing in digital education*

The main purpose of using edge computing in digital education is that it increases the computation and processing *speed*. Edge notes are closer to the origin of the data; thus, the edge notes receive the data very quickly and process them accordingly. Instead of sending the data to the cloud, the edge notes process them instantly. Therefore, the speed of the whole system increases automatically. The amounts of data for the edge note are competitively less so it is easy to manage the data for the edge notes.

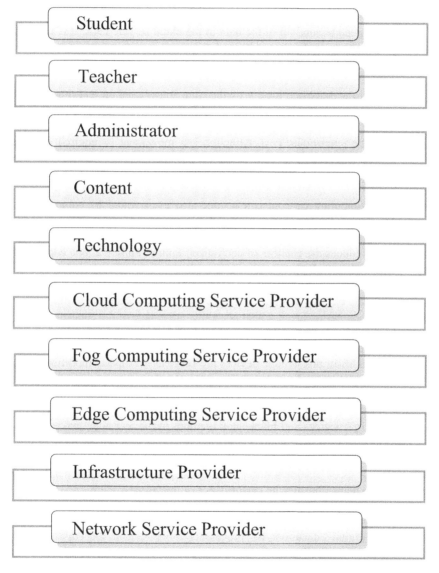

Figure 3.4. *Stakeholders of edge computing in digital education*

Since the data is processed closer to the edge note, the *average response time* is automatically reduced. *Latency time* is the time taken by the data packet to travel from one designated point to another point. Edge computing reduces the number of movements of the data generated from the terminal/device layer to reach the cloud computing layer. Thus, the latency time is automatically reduced by the edge computing concept.

There is no need to send all of the data to the cloud server. Thus, it is indirectly improving the *privacy* of the data. Although the cloud receives a very small amount of data, it reduces the information risk.

Since the data is processed locally by the edge notes based on real-time data, the cloud does not need to be completely involved in the operation. Therefore, the concept of edge computing in digital education has automatically reduced additional *overhead* and the *operational cost*. Although less movement is required, the huge volume of data transferred to the cloud server automatically reduces the *data transmission cost*.

The edge computing concept can be operated even when the communication channels are slow or the Internet connectivity is temporarily lost. It does not need to constantly send the data to the cloud, so it does not need *unnecessary processing* to the cloud so it reduces the chances of centralized failure. Failure at one edge device does not affect the overall performance of the other devices. Thus, it reduces the risk of overall system failure and improves the *reliability* of overall system. Local processing of data ensures an uninterrupted connection between the terminal/device layer and edge computing layer, which is another advantage of the concept.

Edge computing provides a high level of *scalability* to the system. Adding, removing or modifications in edge devices are very easy. Property modified in edge notes may reduce the cloud overhead. Thus, the cloud system is more scalable and more versatile in nature.

The use of IoT devices and blockchain methods at the leaf node makes the *data collection* more efficient. As the data collected and processed nearer to the origin of the data and use real-time data for local processing using many edge nodes, so the data processing speed becomes faster than cloud computing. Less dependency on *Internet service* helps improve the performance of the whole system.

Network optimization and *bandwidth utilization* are major benefits of the edge computing in digital education. By processing more data at the edge node, the overall volume of traffic flow to and from the central cloud server is reduced. Thus, it reduces the whole network traffic and helps to create a congestion free network. It provides the ability to cache high demand content in regional edge servers and puts other contents on a far network. The nodes have the ability to use the entire bandwidth more efficiently.

Data generated by the terminal/device layer may have a lot of noise. Many unnecessary data are also generated. Powerful analytical tools of edge computing technique have tried to classify the data, analyze, process and optimize the data. Before machine-to-machine communication, it has to convert the unstructured data into structured and meaningful data. A well-designed edge computing network combines the local devices with edge computing resources for better management of data.

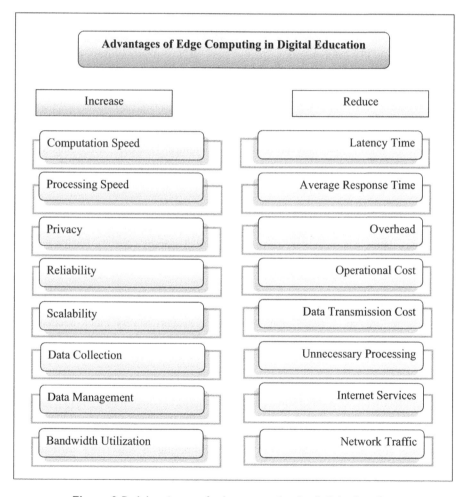

Figure 3.5. *Advantages of edge computing in digital education*

3.6.8. *Challenges of edge computing in digital education*

One of the challenges to implement the concept of edge computing in digital education is that there are some *security risks* at the local level. Although the data is processed at the local level, there is a possibility of revealing valuable information. Since the cloud is a more secure system with a fully virtualization concept, it is very difficult to manage in edge computing. Thus, a very small amount of data is stored in edge storage and critical data is sent to cloud storage.

The *cost of storage* of data inside the cloud is very low. But to establish a new concept is a very challenging task. The initial setup cost of the whole system would be very high. This requires numerous additional components and hardware to be installed. New network establishment costs also have to be considered. Apart from the traditional IT infrastructure, many new ICT infrastructures have to be established. Therefore, to implement the whole system, it needs a strong financial support.

Since the edge computing layer is associated with the *processing of data*, it has the power to discard unnecessary data. There is a possibility that the information, although not useful now, may be useful in the future. However, according to the concept of edge computing in digital education, not all data is stored on the cloud server, so there is a risk of losing valuable data.

It is a big challenge to collect, process and store of data originated in real time. The data is constantly generated and sent to the edge nodes. It is very difficult to store them. Thus, it is necessary to install the most storage capacity for *temporary data storage*.

One of the challenging tasks is the *maintenance* of the system. After the system has been installed, constant monitoring of the system is necessary. There is a chance of system failure, so constant monitoring of the system is very much needed. To upgrade the system regularly, it is necessary to modify the system component. Therefore, the maintenance of the system will be very difficult.

The whole concept is associated with many different components, and different layers interact with each other through ICT technology, which make a very *complex concept*. It is very difficult to distinguish between the processes performed inside the edge computer layer. The interaction between the edge computing with fog computing and fog computing with cloud computing is also very difficult to implement.

In edge computing, edge data storage is mainly designed to store a huge amount of temporary data, so this storage facility does not have a complete core data center infrastructure. Therefore, the *robustness* of the system is very small, which is a major challenge for the edge computer system.

3.7. Conclusion

The concept of edge computing in education is a futuristic concept. After the implementation of the edge computing concept in digital education, the process of the traditional teaching–learning method will be changed. The fastest processing speed and local storage will help the student to interact with the system more efficiently. Real-time local data processing will help to get more accurate results. Less dependency on the Internet will actually help the stakeholders to interact with each other. It will be very easy for the teacher to monitor student performance and identify student difficulties. It will provide a personalized learning experience and will give the student flexibility in learning. A 24-hour availability of the resources will help the learner to learn from anywhere and anytime. It will provide a connected learning, which will help to maintain peer learning. The main advantages of the system are that it is easy to track student progress and to involve the educators and parents in this process. The rapid exchange of information helps us to share knowledge and build self-confidence, which opens up unlimited possibilities for students.

3.8. Acknowledgment

The author expresses his deep gratitude and sincere thanks to Dr. P. K. Paul (for his invaluable guidance, ongoing encouragement) and the whole Informatics Research Group, at the Department of Computer and Information Science, Raiganj University, West Bengal, India.

3.9. References

Al Noor, S., Mustafa, G., Chowdhury, S.A., Hossain, M.Z., Jaigirdar, F.T. (2010). A proposed architecture of cloud computing for education system in Bangladesh and the impact on current education system. *International Journal of Computer Science and Network Security (IJCSNS)*, 10(10), 7–13.

Alabbadi, M.M. (2011). Cloud computing for education and learning: Education and learning as a service (ELaaS). In *2011 14th International Conference on Interactive Collaborative Learning*, IEEE, 589–594.

Chandra, D.G. and Borah, M.D. (2012). Cost benefit analysis of cloud computing in education. In *2012 International Conference on Computing, Communication and Applications*, IEEE, 1–6.

Chandra, D.G. and Malaya, D.B. (2012). Role of cloud computing in education. In *2012 International Conference on Computing, Electronics and Electrical Technologies (ICCEET)*, IEEE, 832–836.

Fernández-Caramés, T.M. and Fraga-Lamas, P. (2019). Towards next generation teaching, learning, and context-aware applications for higher education: A review on blockchain, IoT, fog and edge computing enabled smart campuses and universities. *Applied Sciences*, 9(21), 4479.

Khan, W.Z., Ahmed, E., Hakak, S., Yaqoob, I., Ahmed, A. (2019). Edge computing: A survey. *Future Generation Computer Systems*, 97, 219–235.

Koch, F., Assunção, M.D., Cardonha, C., Netto, M.A. (2016). Optimising resource costs of cloud computing for education. *Future Generation Computer Systems*, 55, 473–479.

Kurelović, E.K., Rako, S., Tomljanović, J. (2013). Cloud computing in education and student's needs. In *2013 36th International Convention on Information and Communication Technology, Electronics and Microelectronics (MIPRO)*, IEEE, 726–731.

Liang, B., Wong, V.W.S., Schober, R., Ng, D.W.K., Wang, L.C. (2017). Mobile edge computing. *Key Technologies for 5G Wireless Systems*, 16(3), 1397–1411.

Liu, S., Liu, L., Tang, J., Yu, B., Wang, Y., Shi, W. (2019). Edge computing for autonomous driving: Opportunities and challenges. *Proceedings of the IEEE*, 107(8), 1697–1716.

Paul, P.K. (2021). Digital education: From the discipline to academic opportunities and possible academic innovations – International context and Indian strategies. In *Digital Education for the 21st Century*, Pal, S., Cuong, T.Q., Nehru, R.S.S. (eds). Apple Academic Press, Palm Bay.

Paul, P.K. and Aithal, P.S. (2018). Computing and information sciences in India: Educational issues, policies & potentialities. *International Journal of Computational Research and Development (IJCRD)*, 2456–3137.

Paul, P.K. and Dangwal, K.L. (2014). Cloud based educational systems and its challenges and opportunities and issues. *Turkish Online Journal of Distance Education*, 15(1), 89–98.

Paul, P.K., Chaterjee, D., Sridevi, K.V., Dangwal, K.L. (2012a). Computer and information science (CIS) education in the universities of India: Emphasizing central universities – A brief study. *International Journal of Marketing and Trade Policy*, 1(04), 277–284.

Paul, P.K., Dangwal, K.L., Chaterjee, D. (2012b). Information technology and advance computing and their interaction for healthy education, teaching and learning: The Ikm approaches. *Asian Journal of Natural and Applied Sciences*, 1(2), 70–77.

Paul, P.K., Bhuimali, A., Aithal, P.S. (2017). Indian higher education: With slant to information technology – A fundamental overview. *International Journal on Recent Researches in Science, Engineering & Technology*, 5(11), 31–50.

Paul, P.K., Bhuimali, A., Aithal, P.S., Rajesh, R. (2018). Digital education and learning: The growing trend in academic and business spaces – An international overview. *International Journal of Recent Researches in Science, Engineering & Technology*, 6(5), 11–18.

Sacco, A., Esposito, F., Marchetto, G., Kolar, G., Schwetye, K. (2020). On edge computing for remote pathology consultations and computations. *IEEE Journal of Biomedical and Health Informatics*, 24(9), 2523–2534.

Satyanarayanan, M. (2017). The emergence of edge computing. *Computer*, 50(1), 30–39.

Sousa, M.J., Carmo, M., Gonçalves, A.C., Cruz, R., Martins, J.M. (2019). Creating knowledge and entrepreneurial capacity for HE students with digital education methodologies: Differences in the perceptions of students and entrepreneurs. *Journal of Business Research*, 94, 227–240.

Stankovski, S., Ostojić, G., Zhang, X., Zečević, I., Stanojević, M. (2021). Challenges with edge computing in mechatronics education. In *2021 20th International Symposium INFOTEH-JAHORINA (INFOTEH)*, IEEE, 1–4.

Sultan. N. (2010). Cloud computing for education: A new dawn? *International Journal of Information Management*, 30(2), 109–116.

Sun, C., Li, H., Li, X., Wen, J., Xiong, Q., Zhou, W. (2020). Convergence of recommender systems and edge computing: A comprehensive survey. *IEEE Access*, 8, 47118–47132.

Xu, X., Xue, Y., Li, X., Qi, L., Wan, S. (2019). A computation offloading method for edge computing with vehicle-to-everything. *IEEE Access*, 7, 131068–131077.

Yadav, K. (2014). Role of cloud computing in education. *International Journal of Innovative Research in Computer and Communication Engineering*, 2(2), 3108–3112.

Edge Computing with Operations Research Using IoT Devices in Healthcare: Concepts, Tools, Techniques and Use Cases

Nowadays, IoT devices generate colossal amounts of data. They are used by scientists and researchers to reveal design patterns associated with them. Edge computing is a technology that uses this colossal volume of data through a distributed computing model. The benefit of this technology is that it reduces data traffic by only sending the relevant data across the network. Operations research is a scientific technique that gives executive departments a quantitative foundation for decisions relating to the operations that are within their purview. Edge computing uses this operations research to make decisions based on the scientific method of analysis. Healthcare is the systematic approach where an individual or a community receives medical care. The Internet of Things is a complex interconnected network. It identifies the system of physical objects that embeds sensors with software. It communicates through the exchange of data with other devices with the help of the Internet. Healthcare service with the IoT has made a profound digital change. Smartphones use edge computing to provide home-centric services like remote patient monitoring, reading heart rate and whole-body scanning. The IoT provides comfort in healthcare. Web application in small handy devices helps hospital management, hospital operations management, operations research and drug suggestion. Other useful tools in use include connected contact lenses, hearing aids, glucose monitoring devices, connected inhalers, blood coagulation testing, medical waste management, GPS smart soles, smartwatches to detect multifunctions, cancer detection, Parkinson patient monitoring, ingestible sensors, surgery assistant robots, hand hygiene monitoring and nurse assistant robots. Vision processing units and neural processing units are the deep learning accelerator's hardware for building intelligent products. Along with edge computing, these units provide remote patient services by distributing workloads in branch data center locations. Waggle, Business Insider and Cisco Fog Director are the tools of edge computing. This chapter gives a systematic review of the reputation of edge computing in healthcare. Today, healthcare relies on machine and

Chapter written by Shalini RAMANATHAN, Mohan RAMASUNDARAM, Tauheed KHAN MOHD and Anabel PINEDA-BRISENO.

deep learning models that are implemented and executed in the cloud environment. Researchers need to address the issues in developing healthcare devices with high power, networking storage and computing power. Healthcare with edge computing will open up numerous new opportunities and challenges for scientists and researchers. Edge computing is the future of digital products, whose outcomes are based on deep learning with cloud technology. Any small IoT device with emerging edge computing technology projects will have a significant impact on society. It can solve the small tasks of physicians.

4.1. Overview

The server is a computer that provides service to another computer and manages access to a centralized resource. Users rely on servers to use computing resources for their development. The edge computing server is a server or a computing resource available close to the users. The content delivery network is a method that uses edge servers to provide services like web and video content to users. This method evolved to host applications called edge computing services, for example, shopping carts, dealer locators and real-time data aggregators.

Edge computing is distributed computing where end-users use the data resources and computing power available in the local server to use low latency. It does compute and have access to resources outside of the cloud, and everything happens at every edge of the entire network. Figure 4.1 shows the basic operation of edge computing. All real-time data processing uses edge computing. IoT devices and sensors, and users generate real-time data (Shi et al. 2016).

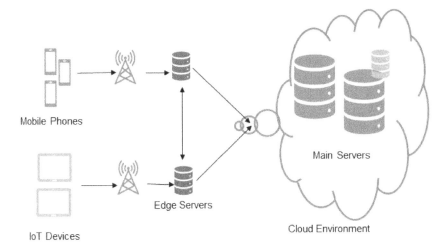

Figure 4.1. *Basic architecture of edge computing. For a color version of this figure, see www.iste.co.uk/chakraborty/smartedge.zip*

The Internet of Things (IoT) entrenches the network of smart devices with software, sensors and other technologies to exchange data and communicate with other devices and systems over the Internet (Lin et al. 2017). Increased IoT devices generate a significant volume of data at the edge of the network. This leads to a bottleneck of high bandwidth, transfer rates and response times. The IoT thus uses operations research techniques to decentralize data and operation proximity to the end-user. It also improves content caching, IoT management, storage and service delivery (Esteva et al. 2021). Operations research is one of the best solutions to complex problems involving the management of large systems of Big Data. Healthcare is an improvement in health status via prevention and rehabilitation. Healthcare practitioners and surgeons deliver it. It is the right way to practice individual healthcare. Health researchers require a laptop or smartphone application to capture, process and track digital data. IoT technology fulfills these requirements (Knight et al. 2021) with the help of operations research. Three typical IoT applications are given below:

1) Internet of Medical Things (IoMT) is an application in an IoT network of smart healthcare devices to connect available medical resources and healthcare services.

2) Remote health surveillance is a telehealth system that helps patients capture Patient Generation Health Information (PGHD) using handheld medical devices and technologies to be sent to healthcare providers to monitor patients in their own or remote venues. This decreases the burden of delivering healthcare.

3) Emergency notification systems are a system to convey emergency information over smart IoT devices to optimize communication during emergencies.

Other IoT healthcare gadgets include heart rate and blood pressure sensors, pacemakers, smart beds and wristbands. There are pros and cons of using healthcare IoTs, which are listed below:

Advantages:

– increases revenue;

– cost-saving for long-term healthcare;

– increases the general well-being and healthy living of people.

Disadvantages:

– security, privacy and integration;

– unauthorized access;

– the cost of implementation is high.

The following sections discuss the systematic review of artificial intelligence techniques used in the edge healthcare system. Three sections of AI, namely machine learning, deep learning and the generative adversarial network, focus on providing detailed descriptions. A short study was conducted about the role of edge computing in essential and trending topics, namely natural language processing and cloud computing.

4.2. The smartness of edge across artificial intelligence with the IoT

Today, the healthcare sector is hugely dependent on IoT devices and has also started moving towards the adoption of augmented reality and artificial intelligence for needs ranging from scanning and diagnosis to treatment and monitoring. It substantially increases the production of patient-generated health data to realize the unlimited potential of these technologies. Healthcare institutes depend on edge computing solutions with IoT networks that work in real time and function at zero latency. These changing demographics and modern technology are driving the healthcare industry upwards; it spent nearly 2.7 trillion dollars per year on IT infrastructure by 2020 (Mahalle and Sonawane 2021; Carvalho et al. 2021). This spending also includes enormous amounts dedicated to data centers. IoT-connected devices such as patient monitoring devices, video capture technology and wearables using healthcare apps for monitoring heart rate and blood sugar levels are ubiquitous. Edge data centers help manage and process this data near the generation point, eliminating any latency and enhancing efficiency.

Edge computing is transforming based on its project deployment. It uses machine learning models to train the network in the cloud. It receives input for the model in real time using end-users edge computing IoT devices. Deploying the training and inference engines at the edge IoT network is increasing. Edge computing with IoT technology is evolving at an astounding pace. This chapter explores the emerging areas of application and the role of brain science in these new fields. With its ground-breaking edge hub, the edge IoT system transforms the face of the health industry. These services are constrained in terms of power, networking, storage, computing, etc. Brain science with edge IoTs demands that physicians, researchers and scientists understand the challenges and find new solutions (Ramanathan and Ramasundaram 2020). However, protection, anonymity and access to the network are all triggering a change in the edge computing paradigm. Table 4.1 provides details about the artificial technologies that have supported the edge computing paradigm in recent years.

AI across edge computing	Items	Description
Artificial intelligence	2	Designing clinical decision systems that are good quality and low cost.
Machine learning	4	Design develops and diagnoses brain diseases, namely Alzheimer's disease. Supervised and unsupervised algorithms are applied in healthcare for safer treatment.
Deep learning	1	Image-based detection enhances edge computing to the next level of advancement.
Generative adversarial network	5	Diagnosis of unusual disorders with Radiological AI.
Natural language processing	2	Healthcare Chatbots – using data extracted from unstructured data.
Cloud computing	3	Monitor and measure the user's physical fitness with small handheld devices.

Table 4.1. *Breakdown of the AI technologies supporting edge computing-based review showing the number of items covered per part*

4.2.1. *Operations research in edge computing*

Operations research in healthcare that produces practically useful knowledge, examples, evidence, findings, information and so on is considered healthcare research. Regardless of whether the research is design-based, methodology-based, or approach-based, operations research can improve program implementation: effectiveness, efficiency, quality, access, scale-up and sustainability. Operations research is increasingly being used in hospital management, resource-constrained operations and treatment planning. Logistics, disease diagnosis, service planning, medical therapeutics, resource scheduling and preventive care are all major issues in healthcare optimization. The approach to conducting operations research in healthcare entails analyzing secondary data as retrospective record reviews and using data generated in the programs. Such data in the field is frequently underused, and many problems and gaps can be identified by reviewing program reports and datasets. Data technology is expanding the number of modeling opportunities available to operations researchers. Modeling these systems can help hospital personnel reduce errors, increase timeliness, cut costs and make appropriate diagnostic and treatment decisions, lowering risk and increasing satisfaction and success (Hassan et al. 2019).

4.2.2. Artificial intelligence and its innovative strategy

Physicians and hospitals are influenced by artificial intelligence. It plays a crucial role in helping the clinical decision system, allowing brain illness detection beforehand and tailored recovery planning to ensure desired outcomes (Saranurak 2021). It shows and educates patients about alternative mechanisms and products of diseases and gives various therapeutic choices. By improving quality and reducing the costs of treatment, AI impacts hospitals and healthcare services (Panch et al. 2019).

4.2.3. Machine learning and its potential application

Machine learning in the healthcare sector has infinite implementations. Machine learning helps streamline business procedures, map and control infectious disorders in hospitals, and personalize healthcare. In a common thread, it provides informatics and medical research. The technology of machine learning introduces advances in brain science research and analyzes complex medical evidence. In this area, many researchers are working to develop new dimensions and functions of the brain network (Chen et al. 2019). Google and Stanford apply machine learning technology to diagnose Alzheimer's disease (Erickson et al. 2017; Katharine 2020). It also provides an algorithm for profound learning in evaluating spinal fluid. Many emerging automated technologies are introduced every year in medical research to deliver safer treatment with machine learning for healthcare. Healthcare learning also includes identifying cardiovascular disease, insulin prediction, liver prediction, robotic surgery, cancer detection and prediction, customized therapy, drug discovery, radiology system instruction, scientific testing, clinical trials and electronic smart health recorders. Using controlled and unsupervised healthcare machine learning will enhance the clinical trial quality and increase the treatment of the patient (Esteva et al. 2019). Other conventional machine learning models such as regression, decision-tab, the Bayesian network, association analysis and clustering analysis use various optimization and probabilistic techniques to distinguish people with normal brain aging.

4.2.4. Deep learning and its significance

Deep learning (DL) transforms the future of healthcare with practical implementations and its experimental outcomes. Artificial intelligence and its benefits for cancer detection and treatment have become widely common. Deep machine vision learning makes medical imaging like MRI, CT, PET and diagnostics more reliable. It stimulates people's healthcare in the visual and auditory context of the external world. Deep learning relies on mass knowledge, so applying smart edge computing technology to analyze the proteins in the blood allows clinicians to predict the concentration of amyloid-beta, a peptide that is a biological marker of Alzheimer's, in spinal fluid (Martinez-Murcia et al. 2019). Here, the data level affects the precision of the analysis of algorithms directly. Deep learning simultaneously improves simulation, natural language processing, and multimedia outcomes; it discovers a new technique to do so without subjecting an Alzheimer's patient to intrusive examinations.

4.2.5. *Generative adversarial network and healthcare records*

Doctors cannot use electronic health record (EHR) data as it requires special diagnostic techniques for the diagnosis of unusual disorders with less available data. Researchers and university students use a profound learning process called the Generative Adversarial Network (GAN) to solve the problem (Goodfellow et al. 2016). GAN is used to generate images, interpret images, generate video and generate reliable evaluations using real and synthetic datasets. The adversarial network uses chronicle details of patients to train the network. GAN has two opposite ANNs: the first is a generator, and the second is a discriminator in the same context. The generator knows the essentials of a given dataset and generates new data instances to make the discriminator feel authentic. The authenticity sets are then tested by the discriminator to see whether they are real or fake, and for authenticity (Kumar and Jayagopal 2020). This method is repeated, compelling the generator to continue practicing having a more robust data model. Recently, scientists have trained several profound learning models to detect Alzheimer's disease with high-precision MRI images. The misdiagnosis rate of disease decreased by 85% with a deep learning algorithm. Hossam Haick was encouraged by his colleague diagnosed with leukemia to develop a kit for cancer therapy (Ramanathan and Ramasundaram 2018).

Based on its design, scientists have developed an artificial neural network model for 17 distinct diseases with an 86% correctness dependent on the patient's breathing, sleeping and thinking structure. Enclitic researchers introduced a system that exceeded a group of specialist radiologists' collective capacity to detect lung cancer nodules in CT panels, achieving a 50% higher detection rate under test conditions. Goyal et al. (2019) trained a neural network model to identify skin cancer by identifying skin lesions' exactness, which is revealed in digital imagery. Google scientists also built a convolutional neural network model to interpret metastasized breast cancer rapidly and reliably from pathology photos. A 99% success rate has been reached by Lymph Node Assistants (LYNA) rather than doctors, with a margin of 38% on specific evaluation slides (Matsumoto et al. 2020). Image reconstruction is a technique used by radiologists to identify disease through

CT and MRI images. Radiological AI has been proven in over 100 hospitals globally to treat over a million patients and has been applied to radiological diagnosis and verified. Brain image reconstruction helps to detect early-stage Alzheimer's (Greffier et al. 2020). All the advanced encoders and decoders are merged into an adversarial network to form a generative structure. This structure makes the image reconstruction more precise to identify brain diseases and disorders.

4.2.6. *Natural language processing and its driving factors*

The health sector easily recognizes the value of statistics, extracting data from EHRs, sensors and other sources. They want operations in a digital system, but 80% of the data is unstructured and of low quality. Natural language processing (NLP) is an approach for data extraction in the healthcare field (Friedman and Elhadad 2014). The data are present today, but with the time and effort taken to be interpreted and reformatted by humans, the data are not very worthy. The need for these unstructured data is more robust in the transition from the service-for-service medical paradigm to value-based medicine. It is where natural language processing and an artificial intelligence sub-category can occur. Several activities happen with NLP chatbots. It acts as a representative of human nature activities. The NLP method facilitates the shift from hospital duty to value-based care for data. NLP-based chatbots can emulate human behavior and execute multiple actions efficiently. The approach can parse data and recover crucial strings of facts to utilize unstructured data when used in a healthcare setting (Hudaa et al. 2019). The value-based approach of NLP is as follows:

– healthcare driving forces are responsible for the increase in clinical results;

– enables value-based patient services and control of the population;

– strengthens EHR relationships with patient and provider;

– improves health awareness of patients;

– superior healthcare quality provision;

– patients who need more care are known.

Radiology is a specific field that needs more attention in healthcare. Here, the NLP uses radiology text files for analysis. It performs two main actions. The first is understanding human expression and the retrieval of meaning. The second is abstracting appropriate values and making this knowledge accessible for decision support and reviewing the unstructured data in records and databases.

4.2.7. *Cloud-based intelligent edge computing infrastructure*

As health and information technologies have evolved exponentially, academics and industry have shown a growing interest in the healthcare sector. However, many hospital facilities cannot respond to patient emergencies and provide a customized resource program for specific people. To solve the dilemma, an intelligent cloud-based edge computing healthcare infrastructure can be deployed (Dang et al. 2019). Users can use edge computing to monitor and measure their physical fitness. It adapts the entire delivery of computing resources to every health threat of the customer for the whole of the edge computer network. The edge tech-based healthcare system provides patients with a better interface. It results in fair optimization of their computer resources and significantly improves the unpredicted hospital emergency survival rates. Due to the very presence of the computing resource request from smartphones as active or inactive devices on the Internet, processing capacity and latency have become critical optimization parameters. The optimal and successful use of the dynamic routing, monitoring and orchestration process of the cloud service is one of the vital challenges. Also, the use of remote computers would encourage the success of the IoT, which would lead to the success of 5G, the fifth generation of wireless technology. They merge the incredible capacity into the conventional cloud or cloud federation to these scattered data structures' idle capabilities. However, it requires effective, dispersed micro-level monitoring of computer resources, management and orchestration, where resources differ in a geographical area and inactivity is still available. The solution to these demands is an edge computing healthcare system. It offers the end-user a dynamic soft pause in storage and storage infrastructure resources to end-users. Capacity and latency have often been critical issues for scientists and clinicians in any network of linked IoT devices. In the next smart era, the number of related devices will expand exponentially, generating a new paradigm change in which the above considerations will become the key criterion for optimization. A business cloud is no longer a viable option because of the rising need for capital. In this case, edge computing is a robust paradigm that fits upcoming trends like 5G technology (Zhong et al. 2019). The architecture aims to include creating business cloud literature of edge computing tools as a necessity. It is a system for universal distribution of capital via the IoT. The business cloud feature's architecture enables the bidirectional sharing of information on the heterogeneous application properties of local computing platforms. The selling method of data exchange for future job makes it more cost-effective to distribute the tools. Cloud resource sharing is consistent with heterogeneous computing devices when determining the feasibility of an operating system.

4.2.8. *Handling security and privacy issues*

Despite the many benefits of using vast volumes of data in EHR applications in patients, risks continue to be present. The recommended approach is "MissingLink" data management. It is an operations research analysis-based method that is useful for organizations in problem-solving and decision-making. Sensitive information is often stored in the EHR databases; people prefer to keep drugs locked away, like before. Hospitals also store non-medical statistics such as patient addresses, debit card numbers and credit card passwords, making these networks the key target of attacks by bad actors. It is essential to protect and retain patients' privacy by providing confidential EHR data and its vulnerability. The primary best possible solution to avoid these attacks is to remove all of the sensitive details from the database for a short period (Jesse 2019; Hathaliya and Tanwar 2020).

4.3. Promising approaches in edge healthcare system

Bringing edge technology into IoT devices opens several new opportunities and challenges for researchers. An edge healthcare system is a promising approach. Its solution partakes in ultra-low latency with a high operator experience, while providing a healthier service to the operator, saving computing capital and achieving high energy proficiency. Through IoT devices and smartphones, edge computing collects a vast amount of data for analysis. Table 4.2 provides a summary of various methods used in medical devices. Healthcare enables IoT to interact dynamically with additional connected objects and acclimate to the present context through unceasing learning from the environment. They can observe, process, identify and excerpt from human information-related and significant patterns. The three different facets of Healthcare IoT are networking, communication and data collection (Alabdulatif et al. 2019). They are described in detail below.

4.3.1. *Software adaptable network*

Healthcare networks are a service driven by complexity, heterogeneity and confidence.

They have specifications for future applications that are gradually self-organized to achieve customer and device goals. They have introduced a "Software Adaptable Network" (SAN) to incorporate the network's basic features and reply to intellectual information (Thomas et al. 2007). It contains the programming application interface called API, edge network status sensors and adjustable edge network components. Since the interface is scalable and extensible, like the other facets of the system, the SAN also has the job of notifying the neural function of network status.

Devices	Methods	Studies	References
IoT device	Software adaptable network	Networking defines the neural function of network status	Thomas et al. (2007) and Wu et al. (2019)
IoT device	Self-learning approach	Communication-responsive IoT products for patients	Muccini et al. (2018)
IoT device	Taking advantage of Big Data	Data collection storage of patients' details with cloud-based Big Data	Bhatt et al. (2017)
Smartphones	Self-assessment software	Monitor, assess and provide results about the human mood such as sleep, anxiety and smiling	Sun and Ansari (2016) and Faurholt-Jepsen et al. (2019)
Smartphones	Medical calculator	Estimate "the foreign fixation indices"	Wu et al. (2011), DeWane et al. (2019), Kerst et al. (2020), Kong et al. (2020) and Larsson et al. (2020)
Smartphones	Resource-controlled edge architecture	Analyze the boundary structure to carry out enduring knowledge valuation	Farahani et al. (2018), Arefin et al. (2019) and Hartmann et al. (2019)
Smartphones	Inertial accelerometer-based architecture and deep feature extraction model	Understand the human gestures with an aggregation model to achieve a final diagnostic outcome	Torous and Roberts (2017), Hassan et al. (2018) and Boukhvalova et al. (2019)
Smartphones	Convolutional neural network	Interpret the unsupervised data with higher accuracy	Lane et al. (2016), Nguyen et al. (2016), Cao et al. (2018), Maresova et al. (2018) and Zhang et al. (2020)

Table 4.2. *Summary of various methods used in medical devices*

The network status is the source of input from the cognitive process, which involves status sensors that contact other intelligent components. Possible local claims are bit error rate, battery life and data rate. The things to consider for non-local are end-to-end delay and clique sizes. If the computer has only a few control points or does not wish to use its control, then the intellectual process must use the characteristics and perceptions of the non-intellectual components of the network to determine machine status. These system states will be attraction basins like a box at the bottom of a pipe, taking multiple starting states. If the system has numerous attractors, and some are stronger than others, a few cognitive control points are enough to detach the system from a single attractor. The water change could be enough to adjust the water flows just a few kilometers downstream of a water change. Any entity or part is included in a network and customizable components, but all SAN variables are unlikely to be changed. Each element should have public and private API interfaces that allow both the SAN and the cognitive mechanism to be exploited. A collection of states can run the adaptable components. The framework would be hypothetically reset by a healthcare strategy for some multi-state aspects. The best approach for the state is the optimal cognitive system – the right way to handle a mental state (Wu et al. 2019).

4.3.2. Self-learning healthcare IoT

Humans receive inputs from various senses like touch, smell and vision. Likewise, the IoT receives inputs in different forms by IoT products attached to humans and the environment. The incorporation of healthcare technology into IoT machines makes them intelligent and responsive, just like humans. These machines can read, think and grasp personal and cognitive worlds by themselves. Advanced healthcare IoT can communicate with patients by knowing and using their human language individually and specifically. They adapt their response to the communication processes and the evolving emotions during the learning process, based on their previous contact objectives (Muccini et al. 2018).

4.3.3. Towards Big Data in healthcare IoT

Big Data is not just a table in a spreadsheet anymore – a tremendous amount of digital evidence generated by the advent of many medical devices used by patients. The capacity to maintain this scale of data is missing. It is a great challenge to the process, this massive volume of data, the results from research studies and experience, data consistency and the regulator's anticipation need to be recognized. The most acceptable solution is cloud-based data. It increases the production of detailed patient results and makes the clinical trial process even more predictable. Big Data platforms handle massive files, so it still has technological limitations and inadequate conditional statements in programming like the Hadoop environment (Bhatt et al. 2017). The specific merits and demerits of Big Data are listed in Figure 4.2.

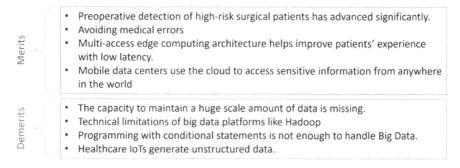

Figure 4.2. *Merits and demerits of Big Data*

4.4. Impact of smartphones on edge computing

Smartphones are more than just a phone. They have more applications, features and capabilities, and have an operating system and storage to manage the computation and communication between hardware and software (Sun and Ansari 2016). Healthcare-related software in smartphones has opened up an entirely new era of health communication. The number of smartphone users in healthcare is increasing day by day. Physicians use smartphone apps to get clinical support information, which reduces medical errors and improves patient care quality. This section describes the rise of smartphone-based healthcare technology and discusses the classification of mobile device applications according to their functionalities. The medical calculator, drug discovery, disease treatment and diagnosis are the most used applications by nursing students, healthcare professionals and medical advisors.

4.4.1. *Use in clinical practice*

In traditional manual therapies, mobile devices have useful features. For example, self-assessment software can help patients identify and track symptoms. In the treatment process, tests can be communicated, monitored over time and shown to characterize clinical results in an excellent graphic display. In the self-assessment process, smartphone applications respond to the essential items for autodetecting severe distress. "eMoods Bipolar Mood Tracker" software consists of a daily monitoring scheme that allows users to enter an automated mood newspaper and monitor subjective mood scores. The software also tracks hours of sleep, anxiety and opioid use and will report to a family member, caregiver or clinician (Faurholt-Jepsen et al. 2019).

4.4.2. *Application for healthcare professionals*

Mobile applications are software that run on a mobile device. Medical professionals in hospitals use numerous applications. These uses include diagnostic disorders, pharmacy reference, medical computers, literature analysis, health correspondence, HIS customers and medical staff teaching. With a few touches on a smartphone, disease diagnosis systems capture diagnosis and therapeutics knowledge. Handheld models are available for smartphones with print medical references, including details on infectious disorders, viruses, diagnostics, therapies, medicines, differential diagnoses, etc. Sanford Antimicrobial Therapy Handbooks, the ePocrates ID, the Johns Hopkins Antibiotic Reference, the 5-minute consultation, the "5-minute consultations on respiratory disorders", infectious diseases and infectious diseases are the most famous examples. These apps also offer functional integration for fast browsing and scanning (Wu et al. 2011). "SafeMed Pocket" is intended to catalogue approved drugs to sell in certain countries. It has been integrated into a support framework for medication for geriatric treatment professionals to warn about interactions, pharmaceutical drugs and clinical duplicates (Kerst et al. 2020). The use of smartphones makes it easier for doctors to access the personal computer and the web version of clinical calculator tools. This medical calculator (Kong et al. 2020) is an application that measures the body mass index, the surface region of the body, the likelihood of coronary heart disease, single medicine dosing, etc. Therapeutic scores or calculating indices usually involve complex, multi-input equations. Consumers do not use or know the precise method to estimate a medicinal rating or score. Medical calculators typically have a user interface to enter parameters and use a standard procedure for evaluating the results. For example, the body mass index (BMI) is called "the Quetelet Index", which is the most common foreign fixation index (DeWane et al. 2019; Larsson et al. 2020).

4.4.3. *Edge computing in cutting edge devices*

Smartphones are the most popular gadgets globally, which renders them omnipresent in our everyday lives as they have many applications. Moreover, smartphones have a wide variety of conceptual data collection sensors, sophisticated operating systems that can work complex algorithms and different networking options, such as Bluetooth, Wi-Fi, infrastructure, cellular radio and more, including conventional IoT systems. In addition to these modules, smartphones have IoT apps that enable users to communicate with IoT solutions. These are from lightweight to increasingly complex smartphones for the application of IoT solutions (Hartmann et al. 2019). However, by receiving data from sensors to solve real-world problems, an enormous amount of the dataset is provided using IoT devices.

Simultaneously, smart IoT devices can take care of anonymity, resources and data security when processing data. For the traditional IoT data analysis, sensor data sent to the cloud needs further review. This chapter addresses IoT implementations on portable handheld mobile devices. It also discusses the use of emerging techniques for creating and storing templates through blockchain, and the joint optimization of computer-based IoT frameworks for cutting-edge devices.

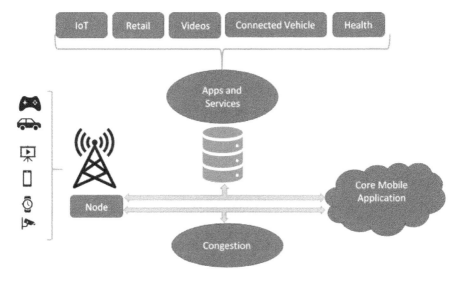

Figure 4.3. *An architecture of mobile edge computing*

However, consider the download of cloud computer activities to complement the resource-controlled edge interface (smartphone) on the network periphery in this architecture. The challenge for researchers in designing powerful models that also fulfill the characteristics of base edge analytics systems is to create and upgrade models for a mobile IoT device. Compared to traditional IoT systems, each mobile functionality is on the same computer, meaning a deep learning model can be generated and implemented easily on mobile. It illustrates the significance of developing IoT applications using this framework and hence the need for that type of architecture. Nevertheless, the framework proposed requires a cloud to build a prototype, update and maintain the features' basic analytical boundary structures. Figure 4.3 shows the default architecture of the mobile edge computing fitted model of a smartphone connected to an IoT network. It means that the edge sensor-based

IoT framework starts with a default model, which is modified gradually by re-equipping the smartphone sensors with real-time data. The consistently refreshing model and the critical device bear on the identical cellular phone alongside the IoT program. It will have a structure that carries out ongoing knowledge assessments and other intuitive explanatory knowledge. Evaluations at the edge of the enterprise are more considerably efficient. Nevertheless, there are numerous customer groups for a particular IoT application, and any application should consequently represent the attributes of the various categories in the applicable subsection. One of the key questions, considering all the information for standardized cloud models, is that the generated model does not represent the particular characteristics of these different classifications. This would result in templates opting for incorrect options or even hilarious conclusions for the other classes, which would corrupt the submission's public display. The program subspace partition into each of its classifications and a dynamic model made for each are used to stay away from this in the proposed architecture in Figure 4.2. New consumers are included for their styles and frontiers in these classifications, and their mobile phone schedules (Farahani et al. 2018; Arefin et al. 2019).

4.4.4. Robust smartphone using deep learning

Mobile fog computing related to edge computing becomes a widespread technology and a link between healthcare professionals and patients. It also moves towards the automated and intelligent monitoring of human well-being. Recognizing human activity is one of the pioneering smartphone technologies in health surveillance. Built-in multifunctional sensors allow smartphones to be an all-round data gathering and processing medium, and make detecting people's actions simpler. The integrated handheld accelerometer is used to understand human gestures. Nevertheless, these conventional approaches do not distinguish dynamic and real-time sensor data.

A solution is a smartphone inertial accelerometer-based architecture to understand this form of human behavior (Hassan et al. 2018). Figure 4.4 shows the input extracted from multiple IoT devices and the model built using a deep neural network. When citizens perform standard everyday tasks, the mobile records the sensory dataset extracts feature with high performance from the initial data and then gathers data from numerous tri-axis accelerometers from people's health behaviors. Data are pre-processed by denoise, standardization and segmentation to remove useful vectors. Multiple sclerosis affects nearly two million people globally in the healthcare field of neurology. Multiple sclerosis causes neuronal defects that reduce neurons' capacity to relay information, which contributes to various effects such as sensational changes in mobility, coordination, vision and comprehension.

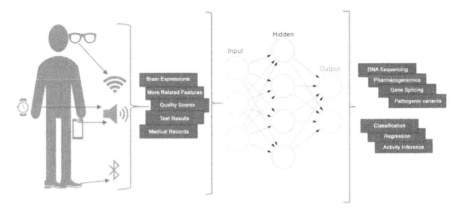

Figure 4.4. *Deep feature extraction and model building for healthcare. For a color version of this figure, see www.iste.co.uk/chakraborty/smartedge.zip*

Multiple sclerosis diagnosis requires empirical confirmation of distribution in time and space of two central nervous system lesions. Naturally, the practitioner will use a combination of clinical calculations to analyze cerebrospinal fluids, blood samples and visualization to remove other disorders with typical symptoms. Only medications are available for multiple sclerosis since there is no fair treatment (Torous and Roberts 2017). It significantly controls multiple sclerosis signs and increases long-term outcomes. For patients, an adequate diagnosis is incredibly necessary. Smartphone experiments are conducted over long stretches to measure various signs of sclerosis in the wild. The fact that mobile analysis yields vast volumes of high-resolution data from various symptom groups is primarily problematic for applying mobile data to diagnose multiple sclerosis. Therefore, both doctors and machines can precisely and promptly classify the critical input segments and achieve a clinically relevant inference from raw sensor data. The machine learning paradigm deals with this dilemma and differentiates mobile data from people with and without multiple sclerosis. At its core, a cautious aggregation model combines numerous experiments over time to achieve a final diagnostic outcome. It will also calculate each independent test's value for model performance by integrating neural attention into the model. This model, with real-world mobile data, tracks the baselines. The mobile data may theoretically derive automated biomarkers for multiple sclerosis diagnosis, helping detect specific trends (Boukhvalova et al. 2019).

4.4.5. *Smartphone towards healthcare IoT*

After a good computer vision, the first applications of deep learning to clinical data are in the processing of images, particularly in analyzing MRI scans to predict variations in Alzheimer's disease. In other medical areas, CNNs are used to deduce the low-field knee MRI representation in section cartilage and immediately foresee osteoarthritis. This technique uses 2D pictures and obtains better results than a sophisticated process, with manually chosen 3D multi-scaling features. Deep learning is spread over the section of several 3D MRI multi-channel sculpting lesions and the diagnosis of variation between benign and malignant ultrasound breast nodules. In recent years, Gulshan et al. (2016) used CNNs in retinal fundus photos to classify diabetic retinopathy with higher sensitivity and accuracy of around 10,000 test pictures of the credentialed ophthalmologist. The success of CNN in the ranking of biopsy-proven clinical images of various skin cancer forms has also come to be equivalent to 21 board-certified dermatologists with a broad range of data from 130,000 pictures. Recently, the focus is on the forecast of unplanted patient readmissions following discharge. Nguyen et al. (2016) suggested "Deepr", a bottom-to-end CNN architecture that identifies therapeutic reasons for longitudinal patient EHRs and integrates those that stratify medical dangers in this area. "Deepr" did better in the six-month time frame when it expected readmission and could see meaningful clinical trends and interpretability. Neural networks in genomics replace traditional machine learning with deep architecture without modifying input features. Schmidt et al. (1992), for example, used a Feedforward neural network with random weights; it applies to forecast the splicing behavior of individual exons of dementia patients (Cao et al. 2018; Maresova et al. 2018). The model uses more than 1,000 pre-set features derived from the candidate exon and neighboring introns. The precision in this process was higher than that of simple methods. Sensor-equipped smartphones and wearables converted several mobile applications for health tracking, like for dementia patients. The disparity between wearable technologies for personal well-being and medical equipment is starting to become softer. A single-wear system is now able to track a variety of medical risk factors. These devices will provide patients with direct access to customized analysis, which simplifies prevention, improves their well-being and handles persistent diseases. Deep learning is a pivotal factor in interpreting this new form of data. However, only a few recent works have used profound models in sensing healthcare, often due to hardware constraints. Running a significant and stable deep-flow architecture on a mobile device is still a daunting job that can exhaust device resources to process noisy and complicated sensor data. Various experiments tested strategies for addressing those hardware restrictions. For instance, Lane et al. (2016) suggested a low-performance, low-power neural network engine to use both the central processing unit (CPU) and the mobile digital signal processor (DSP) without creating substantial hardware overburden. They also proposed DeepX, a virtual accelerator able to lower computer resources through deep learning, which is currently a severe smartphone bottleneck. It enabled a large-scale, profound understanding of the efficient operation of mobile devices and cloud offload solutions (Lane et al. 2016; Zhang et al. 2020).

No	Product	Developer	Usage	Link
1.	Mobile health (m-health)	National Institutes of Health (FNIH)	The delivery of healthcare services via mobile communication devices	https://www.nhp.gov.in/-miscellaneous/m-health
2.	Smart Inhaler	FindAir System	Intelligent inhaler to reduce the symptoms of asthma attack	https://findair.eu/
3.	Health Recommender Cloud	OMRON Healthcare India	Home monitor for pressure and other respiratory disorders	https://www.omronhealthcareap.com/in
4.	Healthcare Chatbots	Orfeo Morello	Messaging service for the use of drugs	https://www.safeinbreastfeeding.com/safedrugbotchatbot-medical-assistant/
5.	Wireless capsule endoscopy (WCE)	Mirocam Capsule	Capsule helps to take pictures of the digestive tract for treatment	https://www.intromedicamerica.com/products
6.	Intel OpenVINO	Intel	Optimizer Toolkit implemented in deep learning technology for multiple application such as face recognition and pose estimation	https://software.intel.com/-content/www/us/en/develop/-tools/openvino-toolkit.html
7.	GE POCUS	GE Healthcare	Produces high-quality images for physicians in all disciplines	https://www.gehealthcare.com/-products/ultrasound/point-ofcare-ultrasound/

Table 4.3. *A collection of edge computing-based medical products with their website links*

4.5. Tools, techniques and use cases

Healthcare focuses on a healthier world with more accurate and efficient care. Many tools and products have been developed for diagnosis, drug discovery, patient monitoring, etc. Table 4.3 explains the products used in medical procedures.

4.5.1. *Smart self-monitoring healthcare system*

Healthcare IoT is a medical device for medical use. It is a technology that aims to enhance an individual's health and well-being. It is a huge and ever-growing market. IoT resources in healthcare are growing every day. They are comprised of all types of wearable hardware to ingestible devices, from smart health software to artificial intelligence, from robots to electronic logs, as shown in Figure 4.5. It allows physicists to cure their diseases by calculating and changing the biological properties of patients. There are many other healthcare IoT devices, which include brain–machine interfaces, in vivo imaging photonic systems, decent DNA synthesis along with sequencing, on-chip sensing with imaging, measuring molecular concentrations, construction of implantable biosensors, biostimulators, closed-loop delivery systems, constructing low-cost devices for point-of-care medical applications, measuring and then changing the activity of electrically excitable cells such as neurons, nucleic acid synthesis, sequencing in addition to analysis, differential phase-contrast X-ray imaging, wireless sensing also powering and designing new deep learning algorithms aimed at systems for early cancer screening through detection. It enables healthcare IoTs for discoveries, diagnoses and treatments (Lupton 2013).

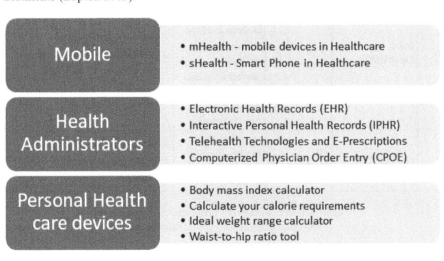

Figure 4.5. *Smart healthcare software for medical practice*

Self-monitoring refers to the capability to control behavior to adapt to social situations. Self-monitoring applications can monitor people's behavioral expression and self-performance. The general population will freely use sensors or software to track and store personal data for self-monitoring applications. It enables personal data analysis to be immediately accessible to the user. Wearable devices are connected to sensors, and tools are available in digital form through mobile device applications. The most popular uses for self-monitoring systems are exercise and wellness surveillance. Self-monitoring systems most notably eliminate the requirement of third-party clinics to conduct both costly and long-term checks. These instruments are a vital advancement in the world of personal health management.

Self-monitoring health devices come in many forms. The Nike Plus Fuel band is a fitness band. It is an example of a modified version of the original pedometer. This kind of computer can be worn on the wrist and help humans to use energy every day. It tracks how many calories are eaten and how many activities are performed per day, while also acting as a clock. The simplicity of the user interface involves the number and indicators that show if the person has accomplished their everyday intent. Finally, it syncs with an iPhone app to log and post personal details and milestones. For most tracking systems, therapeutic importance is greater. A blood glucose meter is a good example. The use of this system is limited to persons only with diabetes and helps users in their bodies to monitor blood glucose levels. It is huge and the findings can be found quickly. However, this unit is not as autonomous as the Nike Plus Fuel band self-monitoring unit, as it requires patient preparation. It relates to the effect of diet and exercise on glucose levels. In addition, users must grasp the procedure tailored according to the findings. In other words, it is not just regular proportions that produce the effects. Since wireless health innovations are becoming more common today, the market for health device self-monitoring has risen. By 2023, 80% of portable medical devices are self-monitoring. The main selling point is the movement of customer knowledge for these products. In the last decade, connectivity to handheld devices such as smartphones, smart devices and tablets has improved markedly. It also allows users to provide real-time data through various devices for end-users (Timmermans 2020). Future enhancements to self-surveillance systems are even more significant. Wearable devices are outstanding in providing real-time data to the individual user. The most important thing to note or consider is the efficient use of these data in a daily routine. The blood glucose monitor does not actively direct the healthcare of a person. However, the patient may act based on data and measures such as pulse rate, electrogastrogram (EGG) signaling and calories. In addition to quantity metrics reported by the instruments, consumers are interested in consistency reviews.

Mobile health (mHealth) identifies wearable devices such as fit bands, time trackers, smartwatches, smart IoT-connected devices and other mobile communication devices, and delivers health facilities, information and data processing for connected edge servers, including the use of notebook computers and personal digital assistants. Notwithstanding financial capacity, everybody needs access to a superbly decent level of health. It has thus been an effective endeavor to build the clinics' operating system that connects to a smartphone app that generates the whole ecosystem. To consult the doctor, the tablet helps people to avoid a "waiting room". It often offers a response, to the frustration of a group of other sick people waiting together. With fewer details in the tablet, encryption and data protection challenges are increased (Ramanathan and Ramasundaram 2019).

The smartphone app provides a self-care symptom monitor and an interactive chat where a child can get helpful advice. This chat service offers valuable information when needed. For effective healthcare, extremely precise knowledge of important symptoms is the most important thing. The accuracy standard should be noted; all medical equipment operates on such measuring instruments from this point of view. The smartphone has now become the integrated ecosystem of communications with the hubs of physicians. A person suffers from an acute brain condition requiring real-time surveillance to live a healthy life at home. The unit acquires biomedical signals such as EMG, EEG and ECG from Smart Healthcare. It delivers these messages to their respective hospital specialist on the core network. Similarly, many individuals around the world are affected by brain disease. Everybody adapts to the new sHealth approach. sHealth is a smartphone-based healthcare approach. Real-time Big Data is the massive data sent through the network, leading to hundreds of megabytes every day for one patient. With so many other patients sending their data concurrently, Big Data started facing network congestion. In turn, doctors' responses to emergencies were delayed. Many other problems also emerged, such as security and privacy issues, because they sent the raw data without encryption. Therefore, the proposed key information is as follows.

The personal edge device, such as a smart mobile phone or a Raspberry Pi, collects biomedical data from the patient. The data gets processed intelligently, the patient condition is understood in context, and hence it is good to reduce the data before it is sent through the core network to the server. What happens internally on the phone? How do we reduce the data? The biomedical signals come from the sensors attached to our patient's body, such as the vibrations that record "EEG" signals. The sensors send the signs to the edge device such as the smartphone or the Pi, where they get classified into different classes depending on the urgency of the data with the patient's status according to their level. Then, the data gets compressed at different ratios. Finally, the appropriate network interface or wireless technology is chosen based on the classified data's urgency.

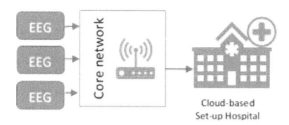

Figure 4.6. *Architecture of high data reduction through cloud environment in hospitals equipped with necessary IoT healthcare devices*

Figure 4.6 shows the architecture of high data reduction through a cloud environment in hospitals equipped with necessary IoT healthcare devices. This architecture achieves high data reduction based on the medical status of the subject. It also achieves benefits such as reducing data and selecting appropriate networks for mobile phone battery consumption. To summarize, the mobile device leads, with up to eight hours more than mHealth and 23 hours more than raw data. Hence, it successfully manages to have the mobile device live longer and the network is much less congested. It succeeded because the amount of data could be significantly reduced by understanding its nature and urgency.

4.5.2. Healthcare development tools

4.5.2.1. Smart inhaler

The inhaler is a respiratory instrument used to transport drugs to the lungs via coughing. A smart inhaler will enable/disable dosing and calculate the dosage given. The cause can be recognized, and the symptoms monitored. It has got GPS tracker units. Both longitudes and latitudes are registered and put in the cloud environment. Physicians use this detail to adapt the care delivery strategy for specific patients. It does not allow a doctor's appointment or a laboratory exam (Saha et al. 2020).

4.5.2.2. Health recommender cloud

The recommendation system is used in many applications of healthcare. A cloud-based healthcare system is one of the recommendation systems. Hospital digital data are stored and maintained in the cloud environment to predict or classify the ICU patients' critical condition for taking immediate actions to reduce the mortality rate. The smartphone's GPS-based system is the recommendation system for senior citizens to monitor cardiovascular disorders (Abbas et al. 2015; Huh and Kim 2019; Ramanathan and Ramasundaram 2021).

4.5.2.3. Healthcare chatbots

Chatbots are smart recommended systems that exploit the various types of available data and related information. They can assist individuals in decision-making in a wide variety of circumstances, from doctors who must make the right diagnoses to patients who may be regularly inspired to attend preventive appointments. Using deep learning algorithms, the chatbot can solve the constraint of classical human–machine interaction, thereby mitigating bias and encouraging the patient to speak more openly and naturally. Text-based healthcare chatbots help patients and healthcare providers enhance people's attitudes and engagement models (Cameron 2018). Common chatbots include HOLMeS, Ada, ABBI, Babylon, Sensely, SafeDrugBota and Florence.

4.5.2.4. Wireless capsule endoscopy (WCE)

A common endoscopy requires moving a long, soft and flexible tube with a video recording camera down the throat or through the rectum. Doctors cannot see the detailed small intestine in these conventional endoscopy procedures. Wireless video capsule endoscopy is a new technique that facilitates the simulation of the entire small intestine mucosa. The primary benefit of wireless capsule endoscopy is that it is the only method used to produce images of the interior of the small intestine (Kasia et al. 2020).

4.5.2.5. Intel OpenVINO

OpenVINO is an AI-based medical tool designed to improve medical imaging, which also promises high efficiency in real-time surgery (Riyanov 2020). Intel QuickAssist Technology is a state-of-the-art technology device that handles and makes the best use of unparalleled quantities of data generated by healthcare IoTs. This technology improves both edge and cloud server performance. It enables compression and decompression of medical files, including MRI and CT scans, as well as recordings such as surgical clips.

4.5.2.6. GE POCUS

This is an AI-enabled point-of-care ultrasound system. The "Point of Care" portfolio is built to suit clinical needs. It is available in all compact console devices, from pocket-sized ultrasound devices to smartphones. It is a great advancement in practice.

4.5.3. Simple use cases

– Rural medicine: the provision of affordable health services to remote rural communities has been a concern throughout history. The rural underserved population needs a primary care facility to assess the physical and mental health symptoms of patients. Long waiting periods will lead patients to miss out on timely disease treatment.

– Patient health records include a wide array of IoT medical equipment, such as blood glucose meters and portable sensors.

– Visiting a doctor must not be a disagreeable or unpleasant experience. Patient interactions are enhanced.

– Supply chain management is one of the really promising situations for edge computing in industry available.

– Operational research in medicine is concerned with the organization of existing clinical techniques and facilities to make them more widely available to patients.

4.6. Significant forthcomings of edge healthcare IoT

Medical devices improve the eminence of people's lives and also help healthcare providers overcome illness or sickness with diagnosis and treatment. These medical devices should be hazardless since they depend on patients' health, which is a sensitive issue. The government should approve and guarantee the device before regulating it in their country. They should acknowledge the safety, security and effectiveness of the concerned devices. The safety of patients is more important when using medical devices.

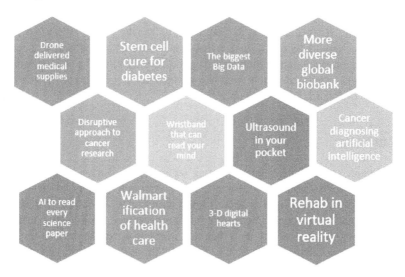

Figure 4.7. *List of future edge healthcare and healthcare IoTs. For a color version of this figure, see www.iste.co.uk/chakraborty/smartedge.zip*

First, practitioners should know how the machine works. They should keep instructions nearby, as well as understand and adequately respond to device alarms. It is crucial to maintain backup through synchronization for emergencies. The general people who choose to use these devices should educate their families and caregivers about the device. Both practitioners and the public should keep all emergency numbers handy. Furthermore, as the associated risk increases, the potential benefit to the patient must also increase. Figure 4.7 provides the list of future modern healthcare systems using edge and IoT technologies.

4.7. Software and hardware companies developing healthcare tools

– GE Healthcare launched a new edge computing technology named "Edison HealthLink", designed for the requirements of healthcare workers.

– Intel presented processors intended for edge computing with features supporting AI, the IoT and security.

– They enable effective, private, fast and offline goods to be produced. For forensic maintenance, irregular identification, mechanical vision, robotics, speech recognition and many other industrial uses, edge tensor processing units (TPU) provide beneficial benefits. In the processing of pharmaceutical products, they are mostly discarded. Edge TPU is an integration model of the LifeLink Chatbots – healthcare workflow. It promotes interactive healthcare services for brands, including picture uploading, moving data, screen recording, snapshots and screen sharing – Telehealth.

– Microsoft Healthcare Cloud builds trustworthy and integrated cloud capabilities to support teams, organize treatment and create feedback that leads to improved patient results and reliability of workflows. It turns the wellness process into healthy and integrated patient interactions and encourages coordination with the health teams to ensure the best possible care.

4.8. Summary

This chapter details the edge computing technology advances in the healthcare sector. IoT collects information from the user through sensors in devices and smartphones. The Cloud helps to store those data quickly and efficiently. Medical practitioners use these technologies to provide a modernized and effective treatment, keeping people updated about their health information for healthy living. Even patients in remote locations get better treatment through the intelligence of edge computing. Engineers are working on security on the one side, and on the other side, they are developing intelligent edge computing products for medical usage.

Artificial intelligence is an advancement in the field of computer science, which helps this edge computing to grow higher in cost and use.

4.9. References

Abbas, A., Bilal, K., Zhang, L., Khan, S.U. (2015). A cloud based health insurance plan recommendation system: A user centered approach. *Future Generation Computer Systems*, 43, 99–109.

Alabdulatif, A., Khalil, I., Yi, X., Guizani, M. (2019). Secure edge of things for smart healthcare surveillance framework. *IEEE Access*, 7, 31010–31021.

Arefin, A.S., Nahiyan, K.T., Rabbani, M. (2019). The basics of healthcare IoT: Data acquisition, medical devices, instrumentations and measurements. In *A Handbook of Internet of Things in Biomedical and Cyber Physical System*, Balas, V.E., Solanki, V.K., Kumar, R., Ahad, A.R. (eds). Springer, Cham.

Bhatt, C., Dey, N., Ashour, A.S. (eds) (2017). *Internet of Things and Big Data Technologies for Next Generation Healthcare*. Springer, Cham.

Boukhvalova, A.K., Fan, O., Weideman, A.M., Harris, T., Kowalczyk, E., Pham, L., Kosa, P., Bielekova, B. (2019). Smartphone level test measures disability in several neurological domains for patients with multiple sclerosis. *Frontiers in Neurology*, 10, 358.

Cameron, G. (2018). Best practices for designing chatbots in mental healthcare – A case study on iHelpr. *Proceedings of the 32nd International BCS Human Computer Interaction Conference*, 32, 1–5.

Cao, W., Wang, X., Ming, Z., Gao, J. (2018). A review on neural networks with random weights. *Neurocomputing*, 275, 278–287.

Carvalho, G., Cabral, B., Pereira, V., Bernardino, J. (2021). Edge computing: Current trends, research challenges and future directions. *Computing*, 103(5), 993–1023.

Chen, P.H.C., Liu, Y., Peng, L. (2019). How to develop machine learning models for healthcare. *Nature Materials*, 18, 410.

Dang, L.M., Piran, M., Han, D., Min, K., Moon, H. (2019). A survey on internet of things and cloud computing for healthcare. *Electronics*, 8, 768.

DeWane, M., Waldman, R., Waldman, S. (2019). Cell phone etiquette in the clinical arena: A professionalism imperative for healthcare. *Current Problems in Pediatric and Adolescent Health Care*, 49, 79–83.

Erickson, B.J., Korfiatis, P., Akkus, Z., Kline, T.L. (2017). Machine learning for medical imaging. *Radiographics*, 37, 505–515.

Esteva, A., Robicquet, A., Ramsundar, B., Kuleshov, V., DePristo, M., Chou, K., Cui, C., Corrado, G., Thrun, S., Dean, J. (2019). A guide to deep learning in healthcare. *Nature Medicine*, 25, 24–29.

Esteva, A., Chou, K., Yeung, S., Naik, N., Madani, A., Mottaghi, A., Liu, Y., Topol, E., Dean, J., Socher, R. (2021). Deep learning-enabled medical computer vision. *npj Digital Medicine*, 4, 5.

Farahani, B., Firouzi, F., Chang, V., Badaroglu, M., Constant, N., Mankodiya, K. (2018). Towards fog-driven IoT eHealth: Promises and challenges of IoT in medicine and healthcare. *Future Generation Computer Systems*, 78, 659–676.

Faurholt-Jepsen, M., Geddes, J.R., Goodwin, G.M., Bauer, M., Duffy, A., Kessing, L.V., Saunders, K. (2019). Reporting guidelines on remotely collected electronic mood data in mood disorder (eMOOD) – Recommendations. *Translational Psychiatry*, 9, 1–10.

Friedman, C. and Elhadad, N. (2014). Natural language processing in health care and biomedicine. *Biomedical Informatics*, 255–284.

Goodfellow, I., Bengio, Y., Courville, A. (2016). *Deep Learning (Adaptive Computation and Machine Learning Series)*. MIT Press, Cambridge [Online]. Available at: https://books.google.co.in/books?id=Np9SDQAAQBAJ.

Goyal, M., Knackstedt, T., Yan, S., Oakley, A., Hassanpour, S. (2019). Artificial intelligence for diagnosis of skin cancer: Challenges & opportunities. arXiv preprint arXiv:1911.11872.

Greffier, J., Hamard, A., Pereira, F., Barrau, C., Pasquier, H., Beregi, J.P., Frandon, J. (2020). Image quality and dose reduction opportunity of deep learning image reconstruction algorithm for CT: A phantom study. *European Radiology*, 1–9.

Gulshan, V., Peng, L., Coram, M., Stumpe, M.C., Wu, D., Narayanaswamy, A., Venugopalan, S., Widner, K., Madams, T., Cuadros, J. et al. (2016). Development and validation of a deep learning algorithm for detection of diabetic retinopathy in retinal fundus photographs. *JAMA*, 316(22), 2402–2410. doi: 10.1001/jama.2016.17216.

Hartmann, M., Hashmi, U.S., Imran, A. (2019). Edge computing in smart health care systems: Review, challenges, and research directions. *Transactions on Emerging Telecommunications Technologies*, e3710.

Hassan, M.M., Uddin, M.Z., Mohamed, A., Almogren, A. (2018). A robust human activity recognition system using smartphone sensors and deep learning. *Future Generation Computer Systems*, 81, 307–313.

Hassan, N., Yau, K.L.A., Wu, C. (2019). Edge computing in 5G: A review. *IEEE Access*, 7, 127276–127289.

Hathaliya, J.J. and Tanwar, S. (2020). An exhaustive survey on security and privacy issues in Healthcare 4.0. *Computer Communications*, 153, 311–335.

Hudaa, S., Setiyadi, D.B.P., Laxmi Lydia, E., Shankar, K., Nguyen, P.T., Hashim, W., Maseleno, A. (2019). Natural language processing utilization in healthcare. *International Journal of Engineering and Advanced Technology*, 8(6S2).

Huh, J.H. and Kim, T.J. (2019). A location based mobile health care facility search system for senior citizens. *The Journal of Supercomputing*, 75, 1831–1848.

Jesse, F. (2019). Query, clone, & stream 45 gigs of X-ray images with MissingLink data volumes [Online]. Available at: https://missinglink.ai/blog/missinglink-features/query-clone-and-stream-45-gigs-of-x-rayimages-with-missinglink-data-volumes/.

Kasia, C., Appannagari, A., Joshi, A., Venu, M. (2020). Safety of wireless capsule endoscopy in patients with implantable cardiac devices. *JGH Open*, 4, 241–244.

Katharine, M. (2020). AI improves Alzheimer's imaging. HAI, Stanford University [Online]. Available at: https://hai.stanford.edu/blog/ai-improves-alzheimers-imaging.

Kerst, A., Zielasek, J., Gaebel, W. (2020). Smartphone applications for depression: A systematic literature review and a survey of health care professionals' attitudes towards their use in clinical practice. *European Archives of Psychiatry and Clinical Neuroscience*, 270, 139–152.

Knight, P., Bird, C., Sinclair, A., Higham, J., Plater, A. (2021). Testing an "IoT" tide gauge network for coastal monitoring. *IoT*, 2, 17–32.

Kong, T., Scott, M.M., Li, Y., Wichelman, C. (2020). Physician attitudes towards – and adoption of – mobile health. *Digital Health*, 6, 2055207620907187.

Kumar, M.P. and Jayagopal, P. (2020). Generative adversarial networks: A survey on applications and challenges. *International Journal of Multimedia Information Retrieval*, 1–24.

Lane, N.D., Bhattacharya, S., Georgiev, P., Forlivesi, C., Jiao, L., Qendro, L., Kawsar, F. (2016). Deepx: A software accelerator for low-power deep learning inference on mobile devices. *2016 15th ACM/IEEE International Conference on Information Processing in Sensor Networks (IPSN)*, 1–12.

Larsson, S.C., Back, M., Rees, J.M., Mason, A.M., Burgess, S. (2020). Body mass index and body composition in relation to 14 cardiovascular conditions in UK Biobank: A Mendelian randomization study. *European Heart Journal*, 41, 221–226.

Lin, J., Yu, W., Zhang, N., Yang, X., Zhang, H., Zhao, W. (2017). A survey on internet of things: Architecture, enabling technologies, security and privacy, and applications. *IEEE Internet of Things Journal*, 4, 1125–1142.

Lupton, D. (2013). The digitally engaged patient: Self-monitoring and self-care in the digital health era. *Social Theory & Health*, 11, 256–270.

Mahalle, P.N. and Sonawane, S.S. (eds) (2021). Internet of things in healthcare. In *Foundations of Data Science Based Healthcare Internet of Things*. Springer, Singapore.

Maresova, P., Tomsone, S., Lameski, P., Madureira, J., Mendes, A., Zdravevski, E., Chorbev, I., Trajkovik, V., Ellen, M., Rodile, K. (2018). Technological solutions for older people with Alzheimer's disease. *Current Alzheimer Research*, 15, 975–983.

Martinez-Murcia, F.J., Ortiz, A., Gorriz, J.M., Ramirez, J., Castillo-Barnes, D. (2019). Studying the manifold structure of Alzheimer's Disease: A deep learning approach using convolutional autoencoders. *IEEE Journal of Biomedical and Health Informatics*, 24, 17–26.

Matsumoto, T., Murayama, Y., Matsuo, H., Okochi, K., Koshiishi, N., Harada, Y., Tanaka, H., Takamatsu, T., Otsuji, E. (2020). 5-ALA-assistant automated detection of lymph node metastasis in gastric cancer patients. *Gastric Cancer*, 23, 725–733.

Muccini, H., Spalazzese, R., Moghaddam, M.T., Sharaf, M. (2018). Self-adaptive IoT architectures: An emergency handling case study. *Proceedings of the 12th European Conference on Software Architecture: Companion Proceedings*, 1–6.

Nguyen, P., Tran, T., Wickramasinghe, N., Venkatesh, S. (2016). Deepr: A convolutional net for medical records. *IEEE Journal of Biomedical and Health Informatics*, 21, 22–30.

Panch, T., Mattie, H., Celi, L.A. (2019). The "inconvenient truth" about AI in healthcare. *Digital Medicine*, 2, 1–3.

Ramanathan, S. and Ramasundaram, M. (2018). Drugs relationship discovery using hypergraph. *International Journal of Information Technology and Computer Science (ITCS)*, 10, 54–63.

Ramanathan, S. and Ramasundaram, M. (2019). Hypergraph learning for fundamental shape detection. *Procedia Computer Science*, 165, 343–348.

Ramanathan, S. and Ramasundaram, M. (2020). Uncovering brain chaos with hypergraph-based framework. *International Journal of Intelligent Systems & Applications*, 12, 4.

Ramanathan, S. and Ramasundaram, M. (2021). Accurate computation: COVID-19 rRT-PCR positive test dataset using stages classification through textual big data mining with machine learning. *The Journal of Supercomputing*, 3, 1–5.

Riyanov, N.A. (2020). Analysis of the acceleration of neural networks inference on intel processors based on OpenVINO toolkit. *Systems of Signal Synchronization, Generating and Processing in Telecommunications (SYNCHROINFO)*, 1–5.

Saha, D., Sharma, D., Nandal, A., Patel, A., Prasad, S.N. (2020). Health monitoring system for asthma patients. *Health*, 29, 4466–4471.

Saranurak, T. (2021). A simple deterministic algorithm for edge connectivity. *Symposium on Simplicity in Algorithms (SOSA), Society for Industrial and Applied Mathematics*, 80–85.

Schmidt, W.F., Kraaijveld, M.A., Duin, R.P.W. (1992). Feedforward neural networks with random weights. *Proceedings., 11th IAPR International Conference on Pattern Recognition. Vol.II. Conference B: Pattern Recognition Methodology and Systems*, The Hague, Netherlands, 1-4. doi: 10.1109/ICPR.1992.201708.

Shi, W., Cao, J., Zhang, Q., Li, Y., Xu, L. (2016). Edge computing: Vision and challenges. *IEEE Internet of Things Journal*, 3, 637–646.

Sun, X. and Ansari, N. (2016). EdgeIoT: Mobile edge computing for the Internet of Things. *IEEE Communications Magazine*, 54, 22–29.

Thomas, R.W., Friend, D.H., DaSilva, L.A., MacKenzie, A.B. (2007). Cognitive networks. *Cognitive Radio, Software Defined Radio, and Adaptive Wireless Systems*, 17–41.

Timmermans, S. (2020). The engaged patient: The relevance of patient–physician communication for twenty-first-century health. *Journal of Health and Social Behavior*, 61, 259–273.

Torous, J. and Roberts, L.W. (2017). Needed innovation in digital health and smartphone applications for mental health: Transparency and trust. *JAMA Psychiatry*, 74, 437–438.

Wu, L., Li, J.Y., Fu, C.Y. (2011). The adoption of mobile healthcare by hospital's professionals: An integrative perspective. *Decision Support Systems*, 51, 587–596.

Wu, J., Dong, M., Ota, K., Li, J., Yang, W., Wang, M. (2019). Fog-computing-enabled cognitive network function virtualization for an information-centric future Internet. *IEEE Communications Magazine*, 57, 48–54.

Zhang, M., Zhang, F., Lane, N.D., Shu, Y., Zeng, X., Fang, B., Yan, S., Xu, H. (2020). Deep learning in the era of edge computing: Challenges and opportunities. *Fog Computing: Theory and Practice*, 67–78.

Zhong, M., Yang, Y., Yao, H., Fu, X., Dobre, O.A., Postolache, O. (2019). 5G and IoT: Towards a new era of communications & measurements. *IEEE Instrumentation and Measurement Magazine*, 22, 18–26.

5

Performance Measures in Edge Computing Using the Queuing Model

Many electronic devices produce large amount of data that should be processed within an efficient time. Nowadays, edge computing is seen as a relevant and appropriate solution to this open challenge to process vast data efficiently. All requests go into the cloud in form of queue. Therefore, all users have to wait until the ongoing request is processed. The edge computing user sends requests to the edge computing service provider to use the resources. If the user finds that the server is busy, the requests need to enter into a queue (waiting line) until the request completes its service. Therefore, this may create obstruction in the network. Hence, to solve this kind of problem, the queuing model is used. It provides services to users with less waiting time. Otherwise, there is a possibility that the user will leave the queue.

This chapter explains how the queuing model is applied on edge computing and also analyzes the performance of edge–cloud computing. "M/M/1", "M/M/2" and "M/M/4" queuing models are used to improve delay and resource utilization. In this chapter, the aim is to reduce waiting time (delay) and resource utilization to process vast data efficiently. Performance analysis indicates that if the number of edge servers is more, then the waiting time (delay) and resource utilization are reduced.

5.1. Introduction

Computing techniques are increasing rapidly every day with the development of the Internet.

For this reason, tons of data have to be processed in a very short time. Therefore, different types of computing models are developed to increase users' requirements,

Chapter written by Shillpi MISHRRA.

such as cloud computing and edge computing (Chen et al. 2018; Reinsel et al. 2018; Li et al. 2019; Wang et al. 2019).

"Cloud" means the Internet or network. Cloud computing is a computational model and plays a vital role in data processing. The Internet is one such medium through which we can access applications very easily. It is basically the on-demand access of computer resources and allows us to create, configure and customize applications, and access database resources online from anywhere (Wang et al. 2019). The architecture of the cloud computing model is shown in Figure 5.1. The main goal is to reduce maintenance and capital costs. It is a world where things are connected to the Internet of Things (IoT).

Due to increasing demand, the IoT-based cloud system faces many problems. Millions of pieces of different information and incomplete data are created by IoT that need to be processed and responded very quickly. Nowadays, the cloud has become very essential to this process. The cloud has been located on the global scale where large amounts of data need to be processed. In addition, the physical distance between the cloud and the user increases, the transmission latency increases and the response time also increases. As a result, users are also stressed. Therefore the processing speed in this environment completely depends on the performance of devices (Shaukat et al. 2016; Du et al. 2018; Guo et al. 2018; Ferdowsi et al. 2019; Song et al. 2019). The solution of this problem is the edge computing platform. To support 5G wireless technology and artificial intelligence, it is able to maintain faster response times, lower latency and maintenance. This is the reason why edge computing has been introduced to the scenario, and it is basically considered as an extension to the cloud (Du et al. 2018).

The edge computing platform is a computational model where applications need to be performed by the edge server that has been placed in between the cloud and user. This allows for the workload to be dropped from the cloud or user device at the location near to the user for processing. At the same time, it speeds up applications that require a low latency response.

There are many articles discussing the mechanism for handling the resource allocation strategy (Ferdowsi et al. 2019).

Resource allocation is a strategic approach for organizations, which provides the procedure of allocating and supervising assets in a specific manner. To enhance the use of limited resources and get a good return on investment, resource allocation is the best option (Anser et al. 2020).

To assign the resources to the users in this environment, various queuing models have been introduced. To fulfill the user's demands, the queuing model increases the productivity of the edge computing environment. Attempts have determined the skilled way to process all users' requests in fruitful way. To obtain an efficient system, two frameworks are designed, such as the single server framework "M/M/1" and the multi-server framework "M/M/C", which are estimated using the delay of the user (Ben-Daya et al. 2019; Leng et al. 2019; Satyanarayanan 2019; Anser et al. 2020; Liu et al. 2020).

In edge computing networks, edge servers can deliver storage resources. The storage resources are limited. To organize and assign resources to ensure optimal resource allocation, practical algorithms are needed. Thus, the systematic allocation strategy is very important, which influences the utilization efficiency of resources (Ben-Daya et al. 2019).

To solve the resource allocation problems, various virtual machines with different working frameworks are engaged. This concept is developed to create and organize by focusing on the CPU, memory and system allocation. To provide services to the users through the Internet, various virtualized computing resources are used. For these issues in the virtual machines, various resource allocation algorithms have been designed to build up the quality of service in the edge system (Satyanarayanan 2019; Liu et al. 2020).

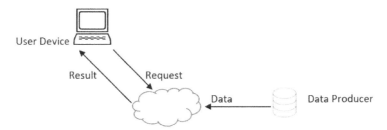

Figure 5.1. *"Cloud computing"*
architecture

All requests go to the cloud in the form of a queue. Therefore, all users have to wait until the ongoing request is processed. An edge computing user sends requests to the edge computing service provider to use the resources. If the user finds that the server is busy, the requests need to enter into a queue (waiting line) until the request completes its service. Therefore, this may create obstruction in the network.

Therefore, to solve this kind of problem, the queuing model is used. It provides services to users with less waiting time. Otherwise, there is a possibility that the user will leave the queue (Jošilo and Dán 2019). If we can use more edge servers in the system, then we can reduce queue length and waiting time.

This chapter explains how the queuing model is applied on edge computing and also analyzes the performance of edge–cloud system. "M/M/1", "M/M/2" and "M/M/4" queuing models are used to reduce delay and resource utilization. In this chapter, the aim is to reduce the waiting time (delay) and resource utilization to process vast data efficiently. Performance analysis indicates that if the number of edge servers is more, then the waiting time (delay) and resource utilization are reduced.

5.2. Methodology

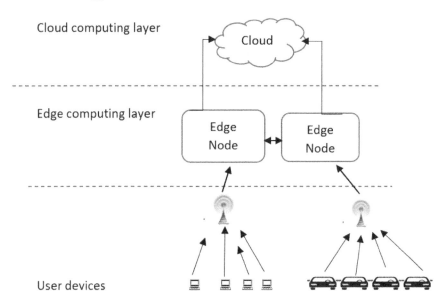

Figure 5.2. *Architecture of the edge–cloud system.*
For a color version of this figure, see
www.iste.co.uk/chakraborty/smartedge.zip

In the edge–cloud computing system, thousands of users provide access rights to the cloud services. The edge–cloud computing system is shown in Figure 5.2. The edge–cloud system can be divided into two layers in a hierarchical manner. The layer of edge–cloud architecture is divided into two sections, namely the "cloud computing layer" and "edge computing layer" (Sohal et al. 2018; Wang et al. 2018; Zhang and Li 2018; Ferdowsi et al. 2019; Han et al. 2019). The "cloud computing layer" depends on the "edge computing layer" to receive requests from user devices. The edge computing layer is the data generation layer. It is a collection of edge devices. These edge devices are provided with sensors, and these collect millions of requests from the user. For processing, it transfers all requests to the cloud computing layer. In this case, edge devices communicate directly with the cloud computing layer and the edge computing layer manages the processing and storing operation of requests. This direct communication between these two layers provides a faster response time and lower transmission latency.

5.2.1. *Queuing theory on edge computing*

Queuing theory is a mathematical model. It is basically used to examine the "arrival rate" and "service time" of a system. Development of queues arises when demand crosses the limited capacity of the system. To calculate the "arrival rate" and "service rate", and to ensure that the request reaches the destination, a queuing model follows mathematical, probabilistic and Markovian models (Gao et al. 2014; Sohal et al. 2018). The queuing system has some components such as:

a) arrival rate: this defines whether the request arrives static or dynamically;

b) service rate: this defines that how many requests can be served when the service is available;

c) number of services: this contains single or multiple services;

d) queue discipline: this defines the way in which the request chooses the service, like first-in first-out (FIFO) and last-in first-out (LIFO).

"M/M/1", "M/M/2" and "M/M/4" queuing models are applied on edge computing. A single server queuing model is shown in Figure 5.4. It is assumed that "x" number of requests, "y" number of demands and "n" number of edge nodes or servers are presented in the system. The structure of the edge computing system after applying three queuing models is shown in Figures 5.3 and 5.5. The requests in the system come from user devices. Assume that n number of user devices are sending data where the rate of request arrival coming from ith user devices is denoted by λ_i. Demands in the scheduler (denoted by k) of the queue are distributed to edge servers and the scheduler controls the scheduling rate.

As shown in Figure 5.3, after applying the queuing model on the edge–cloud system, it is made up of three components, such as "client devices", "edge devices" and the "cloud". The client nodes are denoted by RS_i (where i = 1 to x), which send the requests to the edge. The edge nodes are denoted by ES_i (where i = 1 to y), which are responsible for processing the client's requests to the cloud in the first-in-first-come manner and also responsible for collecting and processing data asynchronously. The edge servers will forward the workflow to the cloud with probability k.

Resource allocation is used to minimize the waiting time. For each queue, turnaround time and waiting time are reduced. Turnaround time is the total time it takes to fulfill a request, and waiting time is the time that processes have to wait in the queue. Here, the resource allocation algorithm is used to reduce the turnaround time and the waiting time for all requests coming from a user's device. It has queues and all requests stored in the linear queue in the FCFS manner (Gao et al. 2014; Shi et al. 2017; Kumar et al. 2021).

"Queuing theory" says that in the first step of the queuing model, the waiting queue is allocated to the scheduler. Then, the waiting time (lower and upper) is calculated for each queue. Finally, the waiting request is designed.

The "M/M/1" queuing model defines Poisson entry for requests denoted by λ. In the Poisson process, the number of services with rate is μ. A single server queuing model is defined in Figure 5.4.

Assume that the request is forwarded to the cloud computing layer. The arrival rate is

$$\lambda = \sum_{i=1}^{n} \lambda_i . \lambda_c$$

Server utilization, $T = \lambda / m\mu$

T<1, for a stable queuing model.

When there are n number of service requests, then the probability S_n is:

$$S_n = \sum_{k=0}^{m-1} (mT)^k / k!$$

In this chapter, we compare resource utilization in the edge computing model using two queuing models, one is "M/M/1" and the other is "M/M/C". The simulations for the single edge server ("M/M/1" queuing model) and multiple edge servers ("M/M/C" queuing model where the number of edge servers is 2 and 4) are defined in Table 5.1. It shows the resource utilization rate. Figures 5.6, 5.8 and 5.10 show the delay. Delay defines the total waiting time for a request.

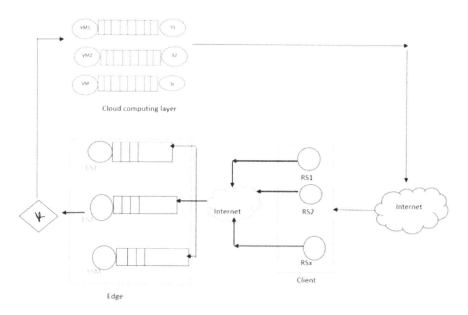

Figure 5.3. *Edge model using queuing theory*

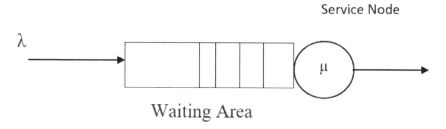

Figure 5.4. *Single server queuing model*

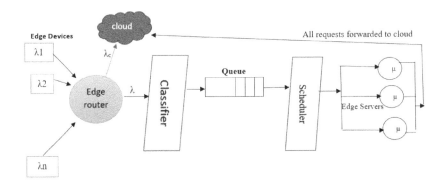

Figure 5.5. *Queuing model for edge computing.*
For a color version of this figure, see
www.iste.co.uk/chakraborty/smartedge.zip

5.2.2. Result

Numerical example

Consider two queuing models for edge computing, M/M/1 and M/M/C, with an arrival rate = 6 and a service rate = 8. We have to measure the performance, i.e. the waiting time on the system and the server utilization.

Model	Number of servers	Server utilization (T)	Delay
M/M/1	C = 1	0.75	0.5
M/M/C	C = 2	0.375	0.145
	C = 4	0.1875	0.1252947

Table 5.1. *Comparison of resource utilization and delay in edge computing using a single edge server, a two edge server and a four edge server queuing model*

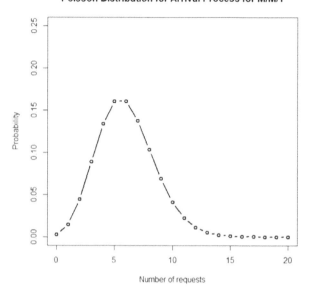

Figure 5.6. *Poisson's distribution for the arrival process for the M/M/1 queuing model*

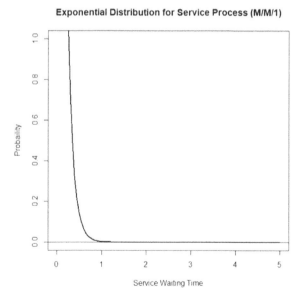

Figure 5.7. *Calculation of the service waiting time (delay) using the M/M/1 queuing model*

Poisson Distribution for Arrival Process for M/M/C

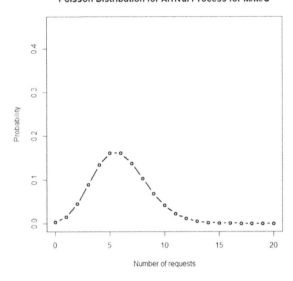

Figure 5.8. *Poisson's distribution for the arrival process for the M/M/C queuing model when C = 2*

Exponential Distribution for Service Process (M/M/C)

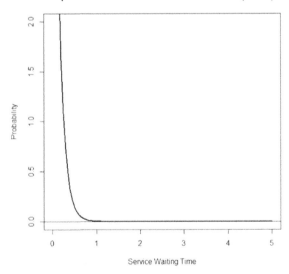

Figure 5.9. *Calculation of the service waiting time (delay) using the M/M/C queuing model when C = 2*

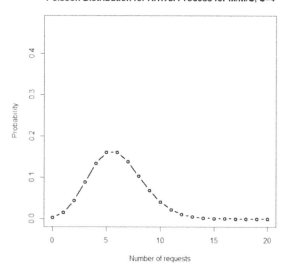

Figure 5.10. *Poisson's distribution for the arrival process for the M/M/C queuing model when C = 4*

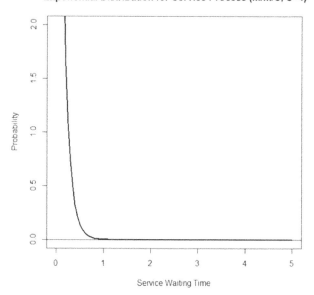

Figure 5.11. *Calculation of the service waiting time (delay) using the M/M/C queuing model when C = 4*

First, we apply the M/M/1 queuing model to the edge–cloud system model and find the performance delay that is 0.5 and resource utilization (T) that is 0.75. In Figure 5.6, the x-axis represents the number of requests and the y-axis represents S_n (probability). This figure shows the Poisson distribution for the arrival process for the M/M/1 queuing model. Figure 5.7 shows the service waiting delay (delay). Then, we apply the M/M/C queuing model to the edge–cloud system model. Here, the number of servers is 2 and 4. We find that the performance delay is 0.145 and the resource utilization (T) is 0.375 when the number of servers (C) = 2. In Figure 5.8, the x-axis represents the number of requests and the y-axis represents S_n (probability). This figure shows the Poisson distribution for the arrival process for the M/M/C queuing model when C = 2. Figure 5.9 shows the service waiting delay (delay) for M/M/2. The same process is also applicable for C = 4. When the number of servers (C) = 4, the performance delay is 0.1252947 and the resource utilization (T) is 0.1875. Figure 5.10 shows the Poisson distribution for the arrival process for the M/M/C queuing model when C = 4. Figure 5.11 shows the service waiting delay (delay) for M/M/4. Table 5.1 and Figure 5.12 show the comparison between the performance delay and resource utilization of "M/M/1", "M/M/2" and "M/M/4" queuing models. From the numerical values, we analyze that when we have more edge servers, the waiting time will be reduced and the resource utilization will also be reduced. We can conclude that the dynamic behavior of the servers gives good improvement.

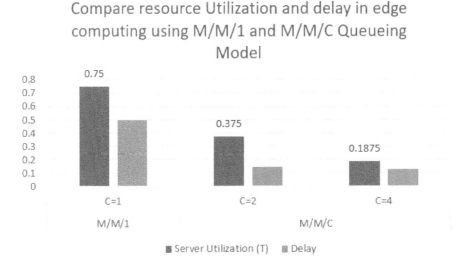

Figure 5.12. *Comparison between resource utilization and delay in edge computing using a single edge server, two edge servers and four edge servers. For a color version of this figure, see www.iste.co.uk/chakraborty/smartedge.zip*

5.3. Conclusion

In this chapter, our aim was to measure the performance of the edge computing system using the queuing model. "M/M/1", "M/M/2" and "M/M/4" queuing models were applied to the edge–cloud system model to improve delay and resource utilization. The performance of these three-queuing models was compared. The analysis showed that when more edge servers were presented on the edge–cloud system model, the waiting time (delay) and resource utilization were reduced. We can conclude that the dynamic behavior of the servers gives good improvement.

5.4. Future scope

Everyone knows Alexa. Suppose you ask Alexa what day it is today? Alexa sends your request, which becomes a compressed file of your speech and sends it to the cloud. Now, the cloud decompresses your request and gets the necessary information from the calendar. The answer is then sent back from the cloud. It takes a lot of effort to find out today's date. It is easy for one Alexa to pass on your request to the cloud through the network, but what about thousands of another Alexas? And what about the billions of other IoT devices that also pass on large amounts of data to the cloud and obtain data in return? IoT devices produce many data. If the physical data storage devices have huge distances from where the data is collected, then it is very costly to transfer this data due to the bandwidth costs and data latency. Hence, edge computing comes in!

In the future, edge computing is going to make the world much better, and it will break the limitations and boundaries by cloud computing for future generations. The future of edge computing will improve contiguous modern networks such as 5G and artificial intelligence. For better access, more capacity, power, global networks such as 5G, satellite, we can use edge computing.

5.5. References

Anser, M.K., Khan, M.A., Awan, U., Batool, R., Zaman, K., Imran, M., Sasmoko, Indrianti, Y., Khan, A., Bakar, Z.A. (2020). The role of technological innovation in a dynamic model of the environmental supply chain curve: Evidence from a panel of 102 countries. *Processes*, 8(9), 1033.

Ben-Daya, M., Hassini, E., Bahroun, Z. (2019). Internet of things and supply chain management: A literature review. *International Journal of Production Research*, 57(15–16), 4719–4742.

Chen, M.-H., Dong, M., Liang, B. (2018). Resource sharing of a computing access point for multi-user mobile cloud offloading with delay constraints. *IEEE Transactions on Mobile Computing*, 17(12), 2868–2881.

Du, J., Zhao, L., Feng, J., Chu, X. (2018). Computation offloading and resource allocation in mixed fog/cloud computing systems with min-max fairness guarantee. *IEEE Transactions on Communications*, 66(4), 1594–1608.

Ferdowsi, A., Challita, U., Saad, W. (2019). Deep learning for reliable mobile edge analytics in intelligent transportation systems: An overview. *IEEE Vehicular Technology Magazine*, 14(1), 62–70.

Gao, Y.Q., Bguan, H., Qi, Z.W. (2014). Service level agreement-based energy-efficient resource man agreement in cloud data centers. *Computers and Electrical Engineering*, 40, 1621–1633.

Guo, F., Zhang, H., Ji, H., Li, X., Leung, V.C.M. (2018). An efficient computation offloading management scheme in the densely deployed small cell networks with mobile edge computing. *IEEE/ACM Transactions on Networking*, 26, 2651–2664.

Han, B., Wong, S., Mannweiler, C., Crippa, M.R., Schotten, H.D. (2019). Context-awareness enhances 5g multi-access edge computing reliability. *IEEE Access*, 7, 21290–21299.

Jošilo, S. and Dán, G. (2019). Selfish decentralized computation offloading for mobile cloud computing in dense wireless networks. *IEEE Transactions on Mobile Computing*, 18(1), 207–220.

Kumar, U., Verma, P., Abbas, S.Q. (2021). Bringing edge computing into IoT architecture to improve IoT network performance. *2021 International Conference on Computer Communication and Informatics (ICCCI)*, IEEE, 1–5.

Leng, K., Jin, L., Shi, W., Van Nieuwenhuyse, I. (2019). Research on agricultural products supply chain inspection system based on internet of things. *Cluster Computing*, 22(S4), 8919–8927.

Li, W., Chen, Z., Gao, X., Liu, W., Wang, J. (2019). Multimodel framework for indoor localization under mobile edge computing environment. *IEEE Internet of Things Journal*, 6(3), 4844–4853.

Liu, C., Feng, Y., Lin, D., Wu, L., Guo, M. (2020). Iot based laundry services: An application of big data analytics, intelligent logistics management, and machine learning techniques. *International Journal of Production Research*, 58(17), 5113–5131.

Reinsel, D., Gantz, J., Rydning, J. (2018). Data age 2025: The digitization of the world from edge to core. IDC White Paper Doc#US44413318, 1–29.

Satyanarayanan, M. (2019). How we created edge computing. *Nature Electronics*, 2(1), 42.

Shaukat, U., Ahmed, E., Anwar, Z., Xia, F. (2016). Cloudlet deployment in local wireless networks: Motivation, architectures, applications, and open challenges. *Journal of Network and Computer Applications*, 62, 18–40.

Shi, W., Sun, H., Cao, J., Zhang, Q., Liu, W. (2017). Edge computing – An emerging computing model for the Internet of everything era. *Journal of Computer Research and Development*, 54(5), 907–924.

Sohal, A.S., Sandhu, R., Sood, S.K., Chang, V. (2018). A cybersecurity framework to identify malicious edge device in fog computing and cloud-of-things environments. *Computers & Security*, 74, 340–354.

Song, F., Zhou, Y.T., Wang, Y., Zhao, T.M., You, I., Zhang, H.K. (2019). Smart collaborative distribution for privacy enhancement in moving target defense. *Information Science*, 479, 593–606.

Wang, T., Zhou, J., Chen, X., Wang, G., Liu, A., Liu, Y. (2018). A three-layer privacy preserving cloud storage scheme based on computational intelligence in fog computing. *IEEE Transactions on Emerging Topics in Computational Intelligence*, 2(1), 3–12.

Wang, Y., Tao, X., Zhang, X., Zhang, P., Hou, Y.T. (2019). Cooperative task offloading in three-tier mobile computing networks: An ADMM framework. *IEEE Transactions on Vehicular Technology*, 68(3), 2763–2776.

Zhang, L. and Li, J. (2018). Enabling robust and privacy-preserving resource allocation in fog computing. *IEEE Access*, 6, 50384–50393.

6

A Smart Payment Transaction Procedure by Smart Edge Computing

Nowadays, smart edge computing is the most promising field for overly controlling other devices. In the future, the entire world may become dependent on edge computing, resulting in Internet of Things devices continuously interacting with other powerful devices to perform computationally intensive tasks. For any transaction-based procedure, blockchain-based technologies will be important for tracking and managing. The data is kept in a blockchain that is protected by a proof-of-work compromise algorithm like Bitcoin. Ethereum's primary value proposal is a fully functional complex business lucidity that may be implemented with the correct programming language. Applications without a trustworthy third party are decentralized, enticing, financial services, identity management, crowdsourcing and gambling. The complex research area of smart contracts includes span disciplines such as programming, consent methods, and cryptography languages for law, government and administration. The state of knowledge in this field is summarized in this book. In this chapter, we provide a technical introduction to Ethereum, a list of current problems and a discussion of the suggested solutions. Substitute blockchains for smart contracts are also discussed. We introduce Ethereum-based edge computing that is cost-effective and more secure for any transactions.

6.1. Introduction

Bitcoin is the first fully decentralized money, invented in 2008 and successfully implemented in 2009. It cleverly combines cryptographic techniques with financial inducements to boost the possibility that balanced participants would respect the rules. The market value of Bitcoin increased dramatically, topping $80 billion in September 2017. Hundreds of rival cryptocurrencies with a similar general architecture have developed since the launch of Bitcoin. To ensure security, early

Chapter written by Animesh UPADHYAYA, Koushik MUKHOPADHYAY, Amejul ISLAM, Shaon Kalyan MODAK and Debdutta PAL.

blockchains purposely kept programming languages basic, such as the Bitcoin scripting language (Nakamoto 2008; Urquhart 2016; Koutmos 2018; De Vries 2020).

The Ethereum platform allows developers to create sophisticated decentralized apps that include built-in economic functionalities. It decreases or eliminates censorship and some counterparty risks while delivering high availability, auditability, transparency and impartiality. Many individuals will come to Ethereum with existing knowledge of cryptocurrencies, particularly Bitcoin. Ethereum has many features in common with other open blockchains, including a peer-to-peer network that connects participants, a Byzantine fault-tolerant consensus algorithm for synchronization of state updates (a proof of work blockchain), the use of cryptographic primitives such as digital signatures and hashes, and a digital currency (ether) (Abd-El-Malek et al. 2005; Buterin 2014; Wood 2014).

Ethereum's primary goal is not to create a digital currency payment network. While the digital currency ether is essential to the operation of Ethereum, it is meant as a utility currency to pay for the usage of the Ethereum platform as the world computer. In contrast to Bitcoin, which has a fairly restricted scripting language, Ethereum is intended to be a general-purpose programmable blockchain with a virtual machine capable of running a code of arbitrary and unfettered length. While the Bitcoin script language is designed for a simple true/false assessment of spending conditions, Ethereum's language is becoming more comprehensive, which means that Ethereum can serve as a general-purpose computer (Buterin 2014).

Ethereum, like all great technologies, solves real-world challenges. It was created at a time when individuals realized the strength of the Bitcoin concept and were looking for ways to expand beyond monetary applications. However, developers were confronted with a dilemma: either build on top of Bitcoin or create a separate blockchain. Building on Bitcoin meant adhering to the intentional constraints of network sizes of data storage, which seemed to limit the types of applications that could run directly on Bitcoin; anything else required additional off-chain layers, which immediately negated many of the benefits of using a public blockchain (Clement et al. 2009).

Around the end of 2013, Vitalik Buterin, a young programmer and Bitcoin enthusiast, began to consider ways to expand the capabilities of Bitcoin and Mastercoin (an overlay protocol that extended Bitcoin to offer rudimentary smart contracts). In October of that year, Buterin offered a more universal approach to the Mastercoin team, one that permitted flexible and scriptable (but not Turing-complete) contracts to replace Mastercoin's proprietary contract language. The Mastercoin team was impressed, but their plan was too extreme to fit inside their development timeline (Buterin 2014).

In December 2013, Buterin started distributing a white paper outlining the Ethereum concept: a Turing-complete, general-purpose blockchain. A few dozen individuals saw this early draught and provided input, assisting Buterin in refining the plan. The writers of this book both obtained an early draught of the white paper and collaborated on it. Andreas M. Antonopoulos was interested by the concept and urged Buterin to refine it (Buterin 2014).

There are several concerns about the usage of a separate blockchain to impose consensus rules on smart contract execution, as well as the ramifications of a Turing-complete language. Antonopoulos continued to monitor Ethereum's growth with great curiosity, although he was in the early stages of authoring his book *Mastering Bitcoin* at the time, and he did not join in with Ethereum directly until much later. Dr. Gavin Wood, on the other hand, was one of the first to contact Buterin and offer to assist him with his C++ programming abilities. Wood was appointed as the cofounder, codesigner and CTO of Ethereum.

Externally owned accounts (EOAs) and contract accounts are the two types of accounts in Ethereum. Users control EOAs, sometimes using software that is not part of the Ethereum platform, such as a wallet program. Contract accounts, on the other hand, are managed by a program code (also known as "smart contracts") that is performed by the Ethereum Virtual Machine. In brief, EOAs are basic accounts with no accompanying code or data storage, whereas contract accounts have both. EOAs are controlled by transactions created and cryptographically signed with a private key in the "real world" external to and independent of the protocol, whereas contract accounts do not have private keys and so "control themselves" in the predetermined way prescribed by their smart contract code (Bezerra et al. 2000; Kranzler et al. 2003). Both types of accounts are identified by an Ethereum address. In this chapter, we will discuss contract accounts and the program code that controls them.

6.2. Related works

Cloud computing is one of the popular platforms by which we can easily use the storage and processing of information from the Internet of Things (IoT) (Zhang et al. 2010). But nowadays, one of the signing procedures is used, which is the alternative process of the previous ones, i.e. the edge computing (Satyanarayanan 2017). Edge computing can effectively utilize a few resources while giving them the instructions for mobile device usage (Satyanarayanan 2009). Chen and Xu (2017) outlined the way that small cell base stations (SBSs) are used in edge computing, which mainly improve the latency and location awareness of resource utilization. They also mentioned the opportunity to create an association of these devices to share their resources, which is mainly performed in the secured network to minimize the risk for the payment procedure. Xiong et al. (2017) described the procedure for creating the mobile chain with the help of edge computing in the field of healthcare, finance, etc. We analyzed the prototype model in their paper; they used it for two different cases: the first one is where the relationship between the optimal edge service and mining rewards is fixed, and the other one is where those are the variable and produce the results which define an optimal resource management policy. Stanciu (2017) described the execution of blockchain-based technology, which supports the distributed control system of the edge computing with the help of Hyperledger Fabric, which is the one of the important factors of the blockchain because it creates functional blocks as a smart container that will be executed by the blockchain and envoy the tasks and resources using the Dockers containers. The smart payment procedure is mainly performed by the smart contracts, as described by Szabo (1997). It basically performs the verification or checking at the time of execution of any contracts with the help of a software implementation. But this implementation can be performed with the help of a Bitcoin protocol (Back and Bentov 2014). The Ethereum protocol, which is mostly used for open blockchain systems (Buterin et al. 2014), is one of the best. It is primarily a state transaction machine that will be processed by a code concurrently with the help of all the miners at the decentralized Ethereum Virtual Machine (Wood 2014). This machine basically works with the principle of the Turing machine. The smart payment, which totally depends on the concept of Ethereum, can be coded through many approaches, but among those approaches, there is a best approach, which is mainly used nowadays, that is solidity. The solidity is basically a specialized programming language (Dannen 2017).

6.3. Ethereum

The original blockchain, essentially Bitcoin's blockchain, keeps track of the status and ownership of Bitcoin units. Consider Bitcoin to be a distributed consensus state machine, where transactions create a global state change, changing coin ownership. After multiple blocks are mined, the state transitions are controlled by consensus rules, allowing all players to (eventually) converge on a shared (consensus) state of the system.

Ethereum is also a distributed state machine. Ethereum, on the other hand, records the state changes of a data store, or a store that may hold any data expressible as a key-value tuple, as opposed to only maintaining the status of currency ownership. In a key-value data storage, random values are kept and each may be retrieved using a key. In some aspects, this is similar to the data storage model of RAM used by the majority of computers. Ethereum contains memory that holds both code and data, and it tracks how this memory changes over time using the

Ethereum blockchain. Ethereum, like a generally stored-program computer, can load and run code, recording the subsequent state changes in its blockchain. Two important distinctions between Ethereum and other computers are that Ethereum state updates are managed by consensus rules and that the state is dispersed worldwide (Mukhopadhyay 2018; Pustišek and Kos 2018).

6.3.1. *Ethereum's four stages of development*

Ethereum's development was strategic in four stages, with significant modifications occurring at each stage. A stage may feature "hard forks", which modify performance in a method that is retrograde companionable.

Frontier, Homestead, Metropolis and Serenity are the four major development stages. Ice Age, DAO, Tangerine Whistle, Spurious Dragon, Byzantium, Constantinople/St. Petersburg, Istanbul and Muir Glacier are the codenames for the intermediate hard forks that have happened thus far (Antonopoulos and Wood 2018). The following chronology, which is "dated" by block number, depicts both the development stages and the interim hard forks:

Block #0

Frontier – Ethereum's first stage, which lasted from July 30, 2015 until March 2016.

Block #200,000

Ice Age – a rigid divergence that provided an exponential difficulty increase in order to encourage a shift to PoS when it is ready.

Block #1,150,000

Homestead – Ethereum's second phase, introduced in March 2016.

Block #1,192,000

DAO – a rigid divergence that divided Ethereum and Ethereum Classic into two competing platforms in order to compensate victims of the compromised DAO contract.

Block #2,463,000

Tangerine Whistle – a rigid divergence that was created to modify the gas computation for some I/O-heavy activities and remove the hoarded assert from a DoS assault that took advantage of those processes' low gas cost.

Block #2,675,000

Spurious Dragon – a rigid divergence that was created to handle additional denial-of-service (DoS) attack trajectories, as well as another state clearing. A reiteration occurrence defense method is also included.

Block #4,370,000

Metropolis Byzantium – Metropolis is Ethereum's third phase. Byzantium, the first phase of Metropolis, was released in October 2017, introducing low-level functions and modifying the block recompence and strain.

Block #7,280,000

Constantinople/St. Petersburg – Constantinople was to be the second half of Metropolis, with comparable enhancements. A significant Bug was uncovered just hours before its activation. As a result, the hard fork was postponed and renamed St. Petersburg.

Block #9,069,000

Istanbul – a supplementary rigid divergence with the equivalent tactic, and identification settlement, as for the prior two.

Block #9,200,000

Muir Glacier – a rigid divergence whose primary goal was to alter the difficulty owing to the Ice Age's exponential rise.

We have also announced two hard forks, Berlin and London, and we are currently in the last phase of Ethereum progress, nicknamed Tranquility. Tranquility requires a significant infrastructure overhaul that will make Ethereum supplementary accessible, safe and supportable. It is marketed as "Ethereum 2.0", the second edition of Ethereum.

6.4. Ethereum's components

In Ethereum, the components of a blockchain system are described as follows.

6.4.1. *P2P network*

P2P is a technology that is built on a very simple premise known as decentralization. Blockchain's peer-to-peer design enables all cryptocurrencies to be exchanged globally without the use of a middleman, middlemen or centralized server. Anyone who wishes to participate in the process of verifying and validating blocks on the decentralized peer-to-peer network can set up a Bitcoin node. The ÐƐVp2p protocol is used by Ethereum, which is accessible on the Ethereum foremost system through TCP port 30303 (Kim et al. 2018; Gao et al. 2019).

6.4.2. *Consensus rules*

Ethereum uses a proof-of-stake consensus process, which derives its crypto-economic security from a system of incentives and penalties applied to stacker's capital. This incentive structure encourages individual stakeholders to run honest validators, punishes those who do not and makes attacking the network exceedingly expensive.

Then, there is a system that defines how trustworthy validators are chosen to propose or validate blocks, process transactions and vote for their preferred chain head. There is a fork-choice process that picks blocks that make up the "heaviest" chain, assessed by the number of validators that voted for the blocks weighted by their staked ether balance, in the rare cases where numerous blocks are in the same position near the head of the chain (Ritz and Zugenmaier 2018; Zhu 2019).

6.4.3. *Transactions*

Ethereum transactions are network messages that include (among other things) a sender, recipient, value and data payload.

6.4.4. *State machine*

Ethereum state transitions are processed by the Ethereum Virtual Machine (EVM), a stack-based virtual machine that executes bytecode (machine-language instructions). EVM programs, called "smart contracts", are written in high-level languages (e.g. Solidity) and compiled to bytecode for execution on the EVM.

6.4.5. *Data structures*

Ethereum's state is stored locally on each node as a database (usually Google's LevelDB), which contains the transactions and system state in a serialized hashed data structure called a Merkle Patricia Tree (Bonneau 2016).

6.4.6. *Consensus algorithm*

Ethereum uses Bitcoin's consensus model, Nakamoto Consensus, which uses sequential single-signature blocks, weighted in importance by PoW to determine the longest chain and therefore the current state. However, there are plans to move to a PoS-weighted voting system, codenamed Casper, in the near future (Shurov et al. 2019).

6.4.7. *Economic security*

Ethereum currently uses a PoW algorithm called Ethash, but this will eventually be dropped with the move to PoS at some point in the future (Chiu et al. 2021).

6.4.8. *Clients*

Ethereum has several interoperable implementations of the client software, the most prominent of which are Go-Ethereum (Geth) and Parity (Cai et al. 2020).

6.5. General-purpose blockchains to decentralized applications (DApps)

Ethereum started as a way to make a general-purpose blockchain that could be programmed for a variety of uses. But very quickly, the vision of Ethereum expanded into a platform for programming DApps. DApps represent a broader perspective than smart contracts. A DApp is, at the very least, a smart contract and a web user interface. More broadly, a DApp is a web application that is built on top of open, decentralized, peer-to-peer infrastructure services (Wu et al. 2021).

A DApp is composed of at least:

– smart contracts on a blockchain;

– a web frontend user interface.

Many DApps also have additional decentralized elements, such as:

– a decentralized (P2P) storage protocol and platform;

– a decentralized (P2P) messaging protocol and platform.

6.6. Ether currency units

The currency unit Ethereum is called ether, recognized correspondingly as "ETH" or with the signs Ξ (from the Greek letter "Xi" that appears similar to a stylized capital E) or, less often, ♦: for example, 1 ether, or 1 ETH, or Ξ1, or ♦1.

Ether is broken down into smaller components, all the way down to the lowest conceivable unit, wei. One quintillion wei (1 * 1,018 or 1,000,000,000,000,000,000) equals one ether. We may also perceive the coinage "Ethereum" mentioned; however, this is a typical novice's error. Ethereum is the operating system, while ether is the money.

Internally, in Ethereum, ether is continuously characterized as an unsigned integer value with a wei unit of measure. When we trade 1 ether, the transaction converts the value as 1,000,000,000,000,000,000 wei.

Ether's different values have both a technical term that uses the International System of Units (SI) and a conversational term that recompenses with respect to several of computing's and cryptography's great brains.

Ether quantities and component terms display numerous units, as well as their informal (common) terms and SI designations. In line with the inner illustration of values, all values are displayed in wei (first row), with ether depicted as 1,018 wei in the seventh row (Delmolino et al. 2016).

6.7. Ethereum wallet

The term "wallet" has evolved to signify a variety of things, all of which are connected and, on a daily basis, amount to the same thing. The term "wallet" refers to a software program that assists us in managing our Ethereum account. In a nutshell, an Ethereum wallet serves as our entry point into the Ethereum system. It has access to our keys and may initiate and publish transactions on our behalf. Choosing an Ethereum wallet may be tough due to the abundance of alternatives with varying features and looks. Some are better suited to novices, while others are better suited to specialists. The Ethereum platform is still being upgraded, and the "best" wallets are frequently those that adapt to the changes brought about by platform updates.

We have chosen a few different sorts of wallets to serve as examples during the chapter. Some are designed for mobile devices, while others are designed for desktop computers and are web-based. We picked several wallets since they reflect a wide spectrum of complexity and functionality. However, the selection of these wallets is not an endorsement of their quality or security. They are merely an excellent beginning point.

Remember that a wallet application requires access to our private keys in order to function; therefore, only download and use wallet software from trusted sources. Fortunately, in general, the more widespread a wallet bid is, the more reliable it is. Nonetheless, it is best practice to diversify our Ethereum accounts among many wallets rather than "placing all your eggs in one basket". The following are appetizer wallets.

6.7.1. MetaMask

MetaMask is a wallet that operates as a browser plugin. It is simple to customize and useful for testing because it can connect to a number of Ethereum nodes and test blockchains. MetaMask is a web-based wallet that also has iOS and Android mobile applications (Li et al. 2022).

6.7.2. Jaxx

Jaxx is a full-featured and multicurrency wallet that works on Android, iOS, Windows, macOS and Linux. Because it is meant for simplicity and ease of use, it is frequently an excellent choice for beginners. Depending on where we install it, Jaxx is either a mobile or a desktop wallet (Bari et al. 2021).

6.7.3. MyEtherWallet (MEW)

The main function of MEW is to function as a web-based wallet in any browser. Additionally, iOS and Android are supported. We will examine several of its advanced features in the examples we use (Zhu et al. 2022).

6.7.4. Emerald Wallet

Emerald Wallet is optimized for the Ethereum Classic blockchain, although it is also compatible with other Ethereum-based blockchains. It is a free and open source desktop application that runs on Windows, macOS and Linux. In "light" mode, Emerald Wallet may operate in a complete node or connect to a public remote node. It also comes with a companion application that allows us to carry out all processes from the command line (Antonopoulos and Wood 2018).

6.8. A simple contract: a test Ether faucet

Ethereum supports a wide range of high-level languages, any of which may be used to create contracts and EVM bytecodes. Many of the more notable and fascinating ones may be found in (high-level languages). Solidity is by far the most popular high-level language for smart contract programming. Dr. Gavin Wood designed Solidity, which has become the most extensively used language in Ethereum (and beyond). We will write our first contract in Solidity.

For our first example, we will design a contract that controls a faucet (Faucet.sol: A Solidity contract implementing a faucet). We previously used a faucet to test ether on the Ropsten test network. A faucet is a simple gadget that can be frequently updated and distributes ether to any address that wants it. We can use a faucet as a web-server or user-controlled wallet.

Example 1. A Solidity contract applying a faucet

```
// Version of Solidity compiler this program was written for
pragma solidity 0.6.4;
// Our first contract is a faucet!
contract Faucet {
    // Accept any incoming amount
    receive() external payable {}

    // Give out ether to anyone who asks
    function withdraw(uint withdraw_amount) public {
        // Limit withdrawal amount
        require(withdraw_amount <= 100000000000000000);

        // Send the amount to the address that requested it
        msg.sender.transfer(withdraw_amount);
    }
}
```

This contract is as straightforward as we can make it. It is a faulty contract that has many unethical behaviors and security flaws. Later parts will explore all of its shortcomings so that we can learn from them. Let us examine this contract's functions and operation line by line for the time being. We will immediately note that Solidity has many features in common with the already-existing programming languages like Java, C++ and JavaScript.

The first line is a comment:

// SPDX-License-Identifier: CC-BY-SA-4.0

The executable EVM bytecode does not contain comments since they are intended for human consumption. On occasion we may place them on the same line as the code we are attempting to explain. The beginning of a comment is two forward slashes: //. The initial slash and the remainder of that line are disregarded and are considered as blank lines.

The beginning of our actual contract is a few paragraphs later:

contract Faucet {

This line declares a contract object, much like a class declaration in other object-oriented languages. The contract description consists of all the lines between the curly braces () that describe a scope, much like how curly braces are used in many other programming languages.

The contract is then made capable of accepting any incoming sum:

receive () external payable {}

If the operation that activated the agreement did not identify any of the specified functions in it or did not contain any data and was thus just a basic Ether transmission, the receive function is invoked. One such receive function, which is used to accept ether, may be included in contracts. Since it may receive ether into the contract, it is designated as an external and payable function. The empty definition enclosed in curly brackets () indicates that it does nothing other than receive ether. This method will handle a transaction that delivers ether to the contract address as though it were a wallet.

We then specify the Faucet contract's initial function to be:

function withdraw(uint withdraw_amount) public {

The withdraw function accepts a single unsigned integer (uint) parameter, withdraw amount. Since it has been designated a public function, other contracts may call for it. The function definition is enclosed in curly braces after that. The withdraw function's first section establishes a withdrawal cap:

require(withdraw_amount <= 100000000000000000);

The withdraw amount must be less than or equal to 100,000,000,000,000,000 wei, the base unit of ether (see Ether denominations and unit names), which is equal to 0.1 ether. This test is performed using the built-in Solidity function need. In this case, the need function will stop contract execution and fail with an exception if the withdraw method is invoked with a withdraw amount larger than that amount. Be aware that Solidity requires semicolons to end statements.

This part of the contract is the main logic of our faucet. It controls the flow of funds out of the contract by placing a limit on withdrawals. It is a very simple control, but can give us a glimpse of the power of a programmable blockchain: decentralized software controlling money.

Next comes the actual withdrawal:

msg.sender.transfer(withdraw_amount);

Several intriguing events are currently taking place. One of the inputs that all contracts may access is the message object. It stands for the activity that caused this contract's execution. The transaction's sender address is represented by the property sender. A built-in function called "function transfer" moves ether from the active contract to the sender's address. This, when read backward, refers to a transfer to the sender of the message that caused this contract to be executed. The single argument for the transfer function is an amount. We call the withdraw function, which was declared a few lines earlier, passing the value of the withdraw amount as an argument.

The very next line is the closing curly brace, indicating the end of the definition of the withdraw function.

Just below our default function is the final closing curly brace that closes the definition of the contract Faucet. That's it!

6.9. Ethereum clients

A software program that implements the Ethereum specification and interacts with other Ethereum clients over the peer-to-peer network is known as an Ethereum client. If they adhere to the reference specification and the agreed-upon communications protocols, several Ethereum clients can communicate with one another. Many of these clients all "speak" the same protocol and adhere to the same rules, despite the fact that they were developed by several teams using various programming languages. As a result, they can all be used to function and communicate with the same Ethereum network.

Since Ethereum is an open source project, the source code for all of the main clients is freely downloadable and used for any purpose, and is distributed under open source agreements (such the LGPL v3.0). But open source is more than just freely available. In addition, this implies that anyone can modify Ethereum because it is created by a public community of volunteers. More eyeballs equal more reliable code.

Ethereum is defined by a formal specification called the "Yellow Paper".

In contrast to this, Bitcoin, for example, has no official definition. Ethereum's "specification" is outlined in a paper that includes an English and a mathematical (formal) specification, whereas Bitcoin's "specification" is the reference implementation Bitcoin Core. This formal specification outlines the expected behavior of an Ethereum client in addition to several Ethereum Improvement Proposals. The Yellow Paper is updated as significant alterations to Ethereum are made.

Due to the explicit formal definition of Ethereum, there are a variety of independently created, yet compatible, software implementations of an Ethereum client. More implementations of Ethereum are active on the network than any other blockchain, which is usually viewed as positive. In fact, it has been demonstrated to be a very effective method of thwarting network attacks because, when one client's implementation strategy is exploited, the developers are merely inconvenienced while they work to patch the vulnerability, while other clients keep the network operating largely unaffected (Rouhani and Deters 2017; Kim et al. 2018; Samuel et al. 2021).

6.9.1. *Hardware requirements for a full node*

Make sure you have a machine with enough power to operate a full Ethereum node before we begin. The Ethereum blockchain requires at least 300 GB of storage space to be stored completely. We need at least an extra 75 GB if we also want to operate a complete node on the Ethereum testnet. Working on a fast Internet connection is advised as downloading 375 GB of blockchain data may take a while.

The Ethereum blockchain requires a lot of input/output (I/O) to sync. Solid-state drives are the ideal choice (SSD). We need at least 8 GB of RAM to use as cache if our hard disk drive is mechanical. Otherwise, we may find that our system is too slow to keep up and sync properly.

The minimum requirements are:

– CPU with 2+ cores;

– at least 300 GB free storage space;

– 4 GB RAM minimum with an SSD, 8 GB+ if we have an HDD;

– 8 MBit/sec download Internet service.

The following conditions must be met to sync a complete (but pruned) copy of an Ethereum-based blockchain.

Since Parity's codebase uses fewer resources at the time of writing, it will probably perform better on hardware that is not as powerful.

We need a more powerful machine if we wish to sync in a reasonable period of time and store all the development tools, libraries, clients and blockchains that we describe in this book.

The recommended specifications are:

– fast CPU with 4+ cores;

– 16 GB+ RAM;

– fast SSD with at least 500 GB free space;

– 25+ MBit/sec download Internet service.

6.9.2. *Advantages and disadvantages of full node*

The decision to run a full node results in some minor to moderate expenditures for us, but benefits the networks we connect it to. Let us examine some of the benefits and drawbacks.

Advantages:

– It promotes the censorship resistance and resiliency of Ethereum-based networks.

– It has the ability to communicate directly with any contract on the public blockchain.

– It can organize conventions into the public blockchain directly, without the need for a mediator.

– It can query (read-only) the blockchain status (accounts, contracts, etc.) offline.

– It can enquire about the blockchain without revealing the information we are looking at to a third party.

Disadvantages:

– It demands large, increasing hardware and bandwidth resources.

– Initially, it could take several days to sync completely.

– To stay synchronized, it must be updated, preserved and kept online.

6.9.3. *The advantages and disadvantages of public testnet*

We should probably operate a public testnet node whether or not we decide to run a complete node. Let us examine some of the benefits and drawbacks of using a public testnet.

Advantages:

– In comparison to the mainnet, a testnet node only needs to sync and store approximately 75 GB of data, conditional on the network. A testnet node can sync completely in much less time.

– Test ether, which is needed for transactions and contract deployment, is useful and available for free from a number of "faucets".

– Testnets are open blockchains that have a large user base and active contracts.

Disadvantages:

– On a testnet, test ether is used instead of "real" money. Because there is nothing at risk, we cannot evaluate security against actual enemies.

– Why we cannot feasibly test all components of a public blockchain on a testnet. For example, since gas is free on a testnet, transaction costs, while required to send transactions, are not a factor. Additionally, the testnets do not occasionally encounter network congestion like the open mainnet does.

6.10. Conclusion

We have presented the payment procedure with the help of a computation procedure among the various edge computing devices belonging to the other parties for the exchange of payment. Smart payment is one of the best features of the IoT. Although our present work is entirely based on the proof of work, our future work will be the continuation of smart payment on edge computing.

The data produced by smart toy devices is developing into a new resource as the data exchange industry and the market for smart toys both emerge. Therefore, we must come up with a practical solution to the issue of smart toy data interchange. A more open data interchange mechanism is also necessary for many isolated IoT devices, including various smart toy data platforms.

We have introduced SmartEdge, a brand-new edge computing smart contract built on Ethereum. It enables nodes to pay for access to edge computing resources owned by third parties in return for offloading work in a verifiable way.

We believe that SmartEdge will be a useful tool for IoT applications. Although our present implementation only serves as a proof of concept, we want to continue working on SmartEdge.

6.11. References

Abd-El-Malek, M., Ganger, G.R., Goodson, G.R., Reiter, M.K., Wylie, J.J. (2005). Fault-scalable byzantine fault-tolerant services. *ACM SIGOPS Operating Systems Review*, 39(5), 59–74.

Antonopoulos, A.M. and Wood, G. (2018). *Mastering Ethereum: Building Smart Contracts and Dapps*. O'Reilly Media, Sebastopol, CA.

Back, A. and Bentov, I. (2014). Note on fair coin toss via bitcoin. arXiv preprint arXiv:1402.3698.

Bari, N., Qamar, U., Khalid, A. (2021). Efficient contact tracing for pandemics using blockchain. *Informatics in Medicine Unlocked*, 26, 100742.

Bezerra, M.A., Leal-Cardoso, J.H., Coelho-de-Souza, A.N., Criddle, D.N., Fonteles, M.C. (2000). Myorelaxant and antispasmodic effects of the essential oil of *Alpinia speciosa* on rat ileum. *Phytotherapy Research: An International Journal Devoted to Pharmacological and Toxicological Evaluation of Natural Product Derivatives*, 14(7), 549–551.

Bonneau, J. (2016). EthIKS: Using Ethereum to audit a CONIKS key transparency log. *International Conference on Financial Cryptography and Data Security*, 95–105. Springer, Berlin, Heidelberg.

Buterin, V. (2014). A next-generation smart contract and decentralized application platform. Ethereum White Paper, 3(37), 2–1.

Cai, C., Xu, L., Zhou, A., Wang, R., Wang, C., Wang, Q. (2020). EncELC: Hardening and enriching ethereum light clients with trusted enclaves. *IEEE INFOCOM 2020-IEEE Conference on Computer Communications*, 1887–1896.

Chen, L. and Xu, J. (2017). Socially trusted collaborative edge computing in ultra dense networks. CoRR, abs/1705.03501 [Online]. Available at: http://arxiv.org/abs/1705.03501.

Chiu, W.Y., Meng, W., Jensen, C.D. (2021). ChainPKI – Towards Ethash-based decentralized PKI with privacy enhancement. *2021 IEEE Conference on Dependable and Secure Computing (DSC)*, 1–8.

Clement, A., Wong, E.L., Alvisi, L., Dahlin, M., Marchetti, M. (2009). Making byzantine fault tolerant systems tolerate byzantine faults. *NSDI*, 9, 153–168.

Dannen, C. (2017). *Introducing Ethereum and Solidity*. Springer, Berlin.

De Vries, A. (2020). Bitcoin's energy consumption is underestimated: A market dynamics approach. *Energy Research & Social Science*, 70, 101721.

Delmolino, K., Arnett, M., Kosba, A., Miller, A., Shi, E. (2016). Step by step towards creating a safe smart contract: Lessons and insights from a cryptocurrency lab. *International Conference on Financial Cryptography and Data Security*, 79–94. Springer, Berlin, Heidelberg.

Gao, Y., Shi, J., Wang, X., Tan, Q., Zhao, C., Yin, Z. (2019). Topology measurement and analysis on ethereum p2p network. *2019 IEEE Symposium on Computers and Communications (ISCC)*, 1–7.

Kim, S.K., Ma, Z., Murali, S., Mason, J., Miller, A., Bailey, M. (2018). Measuring ethereum network peers. *Proceedings of the Internet Measurement Conference 2018*, 91–104.

Koutmos, D. (2018). Liquidity uncertainty and Bitcoin's market microstructure. *Economics Letters*, 172, 97–101.

Kranzler, H.R., Pierucci-Lagha, A., Feinn, R., Hernandez-Avila, C. (2003). Effects of ondansetron in early-versus late-onset alcoholics: A prospective, open-label study. *Alcoholism: Clinical and Experimental Research*, 27(7), 1150–1155.

Li, J., Qiang, W., Zhang, Y., Mo, W., Zheng, C., Su, B., Xiong, H. (2022). MetaMask: Revisiting dimensional confounder for self-supervised learning. arXiv preprint arXiv:2209.07902.

Moniruzzaman, M., Chowdhury, F., Ferdous, M.S. (2020). Examining usability issues in blockchain-based cryptocurrency wallets. *International Conference on Cyber Security and Computer Science*, 631–643. Springer, Cham.

Mukhopadhyay, M. (2018). *Ethereum Smart Contract Development: Build Blockchain-based Decentralized Applications Using Solidity*. Packt Publishing Ltd, Birmingham.

Nakamoto, S. (2008). Bitcoin: A peer-to-peer electronic cash system. *Decentralized Business Review*, 21260.

Pustišek, M. and Kos, A. (2018). Approaches to front-end IoT application development for the ethereum blockchain. *Procedia Computer Science*, 129, 410–419.

Ritz, F. and Zugenmaier, A. (2018). The impact of uncle rewards on selfish mining in ethereum. *2018 IEEE European Symposium on Security and Privacy Workshops (EuroS&PW)*, 50–57.

Rouhani, S. and Deters, R. (2017). Performance analysis of ethereum transactions in private blockchain. *2017 8th IEEE International Conference on Software Engineering and Service Science (ICSESS)*, 70–74.

Samuel, C.N., Glock, S., Verdier, F., Guitton-Ouhamou, P. (2021). Choice of ethereum clients for private blockchain: Assessment from proof of authority perspective. *2021 IEEE International Conference on Blockchain and Cryptocurrency (ICBC)*, 1–5.

Satyanarayanan, M. (2017). The emergence of edge computing. *Computer*, 50(1), 30–39.

Satyanarayanan, M., Bahl, P., Caceres, R., Davies, N. (2009). The case for VM-based cloudlets in mobile computing. *IEEE Pervasive Computing*, 8(4), 14–23.

Shurov, A., Malevanniy, D., Iakushkin, O., Korkhov, V. (2019). Blockchain network threats: The case of PoW and ethereum. *International Conference on Computational Science and its Applications*, 606–617. Springer, Cham.

Stanciu, A. (2017). Blockchain based distributed control system for edge computing. *2017 21st International Conference on Control Systems and Computer Science (CSCS)*, 667–671.

Szabo, N. (1997). The idea of smart contracts. *Nick Szabos Papers and Concise Tutorials*, 6.

Urquhart, A. (2016). The inefficiency of Bitcoin. *Economics Letters*, 148, 80–82.

Wood, G. (2014). Ethereum: A secure decentralised generalised transaction ledger. *Ethereum Project Yellow Paper*, 151(2014), 1–32.

Wu, K., Ma, Y., Huang, G., Liu, X. (2021). A first look at blockchain-based decentralized applications. *Software: Practice and Experience*, 51(10), 2033–2050.

Xiong, Z., Zhang, Y., Niyato, D., Wang, P., Han, Z. (2017). When mobile blockchain meets edge computing: Challenges and applications. arXiv preprint arXiv:1711.05938.

Zhang, Q., Cheng, L., Boutaba, R. (2010). Cloud computing: State-of-the-art and research challenges. *Journal of Internet Services and Applications*, 1(1), 7–18.

Zhu, X. (2019). Research on blockchain consensus mechanism and implementation. *IOP Conference Series: Materials Science and Engineering*, 569(4), 042058.

Zhu, H., Niu, W., Liao, X., Zhang, X., Wang, X., Li, B., He, Z. (2022). Attacker traceability on Ethereum through graph analysis. *Security and Communication Networks*, 2022, 1–12.

Statistical Learning Approach for the Detection of Abnormalities in Cancer Cells for Finding Indication of Metastasis

Operational research into cancer has been going on for many years, but it has been very difficult to find out the rate of propagation of this disease and how it spreads abnormally in the different organs of the human body. When the malignant features of this disease spread at an exponential rate in the human body, then the shape and size of cancer cells increase abnormally and the cell concentration decreases gradually due to the presence of rotten holes. Statistical learning (SL) is one of the advanced techniques under operations research to analyze the post-image processing techniques over the cancerous image to understand the status of image assessment parameters, by which we can create an invariant shape descriptor methodology. This shape descriptor tool can easily determine the texture of the cells and other morphological features. Using this SL technique, the analysis of various image assessment parameters can be performed easily, and it is easy to determine whether there is a metastasis stage or not. In this chapter, we introduce the invariant shape descriptor tool with geodesic transformation, as well as z-transformation of carcinoma images. We have also shown the edge computation approaches over these images. The descriptor tool methodology is first applied to different letters of the alphabet, and then to different cancer cells of different organs that are at different stages. All of these results are analyzed and provide information as to whether or not there is a metastasis stage.

7.1. Introduction

Cancer is the most unpredictable disease in which the prediction of healing directions changes abruptly. The abruptness of this disease also affects the progress of a patient's condition. Medical practitioners cannot predict the diagnosis, and sometimes they fail to see if the disease changes direction (Song and Ang 2014;

Chapter written by Soumen SANTRA, Dipankar MAJUMDAR and Surajit MANDAL.

Uttley et al. 2016; Sangeetha and Srikanta Murthy 2017; Makaju et al. 2018). Cancer patients first go for an X-ray, computed tomography (CT) scan or positron emission computed tomography (PET-CT) scan. These image processing techniques give medical practitioners an idea of which region is affected by this disease. X-ray is the first technique that finds the presence of some abnormalities within bone or tissue (Makaju et al. 2018). Generally, it forms a binary image from which the medical practitioner can identify whether the patient's body has a fracture in the bone, a tumor or an organ penetration. Normally, tissues or cells contain water and bones contain calcium. It is because of the presence of these two compositions that the X-ray gives such a special image. Due to the presence of 70% of water in the cell, we cannot properly see whether there are any hidden features in body parts or organs in an X-ray. CT and PET-CT are other image processing techniques that we use to get more details about the malignant features (Webb 2003; Williams et al. 2014; Kumar et al. 2015; Devkota et al. 2018). Here, we inject or import a special kind of nuclear molecule or radiation into a patient's body by which we get irregular shapes and sizes of malign granules. The cell features are classified into two types: benign and malign. Benign means that the cells, tissues or organs are normal, i.e. their shape, size and texture increase normally. The shape of the nucleus or nuclei is normal, and the ratio of the cytoplasm and the nucleus is proportionate. The shape and size of organs and tissues gradually increase, and the ratio of the previous one is defined. However, in malignant cases, all of these parameters are not fixed or defined. The abnormal increase of shape, size and texture and scattered behavior indicates the presence of malignant or cancerous granules in the cell, tissue or organ. Sometimes they have holes that gradually increase and reduce the presence of water in the cell or the relative molecular weight of bone (normally 40, as per calcium) and that of tissue (normally 20). Due to the lack of water and the consequent reduction in molecular weight, the output of X-ray, CT or PET-CT scans in image form is not clearly understandable for the medical practitioner or ordinary people. This kind of computation process-oriented image output depends on many parameters (Webb 2003) such as the width of tissue, i.e. the weight of patient, the radiation angle between the radiated ray and the affected organ in the patient's body, the immunity of the patient and the amount of water present in the affected cell. Therefore, it is not a deterministic process that can be applied in every situation, regardless of the patient's condition. Since the parameters that act as hidden features in this disease can vary from patient to patient, we are trying to find a general methodology that will allow us to understand the patient's condition and the status of the disease.

As shape is one of the significant features of the cancerous cell, we have generally been trying to adopt a shape descriptor tool or technique that will enable us to understand the variance nature of shape. We have already seen different types of homogeneous image transformations such as translation, rotation and scaling (Duffy et al. 1995; Nasreddine et al. 2009). This homogeneous transformation is basically variant in nature. That is, if we subject an image to a translation technique and its shape changes, then the previous translation figure also changes. In the case of rotation, when we rotate an image or any kind of rotation occurs when capturing an image of an affected organ or tissue, the features of the processing image may change. In these cases, the homogeneous transformation is variant in nature. It is very difficult to diagnose an affected region which is variant in nature because the affected region of interest does not match with the area of the processed image of an actual one. Due to this reason, the medical practitioner sometimes cannot get successful results in relation to this disease (Santra and Mandal 2018; Santra et al. 2020).

The cancer disease propagates at a linear rate, but gradually it converts into an exponential nonlinear rate. When it increases as per the exponential nonlinear rate at that time, the affected region varies. Due to this variation, the medical practitioner's prediction fails with the desired conditions. There are various ways to remove this variant nature to create a tool that is invariant in nature. There are many approaches by which we can find out the hidden elements present in the image. The hidden features contain some parameters by which we obtain hidden information and the status of the respective image. Normally, these hidden features are identified using edge detection algorithms (Santra et al. 2021). Many edge detection algorithms are available, and these kinds of algorithms are operated based on statistics methodologies. Statistical learning (SL) is one of the techniques by which we can process the image in the post-image processing duration. The edge is defined as the distinction between two regions and creates a boundary that indicates the lack of discreteness. Many operational methods work based on statistical theory by which we can easily identify the edges present inside an image. The major and minor edges distinguished by some parameters are working as assessment parameters by which we can identify the hidden features of an image (Santra et al. 2019a, 2019b). There are various edge detection algorithms such as Sobel, Prewitt, Robert, Marr Hildreth and Canny. Among these algorithms, Canny is the most significant algorithm as it can detect major and minor edges. When these major and minor edges overlap with each other, there is a conflict regarding information about hidden features. Statistical approaches and derivatives help us to evaluate these kinds of edge computation algorithms smoothly and find out the accuracy and sensitivity of the edges. These operational research methodologies are used to evaluate the quality of the edges and the value of different assessment parameters (Santra and Mali 2016).

These kinds of operations mainly depend on statistical approaches because assessing the parameters of an image is closely related to Big Data processing. When an image is converted into a structured data format, it becomes large-scale data. To process this large-scale data, we require probability distribution, Z-score, chi-squared, machine learning (ML), deep learning (DL), SL, analysis of big volume data, etc. Apart from data science approaches, we also need to analyze algorithms in a cloud platform scenario. Descriptive statistics, inferential statistics, etc. must also be considered when evaluating assessment parameters of large-scale image data. We have already discussed the nonlinear exponential propagation rate of spreading of this disease over the tissues and organs. Therefore, the data stored in it is a kind of Big Data.

Edge computation is a special kind of technology where the data is stored in the cloud platform, and after processing, it will be delivered to the edge devices, such as smart phones. These edge devices work as an interface from which the user gets the output. Since large-scale data is stored and computed in a cloud platform in a heterogeneous environment, and the data acts as real when delivered to the edge devices, there is a mismatch between the processing approaches due to the differences in time complexity and space complexity regarding the aspects of the analysis of algorithms.

Edge computation for light processing is very much significant due to large-scale image processing in a cloud infrastructure with high computation speed and resources. However, when we can access this type of output through our mobile devices, it is not possible to compute such a large-scale image with the same resources and at the same speed. Therefore, in the edge computing era, we will import statistical methodologies into our algorithm to minimize the storage and speed of computation, and make it lighter using thread computation techniques.

Some brand new issues cannot be completely solved with these solutions alone. Applications such as autonomous driving, smart cities, smart homes and even remote medical all have unique requirements that the cloud in its current form cannot always completely provide. To maximize resource usage, cloud computing makes use of tools for cluster management and resource orchestration. A computing architecture at the edge should include these systems. Currently, all significant cloud providers and businesses working to address these use cases develop their applications and services in a uniform, cloud-only manner. Some offer additional features or services than others, such as data manipulation, storage or understanding through data analytics.

With this change, computing power is once again distributed at the network's edge. Programmable automation controllers (PAC), which manage processing, storage and communication, are connected to sensors via an edge network. Using new technologies, procedures, services and applications that are designed to make use of this new infrastructure is the fundamental idea behind edge computing. The main difference of this model is that it runs and is implemented on computing devices that are placed closer to the edge of the network. As a result, it is advancing the concept of cloud computing.

In the year 2012, Google developed the graphical processing unit (GPU) and the tensor processing unit (TPU). After the development of this GPU and TPU, a new era in the edge computation field began. Here, all the large-scale image or Big Data are computed using the GPU and the TPU. Our smart edge devices could not process this GPU or TPU. Therefore, statistical approaches essentially help us to control these kinds of operations using the user edge computation methodology. In this edge computation, we usually fold the images and reduce the size of the image dataset to reduce the processing unit and enhance easy computation.

7.2. Edge computation: a new era

A distributed computing paradigm known as "edge computing" puts business applications closer to data sources such as Internet of Things (IoT) gadgets or regional edge servers. By doing this, response times are enhanced, and bandwidth is conserved. It relates to technology, particularly architecture. We will experience quicker insights, quicker responses and more bandwidth availability with this technology. The secret to edge computing is location. In conventional enterprise computing, data is generated by client endpoints like a user's PC. Data is transported from a WAN, such as the Internet, to a corporate LAN, where it is stored and processed by business applications. The client endpoint then receives the results. Most types of commercial applications have used the client–server computing model for many years since it is a proven computing technique. Complex data processing can be done locally and more quickly. It is helpful in a variety of situations, including live lectures, video conferences, medical data analysis, robotics and artificial intelligence, to mention a few. In simpler terms, it transmits computer resources and saved data from the centralized data center to the various storage centers. In this way, the data is processed and evaluated close to where it was collected, and only the pertinent information is forwarded to the main hub for business forecasts and analyses.

To get computer vision to the edge, we must complete a few tasks. First, we need a piece of equipment that can serve as an edge device. To recognize and analyze images for computer vision, edge devices must be equipped with GPUs or VPUs, whereas those without a GPU are not particularly useful. We refer to IoT devices when discussing edge devices. When it comes to computer vision analysis, a device that can gather visual data and analyze the world around it can act as an edge device. A subfield of artificial intelligence (AI) known as computer vision uses digital photos, movies and other visual inputs to generate and analyze relevant data. Information about these devices and systems can be used to formulate suggestions and select the best course of action. Here, SL is one of the subfields of AI used in operational methodologies in work.

7.3. Impact of edge computation in cancer treatment

Nowadays, edge computation is an interesting subject that allows us to reduce the network tolerance and large-scale computation effort. It is a new type of network model where the terminal or edge devices relate to the cloud deployment model. As we know, the cloud platform uses large-scale data and provides Software as a Service (SaaS), Platform as a Service (PaaS) and Infrastructure as a Service (IaaS). Therefore, when we try to create a cloud model for unfolding an image dataset at that time, we must consider an app-based mobile device or such type of network edge device. This new era reduces the network latency and tolerance due to quick output response in smart devices through app-based technologies. Normally, for large-scale images, we first divide the whole image into segments. This is one of the precomputation techniques. Then, all the segments process according to the algorithms, and after computation, all processed outputs are merged into a new output.

There is a connection between edge computations and the statistical approaches of image processing techniques. Statistical or operational methodologies are those which can reduce the complexity of parallel computation. When a large-scale image is divided into several segments and then processed based on homogeneous or heterogeneous image processing-based algorithms, then all segments process in a parallel way. An image related to a cancer cell or tissue has a lot of information hidden in it. Using the statistical or operational approach, we can obtain more information regarding this. The retrieval of information or hidden features depends on our methodologies. The more we drill down, the greater the possibility of getting information from the scanned image. If we do not explore all the information, then all the image assessment parameters cannot be evaluated, so it is very difficult for the medical practitioner to understand the status of the image (Santra and Mali 2016). Here, to reduce the network tolerance and enhance the multi-factored fluctuations analysis, we enhance the accuracy of statistical approaches.

Using the Gossip-based protocol, each node can find other nodes that are a part of the same cluster. This is performed to scale the entire system. Each node in the cluster can come into contact with any other node to request data, and eventually learns where the data is kept. Binary protocols such as HTTP/2 should be used via the remote procedure call mechanism so that all communication between nodes is as fast as possible (RPC). Every task that executes on these nodes needs to be packaged as a Linux container. This allows for easier orchestration, improved task packing on machines and job separation on a single machine. To avoid data loss, all data saved in a distributed hash table is replicated a user-specified number of times in succeeding nodes. All nodes that are a part of a single cluster are linked together in a single virtual ring, and nodes and data are hashed using consistent hashing principles. We can simply divide data using this straightforward concept such that each node is only in charge of a small amount of the data (Santra and Mali 2015).

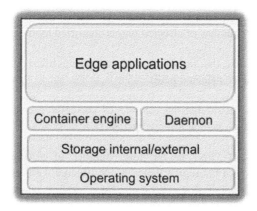

Figure 7.1. *Block diagram of edge computation*

Hashing consistently is advantageous for two reasons: (1) we only need to copy a tiny amount of data across the network when a node joins or leaves a group since each node only manages a small portion of data and (2) we keep identical data (with the same key) in the same location (same node) when we perform calculations because it is quicker. Normally, if we used any cloud-based platform, then due to processing of SaaS, IaaS and PaaS, the complexity of the code increases gradually. But to induce these platforms into mobile devices, we enhance the speed of computation techniques using edge computation technology (Santra et al. 2013, 2014; Santra and Mali 2015, 2016).

There are many image-oriented assessment parameters, some of which are described below.

7.4. Assessment parameters operational methodologies

Various image assessment parameters are listed below:

True positive: denoted as "TP", where we predict the image pixels that are truly affected by cancer.

True negative: denoted as "TN", where we predict the pixels that are truly not affected.

False negative: denoted as "FN", where we did not find the pixels that are really affected.

Accuracy: ratio of the sum of "TP" and "TN" with the sum of all kinds of pixels. It deals with the total number of affected pixels classified by the algorithm.

Precision: evaluates the number of correctly classified affected pixels with respect to total predicted affected pixel.

Recall/sensitivity: evaluates the number of correctly classified affected pixels with respect to the total original affected pixels.

Miss rate: ratio of "FN" to the total number of affected pixels. Here, it determines the portion of the region that was not affected with respect to the affected region.

Specificity: ratio of "TN" to the total number of negative pixels, which indicates the portion of region that was really affected but was not found by the algorithm.

Prevalence: ratio of the total number of affected pixels to the total number of pixels present in the region of interest (ROI).

F1 score: evaluates the equilibrium stages between the precision and recall.

Critical success index: evaluates the ratio of "TP" and the sum of all parameters except "TN".

Positive likelihood ratio: ratio of the true positive rate and the false positive rate. It determines the propagation rate at which the disease spreads. If the value is more than 1, it indicates that the cancer disease spreads throughout the non-affected region.

Negative likelihood ratio: ratio of the false negative rate to the true negative rate. It determines the rate of false detection of the affected pixel with respect to the detection of the normal pixel as the affected one.

Diagnostic odds ratio: ratio of the positive likelihood ratio to the negative likelihood ratio, which indicates how to properly diagnose the disease by detecting the proper affected pixel of the image of the carcinogenic part.

7.5. Shape descriptor analysis: statistical approach

Serial number	Circularity value	Shape
1	<1.53	Rectangle
2	<1.35	Square
3	<1.2	Circle

Table 7.1. *List of circularity values of basic shapes*

Here, we use different formations and orientations of alphabets (A–K), where the dataset is self-generated. According to the statistical approach, we find the list of circularity values of different basic shapes. As we know, the disease propagates at an exponential rate, so the shape of the affected ROI of cells, tissues or organs varies rapidly. Due to shape variation, we focus on the invariant shape descriptor, which is measured by circularity. A circle starts from a point and again ends at the same point, so using this assessment parameter, we can find out the exact shape and the basic shape constituent of the target. Here, we have shown the circularity values of the different forms of shape and given an idea of how basic shapes are present within the target image. Using this parameter, we can also find out the constituent shapes of any form of derived shape, like pentagons or hexagons, or any kind of polygon. This invariant shape descriptor parameter can easily identify the presence of basic shapes from the image of the cancerous segment. All kinds of homogeneous and heterogeneous transformations are possible with this tool. In the results section, we explain all of the types of target shapes based on their different types of formation and orientation. We only focus on the basic shapes, but it is possible to explore more basic shapes beyond these three special fundamental ones. As we know, for a complex image, the shape should be complex, and so we need to explore various types of polygons such as pentagons, hexagons, heptagons and octagons and also different types of holes within the target shape. The invariant shape descriptor tool finds the basic shapes and we then calculate their pixel values and determine the assessment parameters to explore the nature of the target-derived shape.

7.6. Results and discussion

In this section, we show the application of our tool to various forms of alphabets. We first use the alphabets A–K instead of cancerous images and show all of the results. In the case of alphabets, if the orientation changes, we also get the details of the basic shapes. The number of rectangles, circles or triangles present in the target shape is identified. If there is a mixture of basic shapes, then this can also be identified. If there is an image hole present in the shape such as "D" or "F", then this can also be identified. In cancer cells, the shape and concentration of the nucleus and cytoplasm change rapidly due to the presence of carcinoma. Sometimes a hole will be created inside the cell due to the loss of water in malignant cells. Due to the presence of the hole, the concentration ratio of the nucleus and cytoplasm changes and decreases rapidly. This kind of hole can be easily identified through this model. Sometimes, when we diagnose the malign portion, it affects the other surrounding regions. In the case of "F", like the open mouth letter shape, malignant cells, tissues or organs spread to the surrounding areas upon diagnosis or application of medicine. This kind of indication can be found in a few organs, which is also shown here.

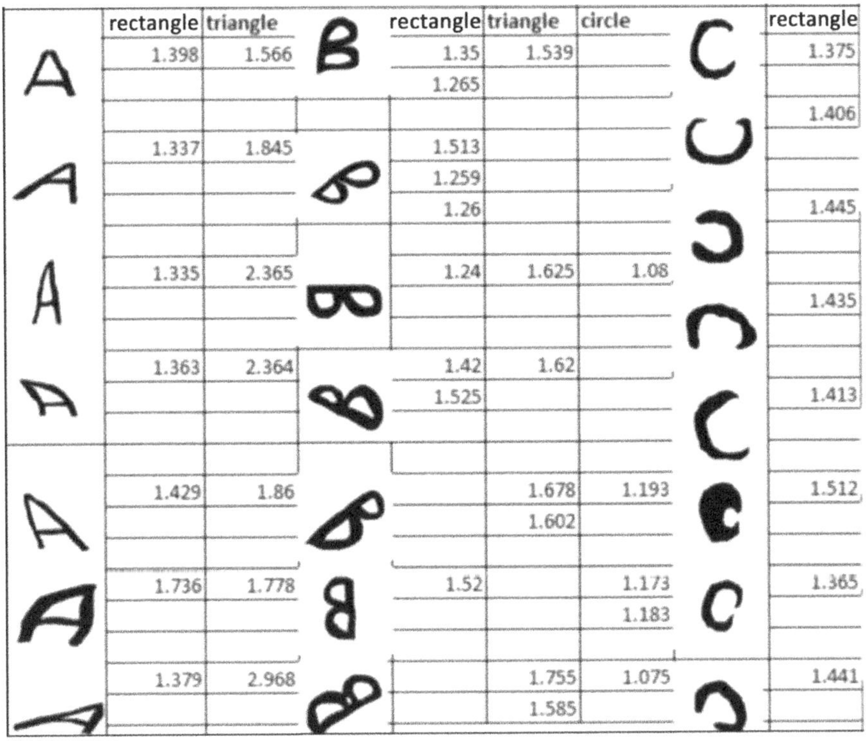

A	rectangle	triangle	B	rectangle	triangle	circle	C	rectangle
	1.398	1.566		1.35 / 1.265	1.539			1.375
								1.406
	1.337	1.845		1.513 / 1.259 / 1.26				1.445
	1.335	2.365		1.24	1.625	1.08		1.435
	1.363	2.364		1.42 / 1.525	1.62			1.413
	1.429	1.86		1.678 / 1.602	1.193			1.512
	1.736	1.778		1.52		1.173 / 1.183		1.365
	1.379	2.968		1.755 / 1.585		1.075		1.441

Figure 7.2. *List of circularity values of the alphabet dataset (A–C)*

rectangle	triangle		rectangle		rectangle	
1.506		E	1.342	f	1.374	
1.293					1.326	
hole fill up					hole not fill	
1.453		e	1.33	f	1.348	
1.411					hole fill up	
1.456		E	1.307	F	1.312	
1.229						
					area>60k	
1.474		E	1.371	F	1.29	
1.207						
					area>60k	
1.418	3.385	e	1.417	f	1.321	
1.381	1.672	Σ	1.308	f	1.298	
1.428	2.914	E	1.36	f	1.344	
1.449	1.835	E	1.389	F	1.292	

Figure 7.3. *List of circularity values of the alphabet dataset (D–F)*

Various formations and orientations of the shape indicate an invariant nature, which can be easily determined using the descriptor tool. Here, in the case of cancer images, since their shapes change rapidly, we need to generate a specific type of shape-invariant descriptor tool that allows us to easily find out any variation in shape. Different image shapes have different types of parameters that need to be identified by the medical practitioner in a dynamic way to help patients clarify their status and find out about the progression of the disease.

Statistical operations such as SL play an important role here, since the confusion matrices can be easily generated after determining the pixel values. Using values such as "TP", "TN", "FP" and "FN", we can easily calculate the other assessment parameters by which the status of the cell, tissue or organ through shape of the image is easily understandable and the propagation rate of the disease is easily understandable. The metastasis stage means the spread of the disease through lymph nodes. Here, the abnormality in shape and the presence of basic shapes in the target image indicate the presence of a metastasis stage therein. Operational methodologies such as SL play a significant role in detecting abnormalities that introduce the metastasis stage and detecting its status.

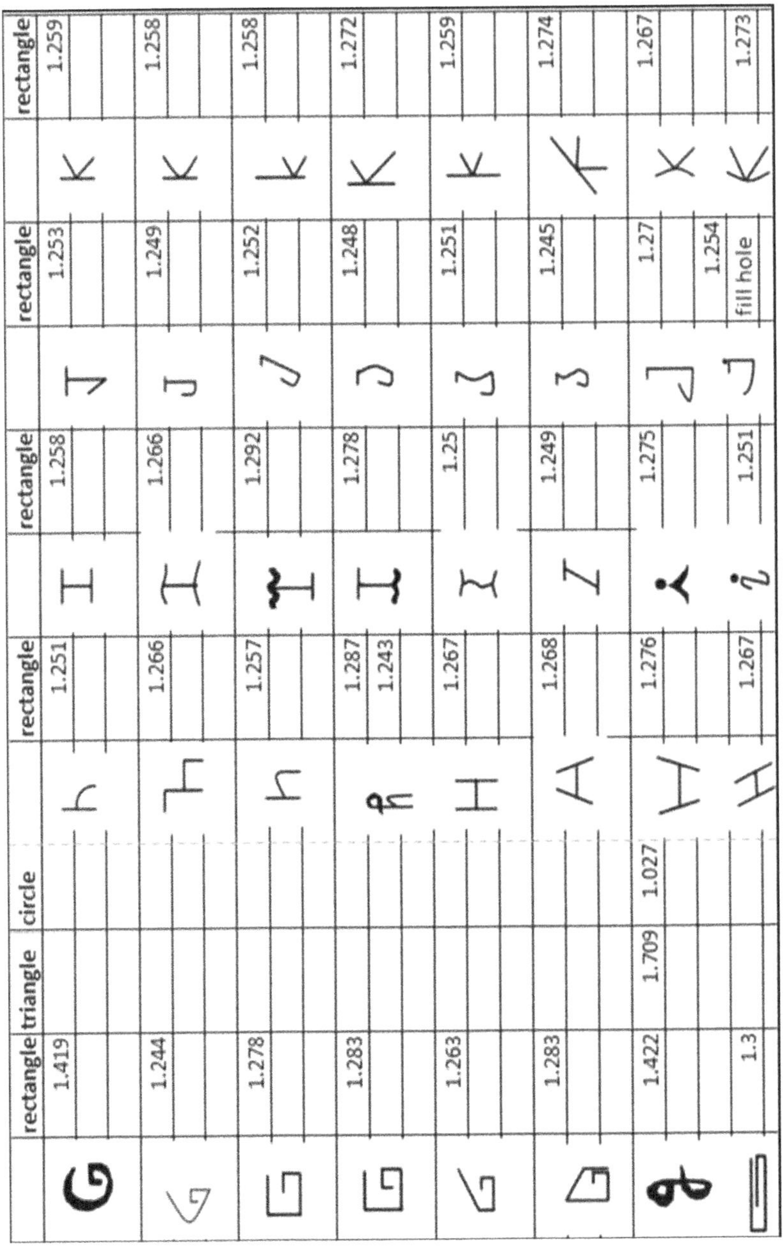

rectangle/triangle	triangle	circle	rectangle	rectangle	rectangle	rectangle	rectangle
1.419			1.251	1.258	1.258	1.253	1.259
1.244			1.266	1.266	1.249	1.249	1.258
1.278			1.257	1.292	1.252	1.252	1.258
1.283			1.287 / 1.243	1.278	1.248	1.248	1.272
1.263			1.267	1.25	1.251	1.251	1.259
1.283			1.268	1.249	1.245	1.245	1.274
1.422	1.709	1.027	1.276	1.275	1.27	1.27	1.267
1.3			1.267	1.251 (fill hole)	1.254 (fill hole)		1.273

Figure 7.4. *List of circularity values of the alphabet dataset (G–K)*

Figure 7.2 shows that our approach can easily obtain the number of basic shapes present in the cancer cell, from which the formation of shape constituents can be easily understood for the application of diagnostic processes such as nuclear medicines, vaccines or radiation to cover the shape of the target ROI. Here, the use image is collected from free resources and applied to the tool. Here, the presence of abnormalities is indicated by the presence of a variety of basic shapes in the target image, indicating the presence of a metastasis stage.

Figure 7.5. *Circularity value measurement of cancerous cells using a software tool. For a color version of this figure, see www.iste.co.uk/chakraborty/smartedge.zip*

7.7. Conclusion

With new applications such as the IoT and autonomous driving, we need to find a new way to solve problems, given the tremendous transition away from centralized computing systems. Although cloud computing has been around for many years, this new class of applications may not be well suited to its centralized nature. We may consider doing pre-processing where data is created, which is at the very edge of the network, rather than wasting time and money on storing, filtering and pre-processing data in the cloud.

In this chapter, we mainly focus on cells, tissues or organs affected by cancer, with our main aim being to explore more information from their scanned images. Operational methodologies represent a new era of edge computation, in which algorithmic approaches attempt to reduce network tolerance and computation time, as well as to reduce costs. Here, statistical methodologies or SL are used to minimize the post-image processing operations and try to find out a maximum amount of hidden information or features for the best possible analysis and diagnosis of the scanned medical image. The invariant shape descriptor tool is a kind of operational methodology that works on the shape of the cell image. As we know, cells affected by cancer have benign features that cause their shape to gradually change, and this change is invariant in nature. Therefore, the invariant shape descriptor tool solves this problem and determines the correct shape or predicts a future shape of the scanned object. This prediction of the shape helps the medical practitioner to better understand the progress of the disease and diagnose the patient more easily. In this cruel disease, locating the correct propagation and finding the affected region which the nuclear medicine needs to be applied to is very helpful.

7.8. References

Devkota, B., Alsadoon, A., Prasad, P.W.C., Singh, A.K., Elchouemi, A. (2018). Image segmentation for early-stage brain tumor detection using mathematical morphological reconstruction. *Procedia Computer Science*, 125, 115–123.

Duffy, S.W., Chen, H.H., Tabar, L., Day, N.E. (1995). Estimation of mean sojourn time in breast cancer screening using a Markov chain model of both entry to and exit from the preclinical detectable phase. *Statistics in Medicine*, 14(14), 1531–1543 [Online]. Available at: https://www.ncbi.nlm.nih gov/PubMed/7481190.

Kumar, R., Srivastava, R., Srivastava, S. (2015). Detection and classification of cancer from microscopic biopsy images using clinically significant and biologically interpretable features. *Journal of Medical Engineering*, 457906. doi: 10.1155/2015/457906.

Lesley, U., Becky, L., Whiteman, H.B., Woods, S., Harnan, S., Philips, S.T., Cree, I.A. (2016). Building the evidence base of blood-based biomarkers for early detection of cancer: A rapid systematic mapping review. *eBioMedicine*, 10, 164–173.

Makaju, S., Prasad, P.W.C., Alsadoon, A., Singh, A.K., Elchouemi, A. (2018). Lung cancer detection using CT scan images. *Procedia Computer Science*, 125, 107–114.

Nasreddine, K., Benzinou, A., Fablet, R. (2009). Shape geodesics for the classification of calcified structures: Beyond Fourier shape descriptors. *Fisheries Research*, 98(1–3), 8–15.

Sangeetha, R. and Srikanta Murthy, K. (2017). A novel approach for detection of breast cancer at an early stage using digital image processing techniques. *International Conference on Inventive Systems and Control (ICISC)*, 19–20 January.

Santra, S. and Mali, K. (2015). A new approach to survey on load balancing in VM in cloud computing: Using CloudSim. *2015 International Conference on Computer, Communication and Control (IC4)*, 1–5. IEEE. doi: 10.1109/IC4.2015.7375671.

Santra, S. and Mali, K. (2016). Pixel variation problem identification in image segmentation for big image data set in cloud platform. *IEEE International Conference on Advances in Computer Applications (ICACA)*, 318–320.

Santra, S. and Mandal, S. (2018). A new approach toward invariant shape descriptor tools for shape classification through morphological analysis of image. In *Computational Advancement in Communication Circuits and Systems*, Maharatna, K., Kanjilal, M, Konar, S., Nandi, S., Das, K. (eds). Springer, Singapore.

Santra, S., Dey, H., Majumdar, S. (2013). A survey with proposed approach on dynamic load balancing: Via VM migration strategy in cloud computing. *IEEE Sponsored Conference CONFLUENCE 2013*, Amity University, Noida, 27–28 September, 27–29.

Santra, S., Dey, H., Majumdar, S., Jha, G.S. (2014). New simulation toolkit for comparison of scheduling algorithm on cloud computing. *2014 International Conference on Control, Instrumentation, Communication and Computational Technologies*, 466–469. IEEE.

Santra, S., Mandal, S., Das, K., Bhattacharjee, J., Deyasi, A. (2019a). A comparative study of Z-transform and Fourier transform applied on medical images for detection of cancer segments. *3rd International Conference on Electronics, Materials Engineering & Nanotechnology (IEMENTech)*, August, 1–4. IEEE.

Santra, S., Mandal, S., Das, K., Bhattacharjee, J., Roy, A. (2019b). A modified canny edge detection approach to early detection of cancer cell. *3rd International Conference on Electronics, Materials Engineering & Nanotechnology (IEMENTech)*, August, 1–5. IEEE.

Santra, S., Mukherjee, P., Sardar, P., Mandal, S., Deyasi, A. (2020). Object detection in clustered scene using point feature matching for non-repeating texture pattern. In *Advances in Control, Signal Processing and Energy Systems*, Basu, T., Goswami, S., Sanyal, N. (eds). Springer, Singapore.

Santra, S., Majumdar, D., Mandal, S. (2021). Identification of shape using circularity approach for medical image analysis. In *Advances in Medical Physics and Healthcare Engineering*, Mukherjee, M., Mandal, J., Bhattacharyya, S., Huck, C., Biswas, S. (eds). Springer, Singapore.

Song, M. and Leong Ang, T. (2014). Early detection of early gastric cancer using image-enhanced endoscopy: Current trends. *Gastrointestinal Intervention*, 3(1), 1–7.

Webb, A. (2003). *Introduction to Biomedical Imaging*. Wiley-IEEE Press, Hoboken.

Williams, I., Bowring, N., Svoboda, D. (2014). A performance evaluation of statistical tests for edge detection in textured images. *Computer Vision and Image Understanding*, 122, 115–130. doi: 10.1016/j.cviu.2014.02.009.

8

Overcoming the Stigma of Alzheimer's Disease by Means of Natural Language Processing as well as Blockchain Technologies

The entire nations throughout the world are suffering from different kinds of chronic diseases. Chronic diseases exert a significant burden on the diagnosed sufferers. Alzheimer's disease (AD) remains such a kind of illness. Self- and other imposed judgments are applied to the sufferers, since no operational therapy or protective measures are taken on behalf of this disease. As a neurodegenerative disease, this disease is also very challenging in nature and it has a significant impact on sufferers' lives. The impact of this disease is far more dangerous than psychological issues, as the fear of being diagnosed with AD can cause people to avoid the initial diagnosis, treatment and even possibilities that could be beneficial to them and help fight against the disease's progression. The attitude and flavor of writing on different social media platforms is analyzed using AI, i.e. artificial intelligence technology in addition to natural language processing (NLP), which is considered a handy tool for measuring public opinion on various topics. These approaches could be used to investigate the public perception of AD. To some extent, a number of medical institutions are very much concerned about the bad and unreliable records, and in these cases, security is not maintained properly. Implementing more secure and localized data movement and different origin techniques, as well as providing patients with greater control over their data, including a blockchain-based method, could help alleviate some of these concerns.

Chapter written by Kaveri BANERJEE, Priyanka BHATTACHARYA, Sandip ROY and Rajesh BOSE.

8.1. Introduction

Chronic diseases are very common issues for entire nations around the world. However, sometimes people are completely unaware of the early indications of these kinds of diseases due to lack of knowledge. As a result, sufferers may die due to the seriousness of these diseases. Electronic medical records (EMR) can be used for the recognition of different indicators to diagnose these kinds of diseases, along with different kinds of control measurements. The different types of control measurements are used to prevent and control the spread of the disease. The description of a conversation between a patient and medical staff regarding the disease, along with the different symptoms of the disease, can be stored in the EMR. The entire process is used for clinical decision support (CDS). However, EMR is often a difficult data process due to inappropriate grammar (Putra et al. 2019). NLP is a very important branch of information technology and data processing. Using this methodology along with artificial intelligence, computers are able to understand text and spoken words like humans. Computational linguistics is the language for expressing things in a computational way, and is combined with NLP. Statistical models, machine learning approaches and deep learning models are used in NLP. Using the above-mentioned NLP technology, human languages are processed by computers in the pattern of voice or text data and, as a result, the meaning of human language is completely understandable by the computer systems. It means that the intention and sentiment of the speaker or writer are completely understandable by the computer system. Because of this, nowadays NLP systems along with machine learning algorithms are very much used for the detection of chronic diseases (Sheikhalishahi et al. 2019). This methodology (Dey et al. 2020) has been used to extract the sentiments of humans, as well as classify them. A very common example of a chronic disease is Alzheimer's, which occurs when nerve cells in the human brain are damaged. The circumferential nervous system of the human body loses its functionality over time. Ultimately, brain cells deteriorate and die due to the severity of this disease. Thinking, behavioral and social skills are impaired in patients suffering from Alzheimer's disease (AD). Patients can even lose their ability to work independently. Acute memory loss is a warning symptom of this disease. Patients are completely unable to look back on their latest memories. Although occasional memory losses may happen due to tremendous mental stress, the early diagnosis of this disease is very difficult. The concept behind the early diagnosis of this disease is very distorted (Armstrong 2019). According to the literature, a survey on the prevalence of AD in couples is conducted every five years after the age of 65. A large percentage of people are affected by this disease after the age of 65. Patients' situations get worse every day. There are no actual methodologies for prevention or healing. The sufferers of the disease are judged and their lives are affected. The early diagnosis of the disease, treatment and research opportunities are hampered due to the reluctant attitude of people. So the impact of this disease is much more dangerous than psychological problems. But the research opportunities are very helpful in the fight against AD and its advancement. Sufferers may benefit from these research opportunities. A total of 55 million people worldwide still suffer from AD. According to a WHO report, 60–70% of geriatric patients have Alzheimer's disease, which is the most common cause of dementia. Nowadays, dementia is a leading cause of death among all other diseases, and this disease may lead the older affected people to complete incapacity and dependency. More than 6 million people of different ages are suffering from AD in the United States; in maximum cases, their ages are 65 and above. In the United States, 80% of them are 75 years old or above. But 200,000 patients in the United States are younger people. Throughout the world, around 44 million people are suffering from AD or dementia. Two-thirds of American people, i.e. approximately 3.3 million people who are diagnosed with this disease are women and 2 million are men (Matthews et al. 2019). This illness grows every 66 seconds in the United States. Every 33 seconds, one person is affected by this mental decay in the United States. It has been projected that by 2050, 16 million people will be affected by this disease (Matthews et al. 2019). Over the years, much research has continued for the warning identification of AD. For the initial detection of AD (Pilozzi and Huang 2020; Gold et al. 2018), many clinical trials in addition to analyses of PET scans or invasive procedures failed to provide a positive outcome. The initial recognition of AD has become a challenge; drugs developed for the disease only decline the development of later symptoms. However, a collaborative effort by IBM and Pfizer promises to be the potential breakthrough for earlier detection of AD. The duo has created an AI model that can detect Alzheimer's based on the linguist patterns of the patient (Gold et al. 2018; Pilozzi and Huang 2020). A systematic literature review was done by some researchers (Petti et al. 2020) for the detection of the above-mentioned disease using automatic language processing. To evaluate the RCT (Randomized Clinical Trial) procedure to distinguish between people with AD and those without AD, word demonstrations from NLP are examined by a group of researchers (Liu et al. 2022). Research work (Adhikari et al. 2022) has established new datasets on low resources language. This dataset consists of a summary of the AD patients and controls normal subjects. A number of algorithms related to machine learning and deep learning are used on the new datasets of AD for the presentation of a model. The speech decline of AD patients is incorporated with the proposed work, and this proposed work is used for the arrangement of AD patients. In this chapter, we describe the difficulties in treating AD sufferers and that the speech narratives of the patients are affected by these difficulties. A group of researchers (Adhikari et al. 2021) have diagnosed Japanese patients with Alzheimer's disease on the basis of word category frequencies. The functionalities of the stop words for expressing the semantic information of the AD-affected patients have been discussed in research work (de la Fuente Garcia et al. 2020). To keep track of the disease (Pandey and Litoriya 2020), artificial intelligence, speech and language processing approaches have been used. For the prognosis of AD, an improved machine learning method has been used (Khan and Zubair 2022). One of the most useful approaches is the verbal fluency method. This sensitive neuropsychological method is used for the recognition and evaluation of cognitive declines in AD. Verbal fluency (VF) is another approach that can be used for the detection of this disease developed by the authors (Soni et al. 2021). For the detection of the risk of AD, random forest (RF), neural network (NN), recurrent NN (RNN) and natural language processing (NLP), along with machine learning techniques have been used by researchers (Soni et al. 2021). They also have used blockchain technology applications, AI and Big Data approaches. The researchers of the project (Chattu 2021; Kaur et al. 2021) have used blockchain technology to frame the data privacy and security issues in electronic healthcare, as well as challenges and remedies adopted by this technology.

The primary goal of this chapter is to explain the contribution of computational methodologies along with natural language processing (NLP) to overcoming the impact of the above-mentioned disease, which is basically representative of chronic diseases. They have summarized the concept of blockchain technology, which is used to secure the entire electronic health record (EHR), as well as different challenges faced by this technology.

A literature survey of Alzheimer's disease is discussed in section 8.2. We discuss different types and classifications of the above-mentioned disease in section 8.3. The application of NLP in chat-bots/AI is clearly depicted in section 8.4. We discuss the proposed methodology using NLP and model objective function as an operations research method for the reduction of stigma in sections 8.5.1 and 8.5.2. The presentation of blockchain technology for data privacy in healthcare and applications of blockchain technology are explained in detail in section 8.6. The conclusion is discussed in section 8.7. Future scope and acknowledgments are given in sections 8.8 and 8.9, respectively.

8.2. Alzheimer's disease

Alzheimer's disease (AD) has been the most prevalent type of dementia, affecting approximately 35 million people worldwide, and the number is increasing. It is a degenerative neurological illness that causes the brain to thin (atrophy) and brain cells to die. Alzheimer's begins with a little amnesia and misperception and progresses with memory loss, trouble making decisions and performing routine day-to-day duties. Such changes are correlated with personality changes, as well as other symptoms including sadness, mood swings, social disengagement and aggression against others. AD is classified differently according to scientific consensus. Some consider AD as a component that contributes to dementia, while others classify the illness as a kind of dementia. AD is categorized into subtypes according to its seriousness, inflammation and manner of onset.

8.3. Alzheimer's disease types

Depending on the seriousness and the severity of its symptoms, AD may be classified into the subgroups of mild symptoms, moderate severity and severe Alzheimer's. AD with mild symptoms entails the onset of consequent dysfunction, which makes it difficult to recall daily activities such as job responsibilities and bill payments, among other things. Since these symptoms are not severe, people at this stage are able to function with difficulties. It takes them longer to do the same activities that they used to do previously, and this develops into a pattern. For AD with moderate severity, the signs of mild Alzheimer's are considerably more severe due to a significant number of neuronal impairments. The disorientation worsens, and as a result of the memory loss, people become more reliant on others. Despite their physical agility, these people are unable to accomplish everyday tasks because their delusions have taken over the sensory processing of their thinking. For severe AD, the brain cells begin to die as plaques and tangles grow throughout the brain. As a result, the brain tissue shrinks. Patients with this illness are usually immobile and have limited communication skills. These classifications are more similar to illness phases, and they commonly progress from mild to severe. The earlier a person is diagnosed, the higher their chances are of being treated and avoiding the disease from developing.

AD is classified into three subcategories depending on the inflammatory response. In response to inflammation, this subtype has a high serum albumin-to-globulin ratio and a high amount of C-reactive protein in addition to behavioral and cognitive symptoms. For non-inflammation, there are no increased inflammatory biomarkers in this subtype of Alzheimer's. However, this syndrome is often associated with other metabolic disorders. A zinc deficiency in multiple areas of the brain causes the cortical subtype. Despite a lack of an inflammatory response, this subtype causes issues with regular brain functioning that contribute to AD.

Early onset Alzheimer's disease is a type of sickness that is prevalent in patients younger than 65 years. This is a relatively rare condition that distresses 5 out of 100 patients affected by this mental decay. Patients often note changes in their late 40s or early 50s. This illness's specific traits are likely to be the outcome of a Chromosome 14 anomaly. The majority of people affected have late onset AD, which afflicts persons over the age of 65. The precise genetic cause has yet to be identified. A range of risk variables have been found by scientists, and further study is ongoing.

AD and dementia continue to be most common in Western Europe (followed by North America) and least common in South Africa. African-American people are twice as likely as white people to develop AD and other kinds of dementia. Hispanic people are roughly twice as likely as white people to develop AD or another kind of dementia.

Blockchain is a novel technology that uses cryptography (Pandey and Litoriya 2020; Shi et al. 2020) to connect a data structure that refers to a collection of items recognized as blocks. The determination of this study remains to present a summary of the existing blockchain-related papers, initiatives and amenities in medicine, as well as neuroscience. Despite the fact that the healthcare segment has accrued massive amounts of data, there are still experiments with data transmission, convenience, comparability, coordination and other preventive factors. It takes a long time for many healthcare systems to transmit, as well as process health information.

Patients and medical personnel may be prepared to communicate with one another and exchange case-relevant data on a decentralized, transparent platform, which could help to unify the overall healthcare experience.

Using a single raised area, it becomes much more stress-free to support patients, exchange proficiency from across the world and seek discussions from diverse professionals.

Despite substantial study about the pathogenesis of AD in the last three decades, no cure has been found for the condition. Little progress has been made in terms of viable treatments or techniques to prevent or cure the disease. Given the enormous increase in the number of AD cases, we may face significant economic and social challenges if no therapy is found in the next few years (Weller and Budson 2018). Furthermore, advancements in AD therapy techniques that result in even minor delays in the development or progression of the disease will greatly reduce the disease's global burden (Weller and Budson 2018).

The capacity to quantify total negative sentiment/stigma consumes consequences on behalf of anti-stigma activities. The great majority of anti-stigma initiatives now lack results measurement; as a result, it is uncertain whether these initiatives are worthwhile and successful, whether properties should be moved somewhere else or whether techniques should be changed. Determining stigma beforehand and after a movement, the launch will allow for a valuable assessment of the effects if adequate facts are gathered or constant observation of sentiment on applicable keywords is done (Bose et al. 2020).

Social integration is a significant issue for Alzheimer's patients and older people in general. It is not just a component of the stigma they are subjected to (Bose et al. 2021), but it appears that it is also affecting their cognitive health. Indeed, social isolation increases with age (Chanda et al. 2020) and the level of isolation has in fact been associated with the intensity of memory loss, as well as an increase in a variety of cognitive decline indicators and symptoms (Chanda et al. 2022).

8.4. NLP in chat-bots/AI companions

Natural language processing (NLP) refers to computer software's capacity to analyze the spoken and written human language, commonly referred to as natural language. AI (artificial intelligence) is a module of it. NLP enables computers to understand natural language in the same manner that people do. Natural language processing, whether verbal or written, uses artificial intelligence to absorb real-world input, study information and create a sense of it in an arrangement that a computer is able to comprehend. Computers contain programs that read and microphones to gather audio, much like people, who have various sensors, including ears for listening and eyes for seeing. In addition, just as people have a brain that allows them to absorb information, computers consume software that allows them to do the same. At a certain point during the handling, the input is transformed into the program, which the computer is able to comprehend. Natural Language Toolkit (NLTK), Genism and Intel Natural Language Processing Architect are three of the most popular natural language processing tools.

AI "chat-bots", which employ natural language processing (NLP) to interpret and answer user queries, may be able to relieve social isolation, while also delivering value to AD patients and older people in general. It is simple to understand why such systems are appealing for offering services to the elderly. The world's population is rapidly aging, but the number of health and social care providers is decreasing in proportion (Pilozzi and Huang 2020). To care for the expanding number of dementia patients, some caregiving tasks, such as general social contact, may need to be automated.

AI deployment is often beneficial in social/companionship jobs. The use of simple animal-like robots was shown to decrease depression among elderly individuals. It has been shown that deploying assistive robots (SAR) for social facilitation enhances the subject's social ties with their peers. The SAR Paro, a communicative robotic baby harpist seal developed in response to users' words and gestures, has been extensively researched, notably with dementia sufferers.

The application of information technology for stigmatization of AD through NLP and AI/Chatbot technologies and blockchain technologies for data security has been clearly shown in Figure 8.1. We have clearly analyzed the procedure of stigmatization through the block diagram.

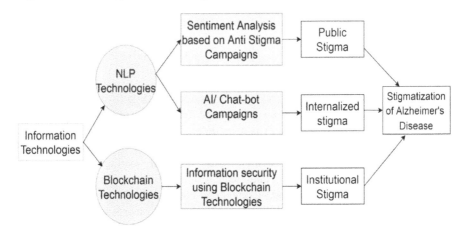

Figure 8.1. *Iconic model for the treatment of Alzheimer's patients. For a color version of this figure, see www.iste.co.uk/chakraborty/smartedge.zip*

In Figure 8.1, we have used an iconic model that is basically an operations research model for stigmatization of AD. In this iconic model, we have used both NLP technologies and blockchain technologies. NLP technology has been used to analyze the data related to this type of the above-mentioned mental illness by using sentiment analysis based on anti-stigma campaigns and AI/chat-bot campaigns. Blockchain technology has been used to maintain the entire data security for institutional stigma, which is basically some policies related to government and private organizations that intentionally or unintentionally limit opportunities for people with mental illness.

Researchers observed that Paro improves mood, decreases loneliness and reduces stress in dementia sufferers. However, some studies reveal that Paro's capacity to reduce aggressiveness and neutral affect is equivalent to a replete toy. Concerns about the expenditure of robot treatments have been expressed. This may be attributed to a lack of complex social connections. The creation of virtual personal assistants accomplished in conversing with humans in actual time is thought-provoking, but it may be valuable. On a daily basis, using their computers, older individuals reported a strong desire to engage with "Wizard of Oz" agents.

Despite the fact that the agent was computer-produced, users commented on the way in which they felt connected with it. While the majority of customers were satisfied and wanted to work through the agent again, others complained about its effortlessness and lack of realism, ultimately failing to create a link. Developing an independent agent for old and Alzheimer's patients brings its own set of challenges; given their proclivity for providing wrong orders, suitable error-recovery techniques are essential to allow for seamless, natural interaction.

It should also be noted that there is now widespread apprehension among the elderly about the idea of a "robot". Despite evidence that they are useful, a group of adults with moderate cognitive impairment (MCI) argued that an automaton could operate by way of a friend owing to the absence of true sentiment/attachment.

People who are more acquainted with robotics and its possibilities, on the other hand, are more optimistic about a social robot's abilities. Furthermore, people have responded favorably to tests with more progressive human SARs accomplished in communication with emotionality, like the "Ryan companion bot" in addition to "Brian 2.1".

Perhaps demonstrating the actual abilities of social robots to worried patients can soothe their anxieties. Surprisingly, having a real figure on behalf of an AI confidant is a tremendous benefit in terms of connection creation. However, mobile human chassis may be somewhat expensive, whereas omitting mobility and other features can dramatically reduce the cost.

Primary care professionals may be able to support the care and management of care for patients when they are diagnosed with cognitive impairment at an early stage. This has the potential to improve results for such a population. However, routinely identifying people with cognitive impairment within clinical settings must have proven logistically difficult. Validated cognitive impairment screening measures, including the Montreal Cognitive Assessment (MoCA), as well as the Mental State Exam (MMSE), remain frequently used in clinical treatment, owing in particular to the conflicting demands for element management in primary care for the elderly. The growth of Big Data analytics and healthcare information technology could have exposed new avenues for diagnosing people with cognitive impairment. Beyond previously used distinct data items such as International Classification of Diseases (ICD) analysis programs, electronic health records (EHR) embrace a massive amount of information. Permitted text documenting by physicians, as well as other health system employees may reveal information about a person's cognitive abilities, ranging from the fundamental to the advanced. Advanced informatics methodologies can be used to harness such data for cognitive impairment studies.

8.5. Proposed methodologies for reduction of stigma

In this chapter, we have described the proposed methodologies for the reduction of stigma of AD. In section 8.5.1, the proposed methodologies using NLP are described in detail. Section 8.5.2 describes the model objective function of AD.

8.5.1. *Proposed methodology using NLP*

Alzheimer's patients will benefit greatly from combining NLP approaches with AI research to produce a relatively dynamic AI assistant capable of providing help and friendship. Patients with AD would have been able to live better independently as a result of decreased social withdrawal and more opportunities for social facilitation. The proposed NLP solutions are summarized in Figure 8.2.

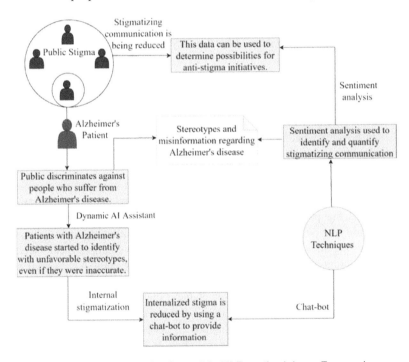

Figure 8.2. *A synopsis of possible NLP methodology. For a color version of this figure, see www.iste.co.uk/chakraborty/smartedge.zip*

It is possible that an NLP-based sentiment analysis may be recycled to detect and ease its implementation of essential anti-stigma programs aimed at eliminating public stigma against Alzheimer's, as well as dementia sufferers. The installation of a chat-bot/AI companion may assist AD patients in living independently while minimizing social isolation, as well as feelings of isolation, both of which encourage self-stigma.

In an ideal environment, people would feel comfortable knowing about their AD status and openly communicating it with others, but this is not always the case. Data privacy is a key worry in today's environment. There is a prevalent assumption that an unintended leak concerning a person's AD status can have serious consequences. The vast majority of AD patients polled believed that being diagnosed with the disease would lead to workplace prejudice. Furthermore, nearly half of those polled believed that healthcare may be restricted based on the health history of a person with AD. These fears are not without merit. Employers and insurance providers have procedures in place to prevent genetic discrimination. Participating in AD-related studies, which may require the presence of certain biomarkers and traits to qualify, puts a person at risk of prejudice even before the onset of any cognitive impairment, because study data is typically included in the participant's medical record (Yaqoob et al. 2022).

8.5.2. Model objective function of Alzheimer's disease

We have used the operations research methodology for stigmatization of the disease. The optimization seeks to minimize (equation [8.1]): (i) the total number of newly affected individuals showing various severity levels of symptoms (asymptomatic, mildly symptomatic and severely symptomatic) and (ii) a penalty term representing the number of deaths of affected individuals who do not get proper treatment, for all locations and over the whole time horizon:

$$
\min \sum_{x \in X} \sum_{j \in J}
\begin{aligned}
&\left(\sigma_x^A \overline{IA_{x,j}} + \sigma_x^{SM} \overline{ISM_{x,j}} + \sigma_x^{SS} \overline{ISS_{x,j}} \right) \cdot \left(\frac{\overline{NA_{x,j}}}{TP_x} \right) + \\
&\sum_{x \in X} \sum_{j \in J} \xi_x^A \left(\left(\overline{ISS}_{x,j} - \overline{ISS}_{x,j}^{|H|} \right) + \left(ISS_{x,j} - ISS_{x,j}^H \right) \right)
\end{aligned}
\qquad [8.1]
$$

In equation [8.1], σ_x represents the transmission rate of the disease at location x, ξ_x^A is the transition rate of severely symptomatic individuals who die without being hospitalized at location x, j is the index of the time period, X is the set of locations, J is the set of time periods, $IA_{x,j}/ISM_{x,j}/ISS_{x,j}$ represent the number of untested affected asymptomatic/mildly symptomatic/severely symptomatic individuals at location x at time j, $NA_{x,j}$ represents the number of untested asymptomatic/symptomatic individuals at location x at time j and TP_x represents the total population at location x.

The proposed objective function seeks to minimize the number of *newly affected individuals* instead of the cumulative number of affected individuals in the population since we consider heterogeneous affection levels that have different characteristics and duration of illness. If the cumulative number of infectious is considered, this would lead to longer disease duration phases with a larger weight in the objective function and a priority to be minimized (e.g. priority to minimize the asymptomatic infectious phase if it lasts longer than the severely symptomatic phase), which is not the desired outcome of the optimization. Therefore, we assume that the policymaker seeks to minimize the total number of newly affected individuals in the population regardless of how long their symptoms will last.

Furthermore, it should be noted that the penalty term is important to consider since, without setting the penalty of minimizing the number of individuals who do not receive treatment, the mathematical programming model does not have a preference between the last different removal states (recovery, death or proper treatment) as they all contribute to minimizing the number of infected individuals in the population. The only relevant factor in this case becomes the values of the transition parameters, which are not sufficient to guarantee a logical outcome of the model, in which the preference is for individuals to be hospitalized rather than leave to die if there is a faster transition of the infected population.

Finally, as it can be seen in equation [8.1], the calculation of newly affected individuals results in a nonlinear term in the objective function, i.e. a function of the disease transmission rates through the community interaction with affected individuals.

8.6. Blockchain technology for securing all medical data

Blockchain is a gathering of computers linked in a peer-to-peer network, also known as a distributed system, a technology that keeps a distributed, time stamped, transparent and fraud-proof digital ledger. The system was improved and more papers were kept within a single block by introducing the Merkle tree structure. Blockchain technology has qualities such as being decentralized, transparent, open-source software, persistent and so on (Fan et al. 2018). The blockchain technology is a public ledger that keeps all data in sets of blocks that make a complete chain of several blocks within which new blocks may be easily added. To secure transactions, this technique implements the distributed consensus mechanism, asymmetric cryptography and blockchain technology, whose major characteristics are decentralization, consistency, privacy and traceability. Because of these characteristics, blockchain is incredibly economical, time-saving and secure. Smart contracts, IoT (Internet of Things), public services, security services and many more sectors wherein blockchain technology is used include digital riches, online payments, remittance, etc. Due to the structure of blockchain technology, once a transaction has started, it cannot even be changed. Blockchain technology functions in a similar way to a cartulary record. It is a chronological transaction of information in the form of blocks that may be characterized as such. It is a growing set of documents identified as blocks. Individual blocks in the network are connected together to use cryptographic technology that uses a mathematical hash function to map any amount of data. This ensures data integrity, non-repudiation and maintaining resource sharing using blockchain in IoT technology. Each member of the network is given a set of the blockchain database (Hort et al. 2021).

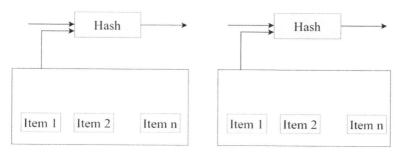

Figure 8.3. *Structure of the blockchain*

We describe the structure of the blockchain along with the concept of the hash function in Figure 8.3.

Because of the security difficulties plaguing the healthcare business, patients are understandably concerned about the protection of their medical information. A recent technological development in data storage/transfer, on the other hand, may be advantageous in mitigating breaches caused by external attackers. Blockchain technology was pioneered by the cryptocurrency "Bitcoin". It was designed to address the problem of double-spending, which arises when a sender initiates two transactions in the same currency at the same time in a decentralized network lacking the traditional central medium that verifies or invalidates transactions and decides transaction order.

B3i is the insurance industry on the blockchain, which includes multinational banks and budgetary authorities. It looks into the potential of blockchain technology in the insurance industry (Singh and Michels 2018). Voting, enhancing agricultural production, increasing supply chain transparency and reducing overfishing are all areas where blockchain may help.

The blockchain arrangement method, named the "minimum vital principle", is used to capture a separate data catalog that preserves the basic mechanisms of the type of transaction. Through the deployment of Ethereum technology for virtual private frameworks and data privacy, blockchain provides a platform to store personal health records (PHR), electronic health records (EHRs) and electronic medical records (EMR), and also manage the data.

In recent periods, blockchain technology has seen significant and exponential growth in a variety of fields. Blockchain technology plays a key role in healthcare information management (Li and Xue 2020), solving a wide range of issues such as counterfeit medicine delivery, future pandemic remedies, data security for clinical trials and point of failure.

Nowadays, there is a great need for safely processing large amounts of data at a minimal price and high efficiency. One method for managing datasets is to store data remotely in the cloud using Cloud Service. The Integrity Management Service is used by the DIaaS framework to deliver cloud services. The first issue with DIaaS is that the Third-Party Auditor does not give the promised dependable services since cloud-based IMS has to afford Data Integrity services crossways multiple stands focused on dynamic IoT data.

The blockchain-based Data Integrity Service platform with IoT data is presented in light of the circumstances. Information integrity is regarded as unique among the most important security concerns regarding data storing, which may take the form of cloud data storage as well as distributed data storage. The most essential approaches in protocols are provable data possession (PDP) and proofs of irretrievability (PoR), which attempt to certify huge stored data integrity on semi-trusted or untrusted servers while minimizing the cost of data integrity. The PDP presents a method for checking most of the data blocks by confirming a minimal sum of blocks, whereas PoR examines the data blocks and determines the data.

Blockchain technology has advanced substantially in fields such as healthcare in recent years. Medical records include private and sensitive information which must be kept secure. Several firms have established unique technologies in the early stages of design and development that have the potential to optimize medical data, including heterogeneous transparency and operational capabilities (Tanwar et al. 2020).

We will discuss blockchain strategies for data privacy in healthcare in section 8.6.1, application of blockchain technologies in section 8.6.2, blockchain application intended for EHR data management in section 8.6.3, different issues related to blockchain security and privacy in section 8.6.4 and different challenges faced by blockchain applications in section 8.6.5.

8.6.1. *Blockchain strategies for data privacy in healthcare*

Datasets are needed for health researchers to better comprehend diseases, learn about biological discoveries and produce medications and strategies based on the patient's situations, heredities and environment. Blockchain would grow by providing up-to-date data on the populaces of individuals receiving medical treatment from medical authorities. The data provided in the context of blockchain makes it simpler to approach patients and exhibits more favorable public results. When compared to existing healthcare service database management systems, blockchain has numerous advantages.

Sections 8.6.1.1, 8.6.1.2 and 8.6.1.3 clearly explain the different areas of healthcare where blockchain strategies are most commonly used.

8.6.1.1. *Blockchain for hospital-patient communication*

Blockchains' decentralized management is appropriate for applications such as hospitals and patients who want to communicate without the involvement of central management.

8.6.1.2. *Utilizing immutable blockchain for insurance claim record*

Blockchains provide unchangeable audit trails, making them suitable for non-changeable databases such as insurance claim records for recording vital information.

8.6.1.3. *Blockchain enhancing data provenance, privacy and security in healthcare*

Blockchain is used to enable data provenance, which is ideal for managing digital assets such as patient information in clinical studies. Only the owner has the ability to modify ownership via cryptographic techniques. Furthermore, the origins of both the records and data could be validated, boosting the reusability of certified data. Blockchains provide data availability and robustness, making them ideal for record retention and ongoing availability. The patient's electronic health records (EHRs) will, for example, be retained indefinitely in the hospital database. Blockchain provides privacy and security for data by encrypting data and decrypting it using the patient's private keys. Even when the network is compromised, it secures the data from harmful parties; there is also no way to read the data.

8.6.2. *Application of blockchain technologies*

Blockchain technology may be used not only in finance, but also in a variety of fields. We will describe the concept of Bitcoin in section 6.2.1, Ethereum in section 6.2.2 and Hyperledger in section 6.2.3.

8.6.2.1. *Bitcoin is a type of digital currency*

Blockchain technology was used to create Bitcoin's data structure and transaction mechanism, providing it with even more digital currency and an online payment system. Using encoded technology, resources may remain sent without depending on a central bank. Bitcoin used public keys to send as well as receive Bitcoin, document the transaction, as well as maintain the personal ID confidential. The operation confirms that the mechanism requires the computing power of other users to reach a consensus, and the transaction is logged into the network.

8.6.2.2. *Ethereum: smart contract*

A smart contract is a digital contract that controls the custom of a user's digital content, but also specifies that participant's privileges and duties. A computer system executes it automatically. In the realm of computer functions, smart contracts can be likened to essential actors responsible for responding to messages, preserving data and transmitting messages or assets to external entities. These intelligent contracts, much like individuals, can be relied upon to temporarily hold assets and execute predetermined instructions as part of their programming. Ethereum is an open blockchain system that combines smart contracts with a decentralized virtual machine for contract management. The digital currency, ETH, may be used to create a wide variety of facilities, applications and contracts. Figure 8.4 shows a view of a hypothetical architecture where medical blockchain keeps an up-to-date version of all health data and uses smart contracts to secure the data.

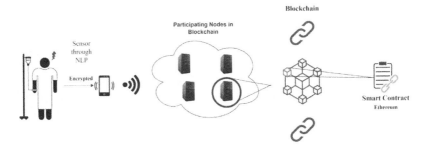

Figure 8.4. *Graphical illustration of a hypothetical architecture in which the medical blockchain keeps an up-to-date version of all health data and uses smart contracts to secure the data. For a color version of this figure, see www.iste.co.uk/chakraborty/ smartedge.zip*

8.6.2.3. *Hyperledger*

Hyperledger was introduced as a proprietary distributed ledger by the Linux Foundation in December 2015. The goal of this technology is to improve the performance and reliability. This technology focuses on several significant financial, supply chain and technical enterprises. A range of independent projects have been presented to demonstrate open standards and protocols by providing a modular framework to enable components for diverse application. A plethora of blockchains will be included, each with their own consensus and repository, as well as specification, authentication and contract management services.

8.6.3. *Blockchain application intended for EHR data management*

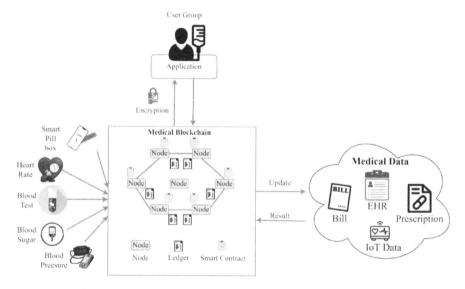

Figure 8.5. *Blockchain-based applications are used to secure medical data by implementing the ledger and smart contract technologies of blockchain. For a color version of this figure, see www.iste.co.uk/chakraborty/smartedge.zip*

A distributed ledger such as blockchain is a feasible choice for personal EHR management. Smart contracts are used to share patient data in the form of tokens. As stated in various research articles, this allows patients to give protection and privacy to their data, as well as build and gather their personal medical records. The goal is to improve communication between caregivers and healthcare organizations so that they can deliver very particular and primary care to patients related to the health-related collected data. For personal EHR management, blockchain is a viable choice. Smart contracts are used to share patient data in the form of tokens. As stated in various research papers, this allows patients to give protection and privacy to their data, as well as build and gather their personal medical records. A healthcare blockchain is a new technological development that encourages cutting-edge clinical research and customized treatment options. It is the finest alternative for giving a patient therapy and communicating with a clinical research rather than instinct. Its key advantages are the aspects of trust, productivity and compliance. Decentralized systems rely on blockchain technology.

Electricity is distributed to all nodes in the system using an established and agreed-upon protocol. The health ledger based on web technology is completely dependent on the network backend as a service. In Figure 8.5, we clearly depict the concept of blockchain-based applications that are used to secure medical data by implementing the ledger and smart contract technologies.

8.6.4. *Issues with blockchain security and privacy*

Many programs do not encrypt transactions since they are widely distributed. When the information is near to home-based information, such as "medical or financial information", organizational and legal concerns arise, notably in Germany. One solution is to save only encoded data in the blockchain, but this raises another problem: if the method for decoding explicit data is destroyed, the data may not have been recovered precisely. Furthermore, if a key is stolen and shared, all of the data inside the blockchain remains decoded indefinitely because the data cannot be altered. However, blockchain can help improve protected cybersecurity measures, particularly in terms of identification and access.

We will discuss the concept of attacks through man-in-the-middle in section 6.4.1, the concept of tampering the data in section 6.4.2, the concept of DDoS attacks in section 6.4.3 and the concept of privacy in section 6.4.4.

8.6.4.1. *Attacks through man-in-the-middle*

Certificate authority (CA) is obtained from the man-in-the-middle (MITM) to also provide public keys to the client (open key replacement MITM assault). MITM is one of the tactics. This can lead to sensitive data being decrypted. In a blockchain technology, customers set the open keys in distributed obstructs and the information is propagated through the participating hubs with links to previous and subsequent squares. As a result, the open key remains intact, making counterfeit keys easier to propagate. Furthermore, the CA, the primary cause of unhappiness, is extensively diffused, meaning that reducing this administration is more necessary.

8.6.4.2. Tampering the data

Individual transactions are labeled and distributed across all hubs related to blockchain, making it almost difficult to control information. A distributed ledger such as blockchain may be used in medical services to create permanent audit trails, ensure the accuracy of health preliminary reports and ensure the integrity of patient data exchanged across multiple clinical situations.

8.6.4.3. DDoS (denial-of-service) attacks

Botnet assaults such as the Mirai botnet would have been easier to stop if the DNS infrastructure was built on blockchain technology. A system of this type would give simplicity and security. The DNS framework could not be concentrated if it was a scattered substructure since the data is allowed and the information portions will not be amended due to the unique character of the blockchain technology. Turtle's research also comprises determining how to control DNS through the use of blockchain technology.

8.6.4.4. Privacy

Blockchain technology is an excellent illustration of the randomized security and protection (at least in the context of permanence). This transaction will be available to all hubs in the system as because of it, it is feasible to build a constant, coated transaction. The most promising inquiry on security issues related to blockchain is zCash on Ethereum. Nowadays, zk-SNARKs are implemented by zCash and Ethereum. The combination of two improvements allows for the implementation of unknown payments, delayed closeouts and a voting mechanism. The mechanisms that underlie zk-SNARKs are too sophisticated to show at this time. The researchers highlight the requirement for improved new approaches for planning and assessing digital projects.

8.6.5. Challenges faced by blockchain applications

Metadata is made whether or not security-enhancing innovation is conveyed. A quantifiable investigation choice finds "a few" data, regardless of whether the data itself is encoded, permitting for plan acknowledgment. Furthermore, because the contract method is now prohibitively expensive, flexibility is a developing test. When money or other assets are transferred over a blockchain-based network, a substantially quicker transfer speed is required. Ethereum now has a data rate of 2.8 data per unit; however, bitcoin has a data rate of approximately 3.2 data per second. The process takes so long because of the extensive agreement procedure for each transaction. Another notable attack is a "higher part hash rate attack" by a 51% assaulter. If an organization or individual holds 51% of hash power, an attacker has the ability to reverse transactions, prohibit deals from gathering confirmations and restrict other miners from mining.

The concepts of privacy and data ownership, legality and security are discussed in detail in sections 6.5.1, 6.5.2 and 6.5.3, respectively.

8.6.5.1. *Privacy and data ownership*

The person is cooperative for completion of interconnection of patient information and utilization, which are significant elements of blockchain. In order to show a blockchain, considerable framework restructuring has been demanded from the Senate and organizations to patients due to moving information ownership. It would inspire individuals to become dynamic experts on their own to give information to seek the best care. The blockchain would also provide users with the single capability to provide data access to multiple providers under control, eliminating the delays associated with present administration and maintaining tolerant security. The features of blockchain continue to provide patients with control over their information, which is a demand in an era where mutualistic and consumer culture thinking specialist connections are becoming the norm. Patients could even use particularly relevant legislation for analysts using blockchain, whether for more significant logical reasons or to focus on their specific problem. Allowing patient and physician associations to securely regulate the use of their information enabled by blockchain would increase the adoption of such platforms and, perhaps, contribute to improved health outcomes. Distribution information can be modified to be disclosed in a framework, but as an inducement, "healthy and developing" patients, meant for design, can be provided with low insurance premiums if there are privacy problems in blockchain. This, and other comparable attitudes, should be used to gauge how successfully they will discover a solution.

8.6.5.2. *Legality*

Individuals can request the deletion of information in accordance with General Data Protection Regulation articles, security regulation for the Organization of Economic Co-Operation, the privacy rule of the Health Insurance Portability Act (HIPAA) and other regulations. If records are not stored in the blockchain, this is indeed possible. Furthermore, regardless of its deletion, a record containing historical data can be added to the chain. The valid question that ascends from this concerns the availability of private, as well as other information about our houses. In any event, the method data in the framework would have been restricted through the patient, and regardless remains a sign of development. Because of information security issues, one approaching constraint is that the use of a privately or consortium-driven blockchain should be intended to make administrations uniform and sellers neutral. For example, HIPAA requires that an organizational assessment board approves the use of data. This significant rescheduling is implausible in any case; thus, adhering to these standards is critical to the success of blockchain.

8.6.5.3. *Security*

Sensitive data necessity can be protected from gatecrashers and busybodies. Disruptions have a detrimental impact on the open perspective of the medical services area and have the potential to sabotage future research by imposing progressively strict administrative restrictions. The WannaCry ransomware attack in May 2017 infected a huge number of computers worldwide, such as those used by the NHS. For authorization of patients, the procedure of inheritance measurement is also used, but blockchain technology is more secure than the inheritance measurement procedure. The above-mentioned technology is capable of achieving this functionality by using a public key encryption technique. Hash is a method that includes generating private and public keys for each client. A single-direction encryption method has been used. Because their private key ensures that only the beneficiary sees data communicated through the blockchain, it is exceedingly improbable that anybody other than the beneficiary would view it. The most serious security flaw that may occur with such a blockchain is randomly produced and occurs while using an open blockchain: programmers may collaborate in an "attack of 51%", causing the chain structure to be modified. Machine learning and blockchain technology have been improved by public blockchain for the system risk of e-healthcare systems. Patients' original identification is avoided by pseudo-missing data for future protection of data. Furthermore, if a corporate or consortium blockchain were used, mining centers could be limited to emergency clinics or other trusted health providers, removing these security flaws. Sharing and capacity of clinical data (creating interoperability) are critical for enhanced security outcomes, especially when it comes to the protection of sensitive data, and this remains a key challenge in social support. The manuscript shows how blockchain can be used through the right organizational regulations and theories in place to manage consented access to EHRs.

In this section, we have discussed some of the most prominent blockchain-based medical and healthcare initiatives and uses. MediBloc is an open-source distributed health data platform. Blockchain technology is used for the benefit of patients, health practitioners and research workers related to health activities. Because of its blockchain technology, all aspects of healthcare have been traced and recorded, such as record modifications and doctor's appointments. An Ethereum Virtual Machine serves as the platform's basis, which is a decentralized software (EVM). MedRec is indeed a blockchain-based, distributed record management solution that provides digital medical information using a Medi Point system (MP), a point-based method. Secrecy, authentication and data accountability are managed by the qualities of this blockchain technology. Empathetic health-related data should be taken into account. HealthCoin is indeed a blockchain-based currency that connects apparently unconnected aspects of preventative healthcare – hospitals, companies, healthcare programs, insurance, governments, non-governmental groups and wellness apps. Health-related information is verified without significant transaction loss using huge database analytics as well as statewide coordination, and a customized program to prevent various diseases is designed. It works by attaching a token to quantifiable health improvements. Some existing solutions are built on a permissioned blockchain network that anyone can connect to. To compensate for the absence of trust, current systems often use native money or transaction fees, which can also consume a significant amount of computing resources. Although some research is based on a permissioned network, it is primarily concerned with the exchange of data related to EMR and is therefore inappropriate for use in a real production environment.

8.7. Conclusion

The stigma associated with AD affects the illness's diagnosis, treatment and prevention. People are stigmatized for signs that may not exist due to the features of a presently incurable and inescapable sickness that affects cognitive function. As a result, many avoid diagnosis and the cultural and organizational challenges that accompany it. Much of the stigma originates from misinformation regarding the ailment and the spread of negative comments on the Internet. Because of the real-world impact of anti-stigma activities, the use of NLP to assess and monitor public opinion can be immensely valuable in evaluating the existence of stigma, as well as monitoring the success of anti-stigma programs. As data security is a main consideration among the general public, particularly among those who wish to keep sensitive health information private, improved cybersecurity, such as that provided by distributed databases such as a distributed ledger-based service, can be exceptionally valuable in overcoming the stigmatization with Alzheimer's disease. Combating Alzheimer's stigma is crucial to improving living conditions and medications for current Alzheimer's patients, and will also be useful for future patients.

8.8. Future scope

Future work in this field of research can be used to analyze the use of different tasks in larger samples of AD and include novel features such as emotional tone to classify groups to improve awareness of this particular disease. This approach will lead to identifying very early linguistic changes for the early diagnosis of AD.

Intellectual IoT and computational intelligence can be used in this research work to improve the early detection of AD.

8.9. Acknowledgments

We completed this chapter in the computer laboratories of the Nopany Institute of Management Studies, the Academy of Technology and Brainware University. We would like to extend our heartfelt thanks to all colleagues and friends at the Nopany Institute of Management Studies, the Academy of Technology and Brainware University, for their continuous support in the completion of this chapter.

Finally, we would like to thank God for allowing us to pass through all difficulties.

8.10. References

Adhikari, S., Thapa, S., Singh, P., Huo, H., Bharathy, G., Prasad, M. (2021). A comparative study of machine learning and NLP techniques for uses of stop words by patients in diagnosis of Alzheimer's disease. *2021 International Joint Conference on Neural Networks*, 1–8.

Adhikari, S., Thapa, S., Naseem, U., Singh, P., Huo, H., Bharathy, G., Prasad, M. (2022). Exploiting linguistic information from Nepali transcripts for early detection of Alzheimer's disease using natural language processing and machine learning techniques. *International Journal of Human-Computer Studies*, 160, 102761–102761.

Armstrong, R.A. (2019). Risk factors for Alzheimer's disease. *Folia Neuropathological*, 57(2), 87–105.

Bose, R., Aithal, P.S., Roy, S. (2020). Sentiment analysis on the basis of tweeter comments of application of drugs by customary language toolkit and TextBlob opinions of distinct countries. *International Journal of Emerging Trends in Engineering Research (IJETER)*, 8(7), 3684–3696.

Bose, R., Aithal, P.S., Roy, S. (2021). Survey of Twitter viewpoint on application of drugs by VADER sentiment analysis among distinct countries. *International Journal of Management, Technology, and Social Sciences (IJMTS)*, 6(1), 110–127.

Chanda, K., Bhattacharjee, P., Roy, S., Biswas, S. (2020). Intelligent data prognosis of recurrent of depression in medical diagnosis. *2020 8th International Conference on Reliability, Infocom Technologies and Optimization (Trends and Future Directions) (ICRITO)*, 840–844.

Chanda, K., Roy, S., Mondal, H., Bose, R. (2022). To judge depression and mental illness on social media using Twitter. *Universal Journal of Public Health*, 10(1), 116–129.

Chattu, V.K. (2021). A review of artificial intelligence, Big Data, and blockchain technology applications in medicine and global health. *Big Data and Cognitive Computing*, 5(3), 41.

Dey, R.K., Sarddar, D., Sarkar, I., Bose, R., Roy, S. (2020). A literature survey on sentiment analysis techniques involving social media and online platforms. *International Journal of Scientific & Technology Research*, 1(1), 166–173.

Fan, K., Wang, S., Ren, Y., Li, H., Yang, Y. (2018). Medblock: Efficient and secure medical data sharing via blockchain. *Journal of Medical Systems*, 42(8), 1–11.

de la Fuente Garcia, S., Ritchie, C.W., Luz, S. (2020). Artificial intelligence, speech, and language processing approach to monitoring Alzheimer's disease: A systematic review. *Journal of Alzheimer's Disease*, 78(4), 1547–1574.

Gold, M., Amatniek, J., Carrillo, M.C., Cedarbaum, J.M., Hendrix, J.A., Miller, B.B., Robillard, J.M., Jeremy Rice, J., Soares, H., Tome, M.B. et al. (2018). Digital technologies as biomarkers, clinical outcomes assessment, and recruitment tools in Alzheimer's disease clinical trials. *Alzheimer's & Dementia: Translational Research & Clinical Interventions*, 4, 234–242.

Hort, J., Vališ, M., Zhang, B., Kuča, K., Angelucci, F. (2021). An overview of existing publications and most relevant projects/platforms on the use of blockchain in medicine and neurology. *Frontiers in Blockchain*, 4(14), 1–8.

Kaur, I., Kumar, Y., Sandhu, A.K. (2021). A comprehensive survey of AI, blockchain technology and big data applications in medical field and global health. *2021 International Conference on Technological Advancements and Innovations (ICTAI)*, 593–598.

Khan, A. and Zubair, S. (2022). An improved multi-modal based machine learning approach for the prognosis of Alzheimer's disease. *Journal of King Saud University – Computer and Information Sciences*, 34(6), 2688–2706.

Li, Q. and Xue, Z. (2020). A privacy-protecting authorization system based on blockchain and zk-SNARK. *Proceedings of the 2020 International Conference on Cyberspace Innovation of Advanced Technologies*, 439–444.

Liu, Z., Paek, E.J., Yoon, S.O., Casenhiser, D., Zhou, W., Zhao, X. (2022). Detecting Alzheimer's disease using natural language processing of referential communication task transcripts. *Journal of Alzheimer's Disease (JAD)*, 86(3), 1385–1398.

Matthews, K.A., Xu, W., Gaglioti, A.H., Holt, J.B., Croft, J.B., Mack, D., McGuire, L.C. (2019). Racial and ethnic estimates of Alzheimer's disease and related dementias in the United States (2015–2060) in adults aged ≥65 years. *Alzheimer's & Dementia: The Journal of the Alzheimer's Association*, 15(1), 17 24.

Pandey, P. and Litoriya, R. (2020). Implementing healthcare services on a large scale: Challenges and remedies based on blockchain technology. *Health Policy and Technology*, 9(1), 69–78.

Petti, U., Baker, S., Korhonen, A. (2020). A systematic literature review of automatic Alzheimer's disease detection from speech and language. *Journal of the American Medical Informatics Association (JAMIA)*, 27(11), 1784–1797.

Pilozzi, A. and Huang, X. (2020). Overcoming Alzheimer's disease stigma by leveraging artificial intelligence and Blockchain technologies. *Brain Sciences*, 10(3), 183.

Putra, F.B., Arman Yusuf, A., Yulianus, H., Pratama, Y.P., Salma Humairra, D., Erifani, U., Basuki, D., Sukaridhoto, S., Nourma Budiarti, R.P. (2019). Identification of symptoms based on natural language processing (NLP) for disease diagnosis based on international classification of diseases and related health problems (ICD-11). *International Electronics Symposium (IES)*, 1(5), 1–3.

Sheikhalishahi, S., Miotto, R., Dudley, J.T., Lavelli, A., Rinaldi, F., Osmani, V. (2019). Natural language processing of clinical notes on chronic diseases: Systematic review. *JMIR Medical Informatics*, 7(2), e12239.

Shi, S., He, D., Li, L., Kumar, N., Khan, M.K., Choo, K.R. (2020). Applications of blockchain in ensuring the security and privacy of electronic health record systems: A survey. *Computers & Security*, 97, 101966.

Singh, J. and Michels, J.D. (2018). Blockchain as a service (BaaS): Providers and trust. *Queen Mary School of Law Legal Studies Research Paper*, 269.

Soni, A., Amrhein, B., Baucum, M., Paek, E.J., Khojandi, A. (2021). Using verb fluency, natural language processing, and machine learning to detect Alzheimer's disease. *2021 43rd Annual International Conference of the IEEE Engineering in Medicine & Biology Society (EMBC)*, 2282–2285.

Tanwar, S., Parekh, K., Evans, R. (2020). Blockchain-based electronic healthcare record system for healthcare 4.0 applications. *Journal of Information Security and Applications*, 50(102407), 2–4.

Weller, J. and Budson, A. (2018). Current understanding of Alzheimer's disease diagnosis and treatment. *F1000Research*, 7(F1000), 1161.

Yaqoob, I., Salah, K., Jayaraman, R., Al-Hammadi, Y. (2022). Blockchain for healthcare data management: Opportunities, challenges, and future recommendations. *Neural Computing and Applications*, 34(1), 11475–11490.

Computer Vision-based Edge Computing System to Detect Health Informatics for Oral Pre-Cancer

Over the last decade, the Internet of Things (IoT) has been the most favorable and promising technology for every growing-edge domain. The IoT is playing an impressive role in new cutting-edge computer applications, showing a new path to leading industries such as healthcare, agriculture, robotics, automotive, home automation and the smart city. Automation in the Industrial Internet of Things (IIoT) is increasing in several industries. The objective of the present study was to assess the clinical correlation between histological changes in the pre-cancerous tissues of subjects with oral submucous fibrosis and the normal control group. This study was conducted on tissue samples from oral submucous fibrosis (n = 20) compared with the healthy group (n = 20). The tissues were stained with special histochemical stains for carbohydrates (periodic acid Schiff (PAS)), lipids (Sudan IV) and collagen (Van Gieson's (VG) stain)) for histochemical characterization analysis.

9.1. Introduction

Cancer is a primary cause of mortality and a major impediment to improving life expectancy in every single republic in the world (Bray et al. 2021). According to the World Health Organization's predictions for 2019, cancer is the primary or second leading cause of death at the age of 70 in 112 out of 183 countries, and the third or fourth leading cause of death in a further 23 countries (WHO 2020).

Chapter written by Animesh Upadhyaya, Vertika Rai, Surajit Bose, Dipankar Bhattacharya and Jayanta Chattopadhyay.

The increasing prevalence of cancer as the leading cause of death is partly due to a significant reduction in mortality rates from stroke and coronary heart disease in several countries compared to cancer (Bray et al. 2021). Oral submucous fibrosis (OSF) is a chronic inflammatory condition with no known cause and has a high risk of developing into cancer. Current methods for diagnosing OSF include clinical evaluation and biopsy using an invasive technique (Rai et al. 2018). The disease must have minimally invasive, specific markers that can be used for risk assessment. Accomplishing this requires a deeper understanding of the complex molecular processes that control disease progression (Varela-Centelles et al. 2017). Early diagnosis increases the survival of oral pre-cancer while reducing incidence and mortality rates (Epstein et al. 2002). Altered histology and morphology, as the disease progresses towards carcinogenesis, is one of the primary distinguishing properties between malignant cells (Rai et al. 2019a). These alterations take place at different stages, all of which lead to reprogramming in cancer histology (Rai et al. 2019b).

Medical imaging is an important data source used in healthcare systems all around the biosphere. Histopathological images are used in pathology for cancer analysis. Nevertheless, these images are extremely complicated, and pathologists have to make significant efforts to analyze them. Medical imaging is an important data foundation used for the study, diagnosis and prognosis of diseases throughout the biosphere. In the broad field of medicine, there are innumerable different types of medical images. Radiology is the discipline of medicine that uses radiation-based images to analyze disorders and chaperone therapy, such as bone X-rays, brain MRIs, cardiac ultrasounds and liver CT scans. On the contrary, pathology studies the causes and consequences of diseases using images such as histology, cytopathology and dermatopathology. Histopathology is the study of diseases using histopathological images of tissue changes. Digital image processing is characterized by medical images of various shapes and sizes. On the contrary, ML and DL are very useful for analyzing cell images. Nowadays, the IoHT (Internet of Healthcare Things) is very popular and conventional. Using IoT methods, we can store the data in a cloud, analyze it in the cloud and collect the results easily.

The remainder of this chapter is organized as follows: section 9.2 reviews the currently available literature. The proposed model and calculations are detailed in section 9.3. The test results are summarized in section 9.4.

Mass spectrometric imaging developed by researchers is a good complement to microscopy-based approaches to visualize tumor heterogeneity. This can contribute to the understanding of tumor biology and the development of future therapeutic techniques (Abramowski et al. 2015). We provide evidence that osteosarcoma origin can proceed following a neutral development model in which many cancer replicas coexist and spread simultaneously (Gambera et al. 2018). An effective method for the clonality of cell research in tissue renaissance and disease is the RGB pattern (Gurcan et al. 2009). After all the exhaustive literature review, there is no research where the histopathological image from a microscope is not uploaded to the cloud and analyzed. Therefore, in this chapter, we developed an application that analyzes RGB color space segmentation depending on cancerous and non-cancerous cells. The histogram for each color component helps us to understand the distribution of brightness, contrast and dynamic range of the color components. We want to perform interpretation on IoT devices, while training is typically performed on mobile applications.

9.2. Related works

In this section, researchers examine the most recent cutting-edge CAD expertise in digital histopathology. Correspondingly, this presentation temporarily highlights the expansion and implementation of unique image analysis technologies for some particular histopathology challenges being performed in the US and Europe (Gurcan et al. 2009). Using the CNN approach, they identified the nucleus from tissue from the histopathological images and segmented the plots (Irshad et al. 2013; Veta et al. 2014; Xing and Yang 2016). They also used the Hough transform (Cosatto et al. 2008), the H-maximum system (Jung and Kim 2010) and the log filtering (Byun et al. 2006; Al-Kofahi et al. 2009; Kong et al. 2013). A similar work with a different technique was developed by the researchers, and the processes they used were fuzzy clustering and multi-phase vector (Hafiane et al. 2008; Bunyak et al. 2011). The researchers discussed the popularity of IoHT and the devices used, as well as cloud connections and data analysis in the cloud resources (Upadhyaya et al. 2022). The researchers developed FastNCA extended parallel execution, which used a dispersed parallelism approach to improve the FastNCA operation (Elsayad et al. 2020).

9.3. Materials and methods

Discarded biopsy slides were collected from Pathology at KSD Jain Dental College & Hospital for the analysis of various stains.

9.3.1. *Microscopic imaging*

Images were captured using a LEICA DM750 microscope (Leica Microsystems, Germany) at 10x magnification (0.25 numerical aperture (NA), with a pixel resolution of 0.63 μm x 0.63 μm and a final magnification of 100x). The images were captured under bright field microscopy with a LEICA ICC50E camera.

9.3.2. *Proposed methodology*

9.3.2.1. *Statistical analysis*

A separate sample t-test was performed to compare the two groups, OSF and normal. The SPSS program was used to analyze the data. Student's t-tests were used to compare the results at a 5% level of significance (p 0.005). The amount in serum that distinguishes between two groups was investigated using the receiver operating characteristic (MedCalc software). The sensitivity and specificity of the markers were assessed using 95% confidence intervals (95% CI).

9.3.2.2. *Histopathological analysis*

Compared to normal, all stained sections showed atrophic and dysplastic alterations in the epithelium. Representative periodic acid Schiff sections on the periodic acid Schiff stained slide showed that the abnormalities were caused by a change in the amount of carbohydrate and glycogen in the tissue sections. Glycogen expression was observed in the suprabasal area of the OSF with the epithelium of the dysplasia group, but was absent in the control group. According to the properties of the stain, glycogen expression was evident in the magenta color in OSF with dysplasia. Increased collagen deposition was observed in the subepithelial region of OSF cases with dysplasia stained with Van Gieson and compared to controls. According to the literature, fibrosis contributes not only to the development of trismus, but also to the stiffening of connective tissue. In Sudan, IV-stained slides showed that OSF with dysplasia had an altered lipid state in contrast to the control group. OSF with the dysplasia group in both the epithelial and subepithelial areas showed the expression of red lipid accumulation. The aforementioned finding confirmed evidence from tissue samples of altered protein, lipid and carbohydrate status.

Literature	Objective	Methodology	Contribution	Remark
Bunyak et al. (2011)	*Nucleus detection*	*Fuzzy clustering with multi-phase vector level set*	*Fully automatic unsupervised approach*	*There are over- and under- segmentation problems.*
Pan et al. (2017)	*Nucleus segmentation*	*Sparse reconstruction and deep CNN*	*The sparse reconstruction technique is used to eliminate the backdrop*	*Since the operation is pixel-based, the processing time is longer.*
Bębas et al. (2021)	*MRI texture analysis*	*SVM, kNN, RF, deep learning*	*Histological subtype of non-small-cell lung cancer using MRI texture analysis*	*Since the operation is pixel-based, the processing time is longer.*

Literature	Objective	Methodology	Contribution	Remark
Benzekry et al. (2021)	*Prediction of immunotherapy efficacy*	*Statistical learning model*	*Non-small-cell lung cancer from simple clinical and biological data*	*Low computational burden*
Luna et al. (2019)	*Predicting radiation pneumonitis*	*Random forest, RUSBoost CART, support vector machines, logistic regression*	*Locally advanced stage II–III non-small-cell lung cancer*	*High computational burden*
Xu et al. (2015)	*Nucleus detection*	*Stacked autoencoder*	*Stacking sparse autoencoder for unsupervised learning*	*High computational burden*
Sirinukunwattana et al. (2016)	*Nucleus segmentation*	*Deep CNN with spatial constraints and a nearby ensemble predictor*	*Local neighboring information is included for better performance*	*High computational burden*
Wang et al. (2016)	*Nucleus segmentation*	*Wavelet breakdown and growth at several scales*	*Wavelet with multiscale region growth for nucleus localization*	*Need further evaluation on large data*

Table 9.1. *Summary of cancer and pre-cancer detection techniques*

9.3.3. *RGB color segmentation*

The proposed methodology consists of two stages: in the first stage, we collect the image through the mobile application and the image is fragmented into such a pixel. Then, the color segmentation is started. In the second stage, the wavelength of the test image is determined with a good cell and the comparison result is sent.

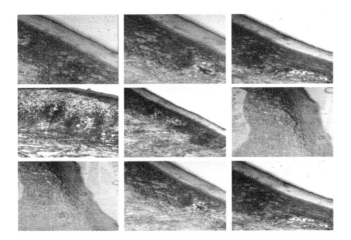

Figure 9.1. *Cancerous cells. For a color version of this figure, see www.iste.co.uk/chakraborty/smartedge.zip*

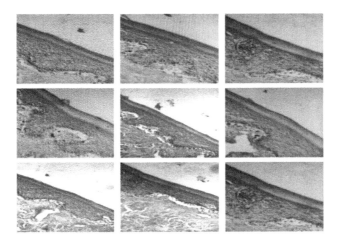

Figure 9.2. *Non-cancerous cells. For a color version of this figure, see www.iste.co.uk/chakraborty/smartedge.zip*

We collected 30 samples, in which 15 samples were cancerous cells (Figure 9.1) and 15 were non-cancerous (Figure 9.2). All samples were collected and analyzed by our mobile application.

9.3.3.1. *Application analysis*

We developed an android application. The application captures the cell, and there are options to select region-wise features and analyze RGB values that are converted into a wavelength nanometer and a color nanometer result.

Figure 9.3. *Application screenshot of cancerous and non-cancerous cells. For a color version of this figure, see www.iste.co.uk/chakraborty/smartedge.zip*

Figure 9.3 shows the analysis of cancerous and non-cancerous cells.

9.3.3.2. *Image filters for color images*

The process of color image smoothing is as follows:

$$f(x,y) = \begin{cases} \dfrac{1}{\gamma} \displaystyle\sum_{(x,y)\in W} R(x,y) \\[2.2em] \dfrac{1}{\gamma} \displaystyle\sum_{(x,y)\in W} G(x,y) \\[2.2em] \dfrac{1}{\gamma} \displaystyle\sum_{(x,y)\in W} B(x,y) \end{cases}$$

Similarly, the process of color image sharpening can be denoted as follows:

$$\nabla^2[f(x,y)] = \begin{cases} \nabla^2[R(x,y)] \\ \nabla^2[G(x,y)] \\ \nabla^2[B(x,y)] \end{cases}$$

Color image edge detection can be done in the following way. Let **r**, **g** and **b** be unit vectors. Assume that these vectors are along the **R**, **G** and **B** axes of an image. The vectors **u** and **v** can be defined as:

$$u = \frac{\partial R}{\partial x}r + \frac{\partial G}{\partial x}g + \frac{\partial B}{\partial x}b$$

and

$$u = \frac{\partial R}{\partial y}r + \frac{\partial G}{\partial y}g + \frac{\partial B}{\partial y}b$$

The following components can be defined as:

$$g_{xx} = u.u = u^T u = \left|\frac{\partial R}{\partial x}\right|^2 + \left|\frac{\partial G}{\partial x}\right|^2 + \left|\frac{\partial B}{\partial x}\right|^2$$

$$g_{xy} = v.v = v^T u = \left|\frac{\partial R}{\partial x}\right|^2 + \left|\frac{\partial G}{\partial x}\right|^2 + \left|\frac{\partial B}{\partial x}\right|^2$$

and

$$g_{xy} = u.v = u^T v = \frac{\partial R}{\partial x}.\frac{\partial R}{\partial y} + \frac{\partial G}{\partial x}.\frac{\partial G}{\partial y} + \frac{\partial B}{\partial x}.\frac{\partial B}{\partial y}$$

The direction of a maximum rate of change is given as:

$$\theta = \frac{1}{2} tan^{-1} \left[\frac{2g_{xy}}{g_{xx} - g_{yy}} \right]$$

And the rate of change along the direction $\theta(x, y)$ is given as:

$$F_\theta(x, y) = \left\{ \frac{1}{2} (g_{xx} + g_{yy}) + (g_{xx} - g_{yy}) \cos 2\theta(x, y) + 2g_{xy} \sin 2\theta(x, y) \right\}^{\frac{1}{2}}$$

9.3.3.3. RGB color space segmentation

This method aims to use a specific color range for segmenting the ROI. Let the average color be denoted by a vector m. Let z be an arbitrary point in the RGB spaces.

For image segmentation, the distance between m and z is computed as:

$$D(x, m) = \|x - m\|$$

$$= \{(x - m)^T (x - m)\}^{\frac{1}{2}}$$

$$= [(x_R - m_R)^2 + (x_B - m_G)^2 + (x_B - m_B)^2]^{\frac{1}{2}}$$

The distance is compared with the threshold value. If $D(x, m) \le$ threshold values, then the points belong to the ROI. Otherwise, they are not part of the ROI.

Another useful generalization is to use the Mahalanobis distance, which has the form:

$$D(x, m) = [(x - m)^T \sum_{0}^{-1} (x - m)]^{\frac{1}{2}}$$

Similarly, the distance between the pixel can also be calculated using the Euclidean distance.

9.4. Results

In Figure 9.4, we analyze the error bar standard deviation and the differences are shown in the red, blue and green plots of cancerous and non-cancerous cells. There is a large error gap between each bar. The gap cannot be seen very clearly in the blue and green bars. Thus, we must say that the wavelength of the cancer cell is moving towards the red bar.

Therefore, we only analyze and plot the red region of cancerous and non-cancerous cells. As shown in Figure 9.5, we confirm that in cancerous cells, the wavelength of the cell area is before the value of 600 nm.

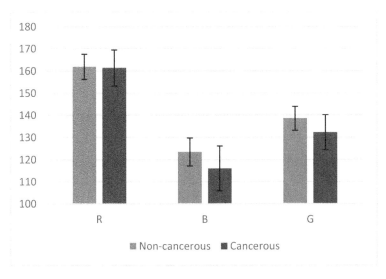

Figure 9.4. *RGB color segmentation analysis of cancerous and non-cancerous cells. For a color version of this figure, see www.iste.co.uk/chakraborty/smartedge.zip*

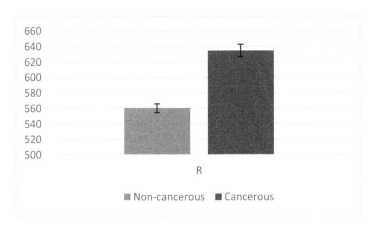

Figure 9.5. *Red color segmentation analysis of cancerous and non-cancerous cells. For a color version of this figure, see www.iste.co.uk/chakraborty/smartedge.zip*

As shown in Figure 9.6, the graph of the cancerous cells always exceeds the 600 nm limit in color segmentation. Some of the non-cancerous cells are about 600 nm, which according to the pathologist, are pre-cancerous cells. Therefore, we can examine the structure of the pre-cancerous cell. The concept is invasive, but without the pathologist's confusion, we are in a complete ML-based application confirmation.

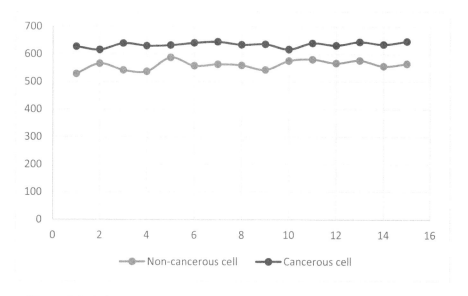

Figure 9.6. *Color segmentation analysis of cancerous and non-cancerous cells. For a color version of this figure, see www.iste.co.uk/chakraborty/smartedge.zip*

9.5. Conclusion

Oral squamous cell carcinoma has a high malignant potential with a high propensity to metastasize to the regional lymph nodes through vascular invasion, resulting in locoregional failure. Various histopathological prognosticators such as vascular invasion, perineural invasion, bone involvement and lymph node involvement help us to predict the outcome and behavior of squamous cell carcinoma. Proper recognition of the histological variants is an important factor in the treatment of squamous cell carcinoma, since verrucous carcinoma requires less aggressive treatment than conventional squamous cell carcinoma.

Our aim is to develop the comparative difference between histochemical analysis and computer vision-based analysis by evaluating a database of cancerous and non-cancerous cell images and a mobile application-based system in which we classify cancerous cells using RGB color space segmentation.

9.6. References

Abramowski, P., Kraus, O., Rohn, S., Riecken, K., Fehse, B., Schlueter, H. (2015). The combined application of RGB marking and mass spectrometric imaging facilitates the detection of tumor heterogeneity. *Cancer Genomics & Proteomics*, 12(4), 179–187.

Al-Kofahi, Y., Lassoued, W., Lee, W., Roysam, B. (2009). Improved automatic detection and segmentation of cell nuclei in histopathology images. *IEEE Transactions on Biomedical Engineering*, 57(4), 841–852.

Bębas, E., Borowska, M., Derlatka, M., Oczeretko, E., Hładuński, M., Szumowski, P., Mojsak, M. (2021). Machine-learning-based classification of the histological subtype of non-small-cell lung cancer using MRI texture analysis. *Biomedical Signal Processing and Control*, 66, 102446.

Benzekry, S., Grangeon, M., Karlsen, M., Alexa, M., Bicalho-Frazeto, I., Chaleat, S., Tomasini, P., Barbolosi, D., Barlesi, F., Greillier, L. (2021). Machine learning for prediction of immunotherapy efficacy in non-small cell lung cancer from simple clinical and biological data. *Cancers*, 13(24), 6210.

Bray, F., Laversanne, M., Weiderpass, E., Soerjomataram, I. (2021). The ever-increasing importance of cancer as a leading cause of premature death worldwide. *Cancer*, 127(16), 3029–3030.

Bunyak, F., Hafiane, A., Palaniappan, K. (2011). Histopathology tissue segmentation by combining fuzzy clustering with multiphase vector level sets. In *Software Tools and Algorithms for Biological Systems*, Arabnia, H. and Tran, Q.N. (eds). Springer, New York.

Byun, J., Verardo, M.R., Sumengen, B., Lewis, G.P., Manjunath, B.S., Fisher, S.K. (2006). Automated tool for the detection of cell nuclei in digital microscopic images: Application to retinal images. *Molecular Vision*, 12(105–107), 949–960.

Cosatto, E., Miller, M., Graf, H.P., Meyer, J.S. (2008). Grading nuclear pleomorphism on histological micrographs. *2008 19th International Conference on Pattern Recognition*, 1–4. IEEE.

Elsayad, D., Hamad, S., Shedeed, H.A., Tolba, M.F. (2020). Gene regulatory network construction parallel technique based on network component analysis. *The International Conference on Artificial Intelligence and Computer Vision*, 850–857. Springer, Cham.

Epstein, J.B., Zhang, L., Rosin, M. (2002). Advances in the diagnosis of oral premalignant and malignant lesions. *Journal-Canadian Dental Association*, 68(10), 617–621.

Gambera, S., Abarrategi, A., González-Camacho, F., Morales-Molina, Á., Roma, J., Alfranca, A., García-Castro, J. (2018). Clonal dynamics in osteosarcoma are defined by RGB marking. *Nature Communications*, 9(1), 1–13.

Gurcan, M.N., Pan, T., Shimada, H., Saltz, J. (2006). Image analysis for neuroblastoma classification: Segmentation of cell nuclei. *2006 International Conference of the IEEE Engineering in Medicine and Biology Society*, 4844–4847.

Gurcan, M.N., Boucheron, L.E., Can, A., Madabhushi, A., Rajpoot, N.M., Yener, B. (2009). Histopathological image analysis: A review. *IEEE Reviews in Biomedical Engineering*, 2, 147–171.

Hafiane, A., Bunyak, F., Palaniappan, K. (2008). Clustering initiated multiphase active contours and robust separation of nuclei groups for tissue segmentation. *2008 19th International Conference on Pattern Recognition*, 1–4. IEEE.

Irshad, H., Veillard, A., Roux, L., Racoceanu, D. (2013). Methods for nuclei detection, segmentation, and classification in digital histopathology: A review–current status and future potential. *IEEE Reviews in Biomedical Engineering*, 7, 97–114.

Jung, C. and Kim, C. (2010). Segmenting clustered nuclei using H-minima transform-based marker extraction and contour parameterization. *IEEE Transactions on Biomedical Engineering*, 57(10), 2600–2604.

Kong, H., Akakin, H.C., Sarma, S.E. (2013). A generalized Laplacian of Gaussian filter for blob detection and its applications. *IEEE Transactions on Cybernetics*, 43(6), 1719–1733.

Kourou, K., Exarchos, T.P., Exarchos, K.P., Karamouzis, M.V., Fotiadis, D.I. (2015). Machine learning applications in cancer prognosis and prediction. *Computational and Structural Biotechnology Journal*, 13, 8–17. doi: 10.1016/j.csbj.2014.11.005.

Leitheiser, M., Capper, D., Seegerer, P., Lehmann, A., Schüller, U., Müller, K.R., Klauschen, F., Jurmeister, P., Bockmayr, M. (2022). Machine learning models predict the primary sites of head and neck squamous cell carcinoma metastases based on DNA methylation. *The Journal of Pathology*, 256(4), 378–387.

Luna, J.M., Chao, H.H., Diffenderfer, E.S., Valdes, G., Chinniah, C., Ma, G., Cengel, K.A., Solberg, T.D., Berman, A.T., Simone II, C.B. (2019). Predicting radiation pneumonitis in locally advanced stage II–III non-small cell lung cancer using machine learning. *Radiotherapy and Oncology*, 133, 106–112.

Pan, X., Li, L., Yang, H., Liu, Z., Yang, J., Zhao, L., Fan, Y. (2017). Accurate segmentation of nuclei in pathological images via sparse reconstruction and deep convolutional networks. *Neurocomputing*, 229, 88–99.

Rai, V., Mukherjee, R., Ghosh, A.K., Routray, A., Chakraborty, C. (2018). "Omics" in oral cancer: New approaches for biomarker discovery. *Archives of Oral Biology*, 87, 15–34.

Rai, V., Bose, S., Saha, S., Chakraborty, C. (2019a). Evaluation of oxidative stress and the microenvironment in oral submucous fibrosis. *Heliyon*, 5(4), e01502.

Rai, V., Bose, S., Saha, S., Kumar, V., Chakraborty, C. (2019b). Delineating metabolic dysfunction in cellular metabolism of oral submucous fibrosis using 1H nuclear magnetic resonance spectroscopy. *Archives of Oral Biology*, 97, 102–108.

Saba, T. (2020). Recent advancement in cancer detection using machine learning: Systematic survey of decades, comparisons and challenges. *Journal of Infection and Public Health*, 13(9), 1274–1289.

Sirinukunwattana, K., Raza, S.E.A., Tsang, Y.W., Snead, D.R., Cree, I.A., Rajpoot, N.M. (2016). Locality sensitive deep learning for detection and classification of nuclei in routine colon cancer histology images. *IEEE Transactions on Medical Imaging*, 35(5), 1196–1206.

Upadhyaya, A., Mistry, C., Kedia, D., Pal, D., De, R. (2022). Applications and accomplishments in the internet of things as the cutting-edge technology: An overview. OSF Preprints. doi: 10.31219/osf.io/p9enu.

Varela-Centelles, P., López-Cedrún, J.L., Fernández-Sanromán, J., Seoane-Romero, J.M., de Melo, N.S., Álvarez-Nóvoa, P., Gómez, I., Seoane, J. (2017). Key points and time intervals for early diagnosis in symptomatic oral cancer: A systematic review. *International Journal of Oral and Maxillofacial Surgery*, 46(1), 1–10.

Veta, M., Pluim, J.P., Van Diest, P.J., Viergever, M.A. (2014). Breast cancer histopathology image analysis: A review. *IEEE Transactions on Biomedical Engineering*, 61(5), 1400–1411.

Wan, N., Weinberg, D., Liu, T.Y., Niehaus, K., Ariazi, E.A., Delubac, D., Kannan, A., White, B., Bailey, M., Bertin, M. et al. (2019). Machine learning enables detection of early-stage colorectal cancer by whole-genome sequencing of plasma cell-free DNA. *BMC Cancer*, 19(1), 1–10.

WHO (2020). Global Health Estimates 2019: Deaths by cause, age, sex, by country and by region, 2000-2019. World Health Organization, Geneva.

Xing, F. and Yang, L. (2016). Robust nucleus/cell detection and segmentation in digital pathology and microscopy images: A comprehensive review. *IEEE Reviews in Biomedical Engineering*, 9, 234–263.

Xu, J., Xiang, L., Liu, Q., Gilmore, H., Wu, J., Tang, J., Madabhushi, A. (2015). Stacked sparse autoencoder (SSAE) for nuclei detection on breast cancer histopathology images. *IEEE Transactions on Medical Imaging*, 35(1), 119–130.

10

A Study of Ultra-lightweight Ciphers and Security Protocol for Edge Computing

With the urge to increase safety and security while transmitting information over the Internet, we need to shift our concern towards the security protocols. A security protocol (cryptographic protocol or encryption protocol) is an abstract or concrete protocol that performs a security-related function and applies cryptographic methods, often as sequences of cryptographic primitives. Cryptographic protocols are widely used for secure application-level data transport. A lightweight protocol refers to any protocol that has a lesser and leaner payload when being used and transmitted over a network connection. As defined by NIST, a lightweight protocol must be within 2,500 gate equivalents (GEs). It is simpler, faster and easier to manage than other communication protocols used on a local or wide area network.

On the other hand, ultra-lightweight protocols are protocols that have a much lower overhead and require minimum hardware and simple operations when transmitted through a network connection. Designing protocols in the ultra-lightweight setting is challenging as it requires approximately 1,500 GEs. It is very likely that a large percentage of tomorrow's interconnected world will consist of ultra-lightweight computing elements. Ultra-lightweight protocols rely only on basic arithmetic and logical operations (modular addition, and, or, xor, etc.). Devices that require low memory, low power supply and have hardware constraints require ultra-lightweight security protocols to ensure high levels of security and privacy. Here, some ultra-lightweight security algorithms such as PRESENT, Piccolo and Hummingbird are studied. We further studied ultra-lightweight protocols such as CoAP, XMPP and MQTT.

10.1. Introduction

The Internet of Things (IoT) has been exploited in numerous application areas. We obtain IoT facilities by linking to numerous servers over numerous types of

Chapter written by Debasmita PAUL, Aheli ACHARYA and Debajyoti GUHA.

networks that expose IoT systems to additional serious safety and confidentiality dangers that involve hardware and software vulnerabilities. Confidentiality jeopardies are generated due to a gathering of confidential data in the IoT environment (Kolias et al. 2019). Authentication is compulsory for user systems (Bae and Kwak 2017). Therefore, protected and lightweight protocols are required by means of small price tags (Avoine et al. 2010). Scientists and researchers are putting an emphasis on ultra-lightweight security protocols.

10.1.1. Evolution of the IoT

Kevin Ashton first suggested the IoT in 1999, which was duly reviewed in 2005 by ITU, and four key technologies were introduced in the IoT, thereby attracting great attention from users (Ashton 2016). These technologies are RFID, nano, wireless sensors and intelligent systems. A lot of devices are being associated with one or many devices worldwide, and several other smart devices are being added to the Internet globally.

People are now frequently joining the smart IoT world using these devices. Most of them usually contain constrained devices with smart handheld devices to electronic user-controlled devices (Sehrawat and Gill 2018). Constrained devices are restricted by storing ability and energy consumption. They are connected to the cloud and managed in wireless sensor networks. Each of them has an exclusive identification number (Suo et al. 2012; Tarish 2018). Protocols are used to connect these devices with other devices (Suo et al. 2012; Tarish 2018).

Block ciphers are crucial for systems that require data integrity, confidentiality and privacy. Low resource devices such as RFID tags and sensor nodes require lightweight cryptography. And thus, the study of designing and analyzing lightweight block ciphers has received a lot of attention.

The main issue of designing lightweight and ultra-lightweight encipher algorithms is to handle the trade-off between safety, rate and performance (Poschmann 2009). Ultra-lightweight cryptographic primitives have become available in recent years, mainly focusing on resource-controlled smart devices.

10.1.2. Content of the review work

The word ultra-lightweight represents a different methodology to cryptographic design by using basic procedures such as xor, + mod n and cyclic shift. It has been developed in recent years in the framework of authentication protocols to deliver very effective and safe solutions.

In this chapter, we will discuss six ultra-lightweight security protocols. A detailed description will be given about their architecture, features and application areas.

RFID arrangements are usually used in high-security applications like access control systems, transaction banking systems and payment systems. The invader tries to mislead RFIDs for unapproved admission to services without payment or to evade safety mechanisms by identifying a secret password. Therefore, how to safeguard successful defense against violations has become the main challenge in RFID systems. Ultra-lightweight cryptography can provide a safety guarantee for defending RFID systems. This chapter presents six ultra-lightweight cryptography algorithms, namely SLIM, Picolo, Hummingbird, LEAP, MIFARE and RFB for RFID systems.

SLIM is a 32-bit block cipher based on the Feistel construction. The key task in designing an ultra-lightweight block cipher is to deal with performance, cost and safety. SLIM uses a similar key for enciphering and deciphering.

Piccolo provides an adequate level of safety against recognized analyses, together with recent related key differential attacks and meet-in-the-middle attacks. Moreover, Piccolo requires just 60 additional gate equivalents to support the decipher function due to its involution structure. Its efficiency on the energy consumption is extraordinary, which makes it a competitive ultra-lightweight block cipher suitable for exceptionally constrained environments such as RFID tags and sensor nodes.

Due to the tight cost and limited resources of high-volume consumer devices such as RFID tags, smart cards and wireless sensor nodes, it is desirable to use ultra-lightweight and specialized cryptographic primitives for many security applications. Hummingbird provides planned safety with smaller block size and is resilient to most common attacks such as linear and differential cryptanalysis.

The lightweight extensible authentication protocol (LEAP) is a Cisco authentication protocol based on EAP, an extension to PPP. This authentication type provides the highest level of safety for wireless networks. By applying EAP to work together with an EAP-compatible RADIUS server, the access point (AP) helps a wireless client device and the RADIUS server to execute mutual authentication and derive a dynamic unicast wired equivalent privacy (WEP) key. The RADIUS server delivers the WEP key to the AP, which uses it for all unicast data signals that it delivers to or receives from the client. The AP also enciphers its broadcast WEP key (entered in the access AP's WEP key slot 1) with the client's unicast key and sends it to the client.

MIFARE Ultralight product-based tickets are perfect for low-priced, high-capacity applications serving as the contactless replacement for magnetic stripe or barcode, addressing the drift of switching entire systems to purely contactless solutions.

RFB ("remote frame buffer") is a simple protocol for remote access to graphical user interfaces. It works at the frame buffer level. It is appropriate for all windowing schemes and applications, including X11, Windows and Macintosh. It is a "thin client" protocol. The remote endpoint where the user sits (i.e. the display plus the keyboard and/or pointer) is called the RFB client or viewer. The endpoint where changes to the frame buffer originate (i.e. the windowing system and applications) is known as the RFB server.

Section 10.2.1 discusses the SLIM ultra-lightweight protocol. Section 10.2.2 deals with Picolo. Piccolo encryption is ultra-lightweight, making it appropriate for enormously constrained surroundings. Section 10.2.3 deals with Hummingbird, an ultra-lightweight encryption scheme whose application areas are a privacy-preserving identification and mutual authentication protocol for RFID applications. At the end of section 10.2.4, a comparative study between the discussed protocols is performed.

Section 10.3.1 discusses the lightweight extensible authentication protocol or LEAP. LEAP is a very prevalent security solution in wireless sensor networks. Section 10.3.2 deals with the MIFARE ultra-lightweight protocol. Section 10.3.3 deals with the remote frame buffer (RFB). RFB is in fact a "thin client" protocol. In the last part of section 10.3, a comparative study between the protocols is performed.

10.2. Ultra-lightweight ciphers

Nowadays, devices have become compact and require less resources. Providing security to such devices requires ciphers that are different from the conventional ones. Ultra-lightweight ciphers provide security to resource-constrained devices efficiently.

In sections 10.2.1–10.2.3, we will discuss a brief outline of the architecture, working, features and applications of some commonly used ultra-lightweight ciphers. Section 10.2.4 consists of a comparison between the three ultra-lightweight ciphers mentioned below.

10.2.1. *SLIM*

In section 10.2.1.1, we will provide a brief overview of the SLIM ultra-lightweight block cipher. In section 10.2.1.2, the working and architecture of the SLIM are discussed. In section 10.2.1.3, we will describe the features and applications of the SLIM.

10.2.1.1. *Brief description*

SLIM is an ultra-lightweight block cipher that was presented by B. Aboushosha in 2020. The security of resource-constrained devices is the biggest concern in today's world. The existing cryptographic algorithms provide protection to high resource devices efficiently, but for RFID systems that are used in high-security applications such as access control systems, transaction banking systems, security against malicious attacks is provided by lightweight algorithms. SLIM provides security to RFID applications with much less power consumption and limited implementation area.

It is a 32-bit block cipher based on the Feistel structure and mostly provides very tight protection for the Internet of Health Things devices. It uses an 80-bit key size through 32 rounds, by using 32 sub-keys, each 16-bit, which are generated from the 80-bit key. It also uses four (4 × 4) S-boxes. It is applicable to both hardware and software environments.

Despite its simple design, SLIM has proven to be effective against all kinds of cryptanalytic attacks, thereby securing the devices.

10.2.1.2. *Architecture and working*

This section describes the architecture of the algorithm. SLIM is a symmetric encryption algorithm where the same key is used for both the encryption and decryption processes, except between two processes, decryption sub-keys are applied in reverse order.

Figure 10.1 shows the Feistel structure of SLIM. It achieves both confusion and diffusion concepts. Confusion is accomplished by using a compact 4-bit S-box with high nonlinearity properties. Diffusion is accomplished by using a combination of various operations. Simplicity is achieved by using a compact S-box, as well as internal simple operations. This algorithm uses a 32-bit plaintext and ciphertext blocks, and is controlled by an 80-bit key. SLIM consists of 32 rounds using 32 sub-keys of 16 bits each, which are generated from the 80-bit key. The input (32-bit) is divided into two parts that go through several rounds (32-round) along with the generated sub-keys. The detailed architecture is as follows:

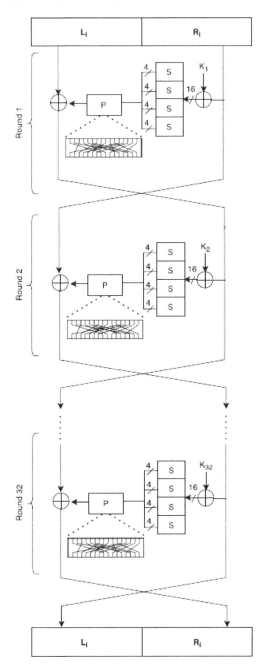

Figure 10.1. *SLIM encryption*

A) Single round processing: the 32-bit input is divided into two equal 16-bit halves-Li and Ri. Equations [10.1] and [10.2] show the overall processing. The right half of the input Ri and the sub-key Ki are XORed. The output of the XORing operation is forwarded to an S-box, and the output of the S-boxes is forwarded to a permutation process. Finally, the output is XORed with the left half to become the right half input of the next round. The right half of the input Ri became the left half input of the next round.

$$\text{Li D Ri1} \tag{10.1}$$

$$\text{Ri D Li1 \_ P .S .Ki \_ Ri1//} \tag{10.2}$$

B) Substitution layer: the poor design of S-boxes makes the algorithm weak. Here, designing the S-box is the most challenging part. SLIM uses S-box (Table 10.1), which is used four times in parallel. The S-box should be strong enough to prevent linear and differential attacks, and 4-bit S-boxes have the lowest footprint. The substitution layer is selected based on linear and differential cryptanalysis performed on a cipher.

x	0	1	2	3	4	5	6	7	8	9	A	B	C	D	E	F
S(x)	C	5	6	B	9	0	A	D	3	E	F	8	4	7	1	2

Figure 10.2. *Substitution layer*

A) Permutation layer: permutation is the last stage of the SLIM function. The permutation box takes 16-bit and permutes them according to certain rules, generating a 16-bit output.

x	0	1	2	3	4	5	6	7	8	9	A	B	C	D	E	F
P(x)	7	13	1	8	11	14	2	5	4	10	15	0	3	6	9	12

Figure 10.3. *Permutation layer*

B) Key generation: 32 sub-keys generated from the 80-bit encryption key are required for 32 rounds and a block of 32-bit.

C) Decryption structure: decryption is done in the same way as encryption. Ciphertext is taken as the input but the decryption sub-key is applied in the reverse order with another sub-key. The decryption round structure is similar to that of encryption, like any symmetric encryption algorithm. In Figure 10.4, the left-hand side indicates the encryption process with the Ki sub-key. The round output consists of n-bits representing the coded message. The right-hand side shows the decryption procedure with the same sub-key Ki. The round function is in the opposite order. The round output consists of n-bits representing the original message.

10.2.1.3. Features and applications

The most important feature of the SLIM algorithm is to have less footprint area suitable for RFID applications.

The algorithm is effective for wireless networks (e.g. wireless sensor networks (WSNs)) and IoT applications. In the future, SLIM will be widely used in the healthcare IoT framework to analyze it for sensitive applications.

10.2.2. Piccolo

In section 10.2.2.1, we give a brief overview of the Piccolo cipher. In section 10.2.2.2, the working and architecture of Piccolo is discussed. In section 10.2.2.3, we will learn about the features and applications of Piccolo.

10.2.2.1. Brief description

In recent years, lightweight cryptography has flourished, as has the designing of lightweight block ciphers. Piccolo is a block cipher that is suitable for the protection of resource-constrained devices such as RFID tags and sensor networks. Piccolo achieves both high security and notably compact implementation in hardware devices that are equipped with limited computation resources and small memory. It has an iterative structure, which is a variant of a generalized Feistel network. In the smallest implementation, the hardware requirements for the 80 and 128-bit key modes are only 683 and 758 GE with 432 and 528 cycles per block, respectively. The Piccolo block cipher achieves good security and very compact implementation, unlike other Feistel-type structure-based lightweight block ciphers.

Therefore, Piccolo, which supports both encryption and decryption functions, is still comparable to other encryption-only lightweight block ciphers.

10.2.2.2. Architecture and working

The architecture of Piccolo is a variant of GFN that can easily support the decryption function without much implementation cost and has light round functions. Piccolo supports 64-bit blocks to fit standard applications, and 80 and

128-bit keys to achieve moderate security levels. The main difference between Piccolo-80 and Piccolo-128 is that Piccolo-80 uses 64-bit blocks with 80-bit keys and 25 rounds, and Piccolo-128 uses 64-bit blocks with 128-bit keys and 31 rounds. The hardware requirements for the 80 and the 128-bit key modes are only 683 and 758 gate equivalents, respectively.

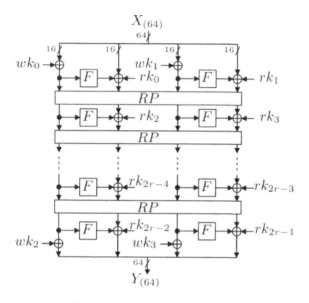

Figure 10.4. *Encryption function*

A) Key schedule: by a permutation-based key scheduling method, the required number of gates can be significantly reduced. Piccolo requires only 60 additional GE to aid the decryption function. The permutation must be carefully chosen to provide immunity against attacks that achieve weakness in the key schedule such as related-key differential and MITM attacks.

B) Round permutation: an 8-bit word-based permutation between rounds is used by Piccolo to improve the diffusion property instead of a 16-bit word-based cyclic shift used in the standard GFN. By destroying the 16-bit word structure, security against strong attacks is achieved.

C) F-function: this has two S-box layers that are separated by a diffusion matrix. The S-box consists of four NOR gates, three XOR gates and one XNOR gate. The structure of the S-box is similar to that of GFN, which is four-round iterative. The S-box of the F-function is appropriate for efficient threshold implementation.

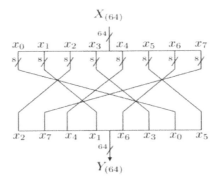

Figure 10.5. *Round permutation*

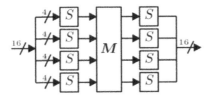

Figure 10.6. *F-function*

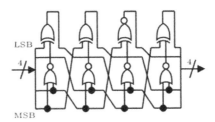

Figure 10.7. *S-box*

10.2.2.3. *Features and applications*

The main feature that makes Piccolo unique is that it has an iterative structure that is a variant of a generalized Feistel network.

Piccolo is suitable for extremely constrained environments such as RFID tags and sensor nodes, as well as devices with low computing power.

10.2.3. *Hummingbird*

In section 10.2.3.1, we give a brief overview of the Hummingbird cipher. In section 10.2.3.2, the working and architecture of Hummingbird is discussed. In section 10.2.3.3, we learn about the features and applications of Hummingbird.

10.2.3.1. *Brief description*

An increasing need to provide security among low resource devices, designing and analyzing lightweight block ciphers has received a lot of attention. Hummingbird is a novel ultra-lightweight cryptographic algorithm proposed for resource-constrained devices such as RFID tags, smart cards and wireless sensor nodes. The design of this algorithm is inspired by the well-known Enigma machine. Block ciphers and stream ciphers combine to make a hybrid structure of Hummingbird, and this is effective against attacks such as differential and linear cryptanalysis attacks. An advantage of this algorithm is that it provides reasonable security with a smaller block size.

10.2.3.2. *Architecture and working*

Hummingbird is quite different from other cryptographic block and stream ciphers. It is a combination of the above block and stream cipher structures with a 16-bit block size, a 256-bit key size and an 80-bit internal state. The architecture provides security to many embedded applications effectively.

A) Initialization process: Figure 10.8 shows the initialization process. Four 16-bit random nonces are selected to initialize the four internal state registers RSi (i = 1; 2; 3; 4), respectively, followed by four consecutive encryptions on the message RS1 _ RS3 by Hummingbird running in initialization mode

B) Encryption process: a 16-bit plaintext block PTi is encrypted after the initialization process by first executing a modulo 216 addition of PTi and the content of the first internal state register RS1. The addition result is then encrypted by the first block cipher Ek1. This process is repeated three more times, and the output of Ek4 is the ciphertext CTi. Figure 10.9 shows the overall encryption process of Hummingbird.

C) Decryption process: the process of decryption is similar to that of encryption. Figure 10.10 shows the overall decryption process.

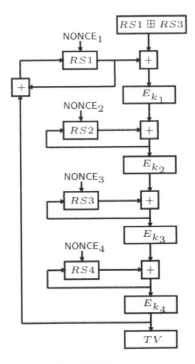

Figure 10.8. *Initialization process*

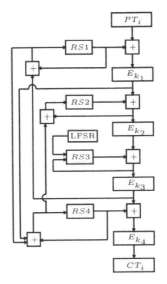

Figure 10.9. *Encryption process*

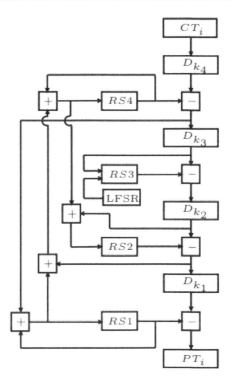

Figure 10.10. *Decryption process*

D) 16-bit block cipher: the 16-bit block cipher is a typical substitution permutation (SP) network with a 16-bit block size and a 64-bit key. It consists of four regular rounds, comprised of a key mixing step, a substitution layer, a permutation layer and a final round that only includes the key mixing and the S-box substitution steps. The substitution layer consists of four S-boxes with 4-bit inputs and 4-bit outputs. The key mixing step is performed using a simple exclusive-OR operation.

10.2.3.3. *Features and applications*

Hummingbird has a hybrid structure unlike other cryptographic block and stream ciphers. It provides security with a small block size.

This cipher is suitable for a large variety of embedded applications.

10.2.4. *Comparison between SLIM, Piccolo and Hummingbird ciphers*

Features	LEAP	MIFARE	RFB
Effectiveness	Good	Good	Good
Power consumption	Successful in using less power	Power consumption depends on used technology and the EDA tool	By replacing four S-boxes with a single one, power requirement is reduced
Structure	It is based on the Feistel structure	It has an iterative structure, which is a variant of a Generalized Feistel Network	Block ciphers and stream ciphers combine to make a hybrid structure of Hummingbird
Applications	Healthcare IoT framework	Sensor nodes	Embedded applications
Cost	Use of compact S-boxes has saved the implantation cost	The underlying GFN structure reduces the implementation cost	Low cost

Table 10.1. *Comparative study of ultra-lightweight ciphers*

Table 10.1 shows the comparative study of some ultra-lightweight ciphers. Each one has applications in various fields, which provide effective security. SLIM is designed carefully with respect to power and area constraints for resource-constrained devices such as RFID tags. Moreover, the use of compact S-boxes has saved memory space and implementation costs. For Piccolo, the power consumption entirely depends on the technology used and the EDA tool. It is proportional to the area requirement at low frequencies. To measure the efficiency with respect to the power consumption in this work, the area requirement, i.e. gate equivalents (GE), is adopted. Piccolo implements several design approaches such as the half-word-based round permutation and the effective permutation for key expanding to avoid known attacks without losing efficiency on power consumption. The hybrid model of Hummingbird provides sufficient security with a small block size and thus it is expected to meet the power consumption requirements and stringent response time for a large variety of embedded applications. By replacing four S-boxes with a single S-box, the power requirements of this cipher are efficiently reduced.

10.3. Ultra-lightweight security protocols

Although the ultra-lightweight system has numerous limitations, it is designed to provide a good solution to security and privacy concerns. Here, we will describe such protocols that are able to provide authorized and encrypted communication to the end-users with a very low computational and storage setting.

In sections 10.3.1–10.3.3, we will give a brief outline of the architecture, working, features and applications of some commonly used ultra-lightweight security protocols. Section 10.3.4 consists of a comparison between the three below-mentioned ultra-lightweight security protocols.

10.3.1. *Lightweight extensible authentication protocol (LEAP)*

In section 10.3.1.1, we will give a brief overview of the lightweight extensible and authentication protocol. In section 10.3.1.2, the working and architecture of the LEAP protocol is discussed. In section 10.3.1.3, we will learn about the features and applications of the LEAP protocol.

10.3.1.1. *Brief description*

In sensor networks, the nodes that are not protected physically in several environments are vulnerable to security threats. Security threats such as sinkhole attacks, wormhole attacks, false nodes, passive information gathering, malicious data, etc. are included. To overcome such security threats, a sensor network is designed with a strong sensor hardware that is more efficient in terms of security and chosen to minimize the effects of the threats and boost the performance of the network. Sometimes it is necessary to increase the cost of protocols and software to ensure strong network security. We will see how the LEAP protocol design provides a solution to the above-mentioned problem.

The lightweight extensible authentication protocol (LEAP) developed by Cisco systems is a proprietary wireless LAN authentication method. Built on the 802.1x authentications, LEAP is a wireless technology mainly designed for local area networks (LANs). The protocol allows the user to not be confined to a specific domain or within the rotation of encrypted security keys. LEAP, being a very popular security key management protocol in wireless sensor networks, provides extensive security and support to the sensor networks. The lightweight extensive authentication protocol was proposed by Zhu et al. (2004). This protocol enables broadcast authentication of the base station using Tesla. It also uses a one-way hash key to authenticate various source packets in the wireless sensor network. In a sensor network, every message that has been broadcasted between different sensor nodes contains different security requirements and is quite different from other messages. On the basis of this above-mentioned point, the LEAP protocol is designed.

Although the protocol is known to be vulnerable to dictionary attacks or base station attacks, it can be secured if sufficient complex passwords are used. However, the use of complex passwords is rare in the real world, as they are difficult for regular general users to use.

10.3.1.2. *Architecture and working*

When exchanging messages, LEAP uses four types of keys, which are assigned to each individual node in the network to meet security requirements. The four types of keys ensure a high level of security when exchanging messages, which are discussed below.

In section 10.3.1.2.1–10.3.1.2.4, we will briefly discuss the four types of keys that are assigned to each node to ensure its security.

10.3.1.2.1. Individual key

To ensure secure communication between a node and its corresponding base station, a unique key called the individual key is used. It is very important to have a secured communication between the base station and node as it helps the node to give necessary information to the base station about any unusual behavior among the surrounding nodes. It even helps the base station to be aware of any false node or attacks from malicious nodes. So, the individual key plays a crucial role in encrypting confidential information, like specifying instructions to a particular node. The following equation is used to construct an individual key:

10.3.1.2.2. Pairwise key

The second type of key used in the LEAP protocol to ensure encrypted communication between a node and its neighboring sensor nodes is the pairwise key. This key ensures the protection of communications that are not authenticated by the source, and the transmission shared between a node and its neighboring node prevents attacks by intruders. After a node is introduced to the network, it can use the individual key to establish communication with the base station and identify its neighbors by sending a message encrypted with the pairwise key to establish a strong and secure connection.

10.3.1.2.3. Group key

The third key used in the LEAP protocol is the group key, which is shared globally by all the sensor nodes present in the network. The base station uses this key to encrypt the message that needs to be sent to all the nodes of the network. The advantage of using this key is that the base station does not have to encrypt the same message for every node using the individual keys. Instead, the base station can broadcast the message using the group key. The key is updated occasionally, which ensures confidentiality and security because if a node stops working or malfunctions, it is removed from the network.

10.3.1.2.4. Cluster key

The cluster key is a special case of a group key where it is generated by a node using a random function and shared within its multiple neighboring sensor nodes. This key is encrypted using the pairwise key to ensure decryption only by authenticated neighbors to get access to the cluster key.

The working of the LEAP protocol is simple and implemented using one base station and randomly situated sensor nodes. An individual key is generated for each node, and each node generates a cluster key that helps to connect to their neighboring nodes using the pairwise keys. The base station generates a group key to communicate through public broadcast with the sensor node of the network.

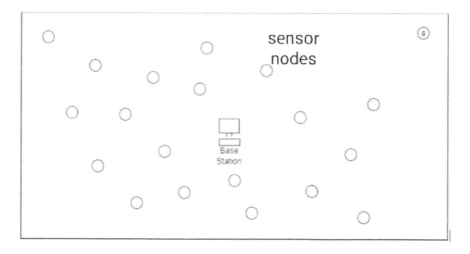

Figure 10.11. *Ideal case scenario for LEAP protocol*

Figure 10.11 shows the ideal case for the LEAP protocol. The base station is in the center and is surrounded by a number of sensor nodes. In an ideal scenario, no nodes are removed from the network. But even in the ideal case, there is the problem of data loss. If a node that is far from the base station wants to communicate, it must transmit through more nodes, resulting in higher bandwidth usage and a high risk of data loss.

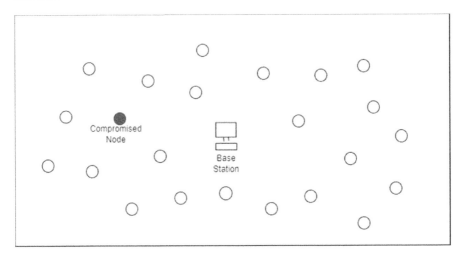

Figure 10.12. *Compromised sensor node scenario for LEAP protocol*

Figure 10.12 shows the case where a node is compromised in the LEAP protocol. The black circles represent the healthy sensor nodes, while the red circle represents the compromised sensor node. The base station is in the center and among the surrounded nodes, one node is colored red and marked as a compromised node, which is the hacked node. In cases where a sensor node has been hacked, the LEAP protocol efficiently acts against such nodes. The LEAP protocol has the advantage of refreshing key schemes in which the keys are updated occasionally, and when a sensor node is unable to decrypt the messages from the updated key, the node is considered malicious and not allowed to participate in the transmission process in the network. The neighboring nodes of the malicious node eventually inform the base station that the hacked node is no longer a part of the network, and the compromised node is removed.

10.3.1.3. *Features and application*

Some important features of the LEAP protocol are as follows: it uses dynamic WEP keys and conducts mutual authentication between the wireless client and radius server. The LEAP protocol also allows the client to re-authenticate frequently by occasionally updating the keys. Whenever a client is successfully authenticated, the client receives a new WEP key that remains live for longer.

The LEAP protocol reduces the participation of a base station. It is a modified authentication protocol in which user credentials are not strongly protected. It can be vulnerable to eavesdropping.

10.3.2. *MIFARE*

In section 10.3.2.1, we will give a brief sketch of MIFARE (derived from the term MIkron FARE Collection System). In section 10.3.2.2, the working, architecture and members of the MIFARE Ultralight system are discussed. In section 10.3.2.3, we will learn about the features and applications of the MIFARE system.

10.3.2.1. *Brief description*

Without cryptographic security, the MIFARE Ultralight only has 64 bytes of memory. The memory of 4 bytes is provided in 16 pages, and the cards based on these MIFARE Ultralight chips are very cheap, which is why they are extensively used in making disposable tickets for events such as the football world cup. They provide maximum pliability for complete system solutions to the system integrators. The solutions are not limited to time-based, zone-based or multiple ride tickets. Single-use tickets are also considered. It provides the system integrators with security features such as one-time programmable (OTP) bits along with a write-lock feature so that it can prevent the rewriting of memory pages. MIFARE Ultralight product-based tickets are ideal as the contactless replacement for magnetic strips or barcodes. Thus, they can transform the system into an entirely contactless solution. The launch of MIFARE Ultralight contactless ICs is extremely useful as it reduces system installation and maintenance costs but is suitable for limited-use applications. These products can be easily integrated into the existing schemes, and some devices, such as those used for standard paper ticket vending, can also be upgraded.

10.3.2.2. *Architecture and working*

The two MIFARE Ultralight family members are as follows.

10.3.2.2.1. MIFARE Ultralight EV1

In the next generation of smart card ICS for paper ticketing, the MIFARE Ultralight EV1 was introduced for some limited applications, mainly for ticketing schemes and also to provide additional security features. It basically comes with intensification and enrichment of the original MIFARE Ultralight. It has 384 and 1024 bits using memory product variants along with OTP, lock bits and configurable counters for improved security. The MIFARE Ultralight EV1 has three independent 24 bit one-way counters, which is extremely beneficial as it stops reloading. However, the main feature is the protected data access through a 32 bit password, which provides intensive security to the system. As it is an integrated original checker, it has an NXP Semiconductors originality signature function and provides effective cloning protection that helps prevent counterfeit tickets.

10.3.2.2.2. MIFARE Ultralight C

The MIFARE Ultralight C IC is part of NXP's low-cost MIFARE product offers with triple DES encryption facility and uses a widely adopted standard that enables easy integration into the pre-existing infrastructures and features. It provides an effective correction against cloning as it is secured by triple DES authentication.

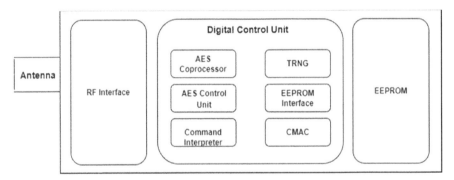

Figure 10.13. *MIFARE Ultralight AES IC*

Figure 10.13 shows the MIFARE Ultralight AES IC, which provides a new level of loyalty for limited-use tickets and key cards by supporting AES cryptographic authentication.

10.3.2.3. *Features and applications*

The MIFARE Ultralight products have an operating distance of up to 10 cm and an operating frequency of 13.56 megahertz. Being an ultra-lightweight product, it has a data transfer rate of 106 KB per second. It has anti-collision schemes, and MIFARE SAM AV2-based security methods are supported.

The MIFARE Ultralight products are used as limited-use tickets in public transport. They are mainly used in disposable ov-chipkaart. MIFARE ultralight has no keys to protect the memory access, and the system depends on read-only and write-once memory for security. It helps in event ticketing such as in stadiums, exhibitions, leisure parks, etc. It ensures loyalty and closed-loop payment schemes.

10.3.3. *Remote frame buffer (RFB)*

In section 10.3.3.1, we will give an overview of RFB. In section 10.3.3.2, the working and architecture of the RFB protocol is discussed. In section 10.3.3.3, we will learn about the features and applications of the RFB protocol.

10.3.3.1. *Brief description*

RFB is the open simple protocol used in virtual network computing to provide remote access to graphical user interfaces. The protocol now has some additional features such as file transfer and more sophisticated compression facilities, as well as security techniques that have been developed over the years, improving the overall feature and accessibility of the protocol. The client and server negotiate a connection so that they can maintain an indefectible cross-compatibility between the different VNC client and server implementations. RFB is applicable to all Windows systems and applications, including excellent Windows and Macintosh systems, because it works at the frame buffer level.

10.3.3.2. *Architecture and working*

In this system, there are two endpoints: the remote end point is for users called the RFB client or viewer and the other endpoint that originates from the frame buffer is the RFB server. Prominence in the design of the protocol is in such a way that the clients can run on the widest range of hardware, and implementation of a client is made very simple and easily accessible as if the protocol makes the client stateless. This feature is very useful in situations where a client, after being disconnected from a given server, again reconnects to the same server and its state of user interface remains preserved. Also, different Arabic lines can be connected through the same server, and as a result, the user in the new endpoint can experience the same graphical user interface as that of the original end point. With this protocol, the user is strongly benefited as they can access their own personal applications whenever there is a suitable network connectivity and the state of these applications is always maintained, even if access changes from location to location. Therefore, the user gets a friendly and uniform view of the computing infrastructure in any location.

Figure 10.14 shows the RFB protocol; the client gives input to the server and the server sends the graphics to be displayed in the remote display of a client.

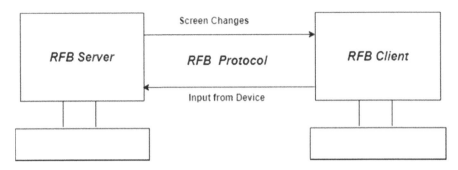

Figure 10.14. *Working structure of RFB protocol*

10.3.3.3. *Features*

Information about the rectangles displayed on the screen is sent by the RFB protocol. The information about the color of the rectangles displayed on the screen is sent as a frame buffer.

The RFB protocol includes security features and compression techniques.

Here, the client uses port 5,900 for server access, whereas the server makes connections in the listening mode on port 5,500.

10.3.4. *Comparison between LEAP, MIFARE and RFB protocols*

Although all of the three protocols have certain features that are extremely beneficial for the use of clients, in Table 10.2, we performed a comparative study on how the three protocols behave in terms of some specific features. In terms of performance, all three protocols perform very well practically. The LEAP protocol has a strong security that ensures encrypted and authorized communication between the nodes and the base station. It also uses dynamic WEP keys to re-authenticate the sensor nodes, but these are vulnerable to base station attacks, whereas in MIFARE, OTP bits are used along with write-lock features to ensure a secured transaction of data. RFB also includes strong security features and compression techniques. The implementation of the LEAP protocol is simple, but to ensure security it uses complex passwords, making it less user-friendly and difficult for regular use. On the other hand, the implementation of MIFARE and RFB are easy and user friendly. The integration of features into the existing system is possible for all of the three protocols. For the LEAP protocol, to work efficiently, the base station and nodes should be in a LAN, while the MIFARE works up to a distance of 10 cm and in the RFB the server and client can be a comparatively longer distance apart as the server is used to display the graphics in a remotely located client. The implementation and use of the LEAP protocol can be cost-effective because many keys are used for authentication purposes, whereas the MIFARE and RFB are quite inexpensive.

Features	LEAP	MIFARE	RFB
Performance	Good	Good	Good
Security	Very strong security (dynamic WEP keys are used for re-authentication)	Very strong security (OTP bits are used along with write-lock features to ensure a secured transaction of data)	Strong security with compression technique.
Ease of implementation	Difficult to implement as it uses complex passwords to ensure security	Easy to implement	Easy to implement
User friendliness	Less user friendly and hard for regular use	Very user friendly	Very user friendly
Working distance	The base station and nodes should be in a LAN	Work up to a distance of 10 cm	The server and client can be a comparatively longer distance apart
Cost-effectiveness	Bit expensive as so many keys are used	Inexpensive	Inexpensive

Table 10.2. *Comparison between LEAP, MIFARE and RFB protocols*

10.4. Conclusion

A full round of Piccolo (25 and 31 rounds for Piccolo-80 and -128) is expected to provide sufficient resistance to differential and linear attacks as it has a large safety edge. A full round of Piccolo is adequately safe against boomerang-type attacks. Therefore, we conclude that a full round of Piccolo is expected to be secure against the unbearable differential attack and a three-subset MITM attack.

In the case of Hummingbird, it appears to be resilient to most public attacks to block ciphers, and it seems to be resistant to the most common attacks to block ciphers and stream ciphers, including birthday attacks, differential and linear cryptanalysis, structure attacks, algebraic attacks, cube attacks, etc. Furthermore, efficient software operations of Hummingbird on 8-bit and 16-bit microcontrollers are presented. It can achieve 99.2% and 82.4% higher throughput for dimension and speed optimized applications, respectively, compared to ultra-lightweight block ciphers such as PRESENT implemented on the same platforms.

LEAP is featured with dynamic WEP keys and mutual authentication between a wireless client and a RADIUS server. LEAP permits clients to re-authenticate frequently. With each successful authentication, clients receive a new WEP key, which is not expected to last long and cannot be cracked. LEAP has well-known safety softness involving offline password cracking. It uses a revised form of the MS-CHAP authentication protocol, where user credentials are threatened. Robust authentication protocols use a salt to reinforce the credentials against spying during the authentication procedure. The softness of LEAP recommends network administrators to force customers to use solid and difficult passwords. Another application is to move to the EAP-FAST authentication protocol developed by Cisco to ensure security. Tools such as ASLEAP validate the ease of receiving unsanctioned admittance in networks endangered by LEAP applications.

In the case of MIFARE, Ultralight C is the leading contactless IC supporting 3DES cryptography in limited-use applications. It offers cryptographic authentication and increases customer convenience, while simplifying the integration into existing infrastructures. MIFARE Ultralight EV1 is the next generation of paper ticketing smart card ICs for limited-use applications, providing solution developers and operators maximum flexibility for their ticketing schemes and additional security options. Enabling easy integration in existing infrastructures is guaranteed by compatibility with MIFARE-based systems. The integrated originality checker is an effective cloning protection that helps to prevent counterfeit tickets.

Features	MIFARE Ultralight C	MIFARE Ultralight EV1
Memory	144 bytes	48/128 bytes
OTP area	32 bit	32 bit
Counter	1 x 16 bit	3 x 24 bit
Access protection	32-bit password + password acknowledgement	

Table 10.3. *Comparative study between MIFARE Ultralight C and Ultralight EV1*

Developers are allowed to add encoding and security types, but they must book unique identification numbers for these with the maintainers of the protocol so that the numbers do not clash. Clashing numbers would cause confusion when handshaking a connection and break cross-compatibility between implementations.

Version	Published	Date	Specification
RFB 3.3	ORL	January 1998	RFB Protocol 3.3
RFB 3.7	RealVNC Ltd	August 2003	RFB Protocol 3.7
RFB 3.8(Current)	RealVNC Ltd	June 2007	RFB Protocol 3.8
IETF RFC (3.8)	RealVNC Ltd	March 2011	RFC 6143

Table 10.4. *Published versions of the RFB protocol*

The VNC protocol is pixel-based. Although this leads to great flexibility, it is often less effective than solutions that better understand the underlying graphical layout. These protocols provide graphical primitives or high-level commands in a simpler form (e.g. open window), while RFB only provides the raw compressed pixel data.

In this chapter, we presented six ultra-lightweight protocols. We also discussed some of the shortcomings of those protocols. The ciphers use several new design methods to avoid known attacks without losing efficiency in both power and energy consumption.

10.5. References

Airehrour, D., Gutierrez, J., Ray, S.K. (2016). Secure routing for internet of things: A survey. *Journal of Network and Computer Applications*, 66, 198–213. doi: 10.1016/j.jnca.2016.03.006.

Avoine, G., Carpent, X., Martin, B. (2010). Strong authentication and strong integrity (SASI) is not that strong. *RFIDSec'10 Proceedings of the 6th International Conference on Radio Frequency Identification: Security and Privacy Issues*, 50–64. doi: 10.1007/978-3-642-16822-2_5.

Bae, W. and Kwak, J. (2017). Smart card-based secure authentication protocol in multi-server IoT environment. *Multimedia Tools and Applications*, 1–19. doi: 10.1155/2019/6452157.

HandWiki (2023). RFB protocol [Online]. Available at: https://handwiki.org/wiki/RFB%20protocol.

Kevin, A. (2016). That "Internet of Things" thing. *RFID Journal* [Online]. Available at: http://www.itrco.jp/libraries/RFIDjournal-That%20Internet%20of%20Things%20Thing.pdf [Accessed August 2016].

Kolias, C., Meng, W., Kambourakis, G., Chen, J. (2019). Security, privacy, and trust on Internet of Things. *Wireless Communications and Mobile Computing*, 6452157.

Poschmann, A. (2009). Lightweight cryptography – Cryptographic engineering for a pervasive world. PhD Thesis, Ruhr-Universitä Bochum.

Sehrawat, D. and Gill, N.S. (2018). Security requirements of IoT applications in smart environment. *Proceedings of the 2nd International Conference on Trends in Electronics and Informatics (ICOEI 2018)*, 324–329. IEEE. doi: 10.1109/ICOEI.2018.8553681.

Suo, H., Wan, J., Zou, C., Liu, J. (2012). Security in the internet of things: A review. *International Conference on Computer Science and Electronics Engineering (ICCSEE)*, 3, 648–651. IEEE. doi: 10.1109/ICCSEE.2012.373.

Tarish, H.A. (2018). Proposed lightweight protocol for IoT authentication. *Iraqi Journal for Computers and Informatics (IJCI)*, 44(1), 27–33.

11

A Study on Security Protocols, Threats and Probable Solutions for Internet of Things Using Blockchain

The Internet of Things (IoT) was invented from various technologies. The development of IoT will improve many everyday processes for both small customers and commercial organizations. Unfortunately, safety remains an ongoing concern in the IoT environment. Since the IoT paradigm encompasses a wide variety of devices and equipment, ranging from small embedded processing chips to large high-end servers, it needs to address security issues at different levels such as low-, intermediate- and high-level security issues. There are probable solutions to address these threats using IoT security algorithms (from common encryption algorithms to lightweight cryptography algorithms) with different requirements. From smart home applications to smart agriculture and from healthcare applications to industrial systems, lightweight cryptography algorithms can be used everywhere by securing devices. Today, IoT systems typically run on a distributed client–server model, where linked devices rely on the central network to determine their behavior. This central hub is typically the key target of IoT-related cyber outbreaks. Whenever there is a security breach at the central authority, the data sent by smart devices can be easily captured by hackers, and most cyber attacks in IoT target this vulnerability. The use of blockchain technology to decentralize the IoT network will make it more scalable, autonomous and endangered against most common attack points. Blockchain technology, which is based on cryptography, decentralization and consensus, provides a data structure with intrinsic security assets and guarantees trust in deals. This chapter conducts a study on different security issues in the IoT and the existing lightweight messaging protocols, namely MQTT, CoAP, AMQP, HTTP, DDS, and XMPP, and compares them. In addition, efforts are made to describe specific attacks associated with one or more layers of the IoT and the countermeasures against these attacks, and finally how blockchain can be effectively used to address the challenges posed by the IoT architecture. Finally, a direction is established to provide new research ideas in the area of lightweight cryptography and blockchain for securing IoT applications.

Chapter written by Debajyoti GUHA.

11.1. Introduction

The Internet of Things (IoT) is an evolutionary skill that gained an intense application in many areas targeted at eradicating human interference. According to the Gartner report, nearly 20 billion IoT smart devices connected to the Internet will exchange massive amounts of data to make people's lives more convenient (Gao et al. 2014; Turner et al. 2018). Aside from our own use, IoT also supports the public needs. Numerous smart objects that execute different operations, namely monitoring surgical procedures, identification of climatic situations, specification of animals using biochips, etc., serve to meet the specific needs of the public (Rouse and Wigmore 2016). The importance of IoT is obvious due to its use in everyday life.

From safety and confidentiality viewpoints, IoT can be measured as a skill that is vulnerable to different attacks that results in data leakage. Stuxnet (Kushner 2019) and Mirai DDoS attack (Arghire 2019) are IoT attacks that show how the whole IoT setup can be affected due to misconfigured IoT devices. The arrival of blockchain technology carries an attractive method to comprise of the distributed transactions in the IoT network. The reason for integrating blockchain into the IoT is to remove centralization and mechanize a protected exchange of real-time data between IoT devices. Blockchain organizes distributed, public ledgers to enable unidentified transactions, shifting current centralized business models to decentralization (Subramanian 2018). Blockchain authorizes individuals to regulate their personal data and allows them to share only with intended recipients under agreed environments (Christidis and Devetsikiotis 2016).

Edge computing is different from conventional cloud computing that performs computing at the edge of the network. Its main principle is to perform computing closer to the data source (Satyanarayanan 2017). Satyanarayana (2017) defined edge computing as: "Edge computing is a new computing model that deploys computing and storage resources (such as cloudlets, micro data centers or fog nodes, etc.) at the edge of the network closer to mobile devices or sensors". Zha et al. (2018) proposed: "Edge computing is a new computing model that unifies resources that are close to the user in geographical distance or network distance to provide computing, storage, and network for applications service." Edge computing is about migrating the cloud network, computing, storage abilities and resources to the edge of the network, and providing intelligent services at the edge to meet the IT industry's critical needs of agile linking, real-time business, data optimization, application intelligence, security and privacy, as well as meeting the requirements of low latency and high bandwidth in the network, which has become a research area nowadays (Internet of Things World Forum 2014; Sun and Ansari 2016; Alrawais et al. 2017; Kang et al. 2018; Mouradian et al. 2018).

This chapter is organized as follows.

Section 11.2 outlines the IoT construction and the safety challenges faced at each layer of the protocol stack organized by the IoT. Section 11.3 classifies the key safety concerns; section 11.4 inspects and defines a mapping of the solutions proposed. Numerous solutions associated with blockchain security are described and analyzed in section 11.5. In section 11.6, IoT messaging protocols are discussed and in section 11.7, edge computing is briefly discussed before concluding this chapter.

11.2. IoT architecture and security challenges

An IoT deployment consists of varied devices with implanted sensors interconnected through a network. IoT devices are solely recognizable and categorized by low power, small memory and limited processing proficiency. IoT-layered architecture includes the standards and protocols for low-rate wireless personal area networks (LR-WPANs) (IEEE 2012) and low-power wide area network-based (LPWAN) protocols. For LR-WPANs, the IEEE standard 802.15.4 defines the physical layer and the medium access control (MAC) layer. The physical layer requirement is associated with communication over wireless channels with various data rates. The MAC layer specification is responsible for mechanisms for channel access and synchronization. As IEEE 802.15.4 uses a small MTU standard, an IPv6 over 6LoWPAN adaptation layer is included above the link layer to enhance the sensor node with IP-based communication capabilities. Each device in the IoT is exclusively specified by an IPv6 network address. The Routing Protocol for Low-power and Lossy Networks (RPL) is used to support 6LoWPAN settings. Due to a limited payload, application design in IoT incorporates the User Datagram Protocol (UDP) (Postel 1980) for communication as it is considered to be more efficient and less complex than the TCP (Transport Control Protocol). Moreover, the UDP header compression may be performed for a better utilization of the limited payload space (Hui and Thubert 2011). The Constrained Application Protocol (CoAP) (Shelby et al. 2014) provides a request–response-based model for Low-power Lossy Networks existing in constrained environments. The LPWAN allows for a long-range communication of "things" in the IoT. In contrast to a wireless WAN, which requires more power to work with a high bit-rate, it supports low-power communication with low bit-rate. The LPWAN uses the LoRaWAN protocol for communication between gateways and the end devices while supporting varying data rates in a network of battery-operated things.

Security threats related to the IoT deployment architecture are described as follows:

– low-level security threats;

– intermediate-level security threats;

– high-level security threats.

11.3. Security threat classifications[1]

11.3.1. *Low-level security threats*

The first level of security is concerned with the security issues at the physical and data link layers of communication as well as the hardware level, as detailed below.

Jamming adversaries: jamming attacks on wireless devices in IoT aim to deteriorate networks by emitting radiofrequency signals without following a specific protocol (Pirzada and McDonald 2005; Wang et al. 2008; Ahmed and Ko 2016; Wazid et al. 2016). The radio interference severely impacts the network operations and can affect the sending and receiving of data by legitimate nodes, resulting in malfunctioning or unpredictable behavior of the system.

Insecure initialization: a secure mechanism of initializing and configuring IoT at the physical layer ensures a proper functionality of the entire system without violating privacy and disruption of network services (Noubir and Lin 2003; Xu et al. 2005). Communication between physical layers also needs to be secured to make it inaccessible to unauthorized receivers.

Low-level Sybil and spoofing attacks: Sybil attacks in a wireless network are caused by malicious Sybil nodes that use fake identities to degrade the IoT functionality. On the physical layer, a Sybil node may use random forged MAC values in order to masquerade as a different device while aiming to deplete the network resources (Chen et al. 2007). Consequently, the legitimate nodes may be denied access to resources.

Insecure physical interface: several physical factors compound serious threats to proper functioning of devices in IoT. The poor physical security, software access through physical interfaces and tools for testing/debugging can be exploited to compromise nodes in the network.

---

1 See: Khan and Salah (2018).

Sleep deprivation attack: energy constrained devices in IoT are vulnerable to "sleep deprivation" attacks by causing the sensor nodes to stay awake. This results in the depletion of the battery when a large number of tasks are set to be executed in the 6LoWPAN environment.

11.3.2. Intermediate-level security threats

Intermediate-level security issues are mainly concerned with the communication, routing and session management taking place at network and transport layers of IoT, as described below.

Replay or duplication attacks due to fragmentation

The fragmentation of IPv6 packets is required for devices conforming to the IEEE 802.15.4 standard, which is characterized as having small frame sizes. A reconstruction of the packet fragment fields at the 6LoWPAN layer may result in the depletion of resources, buffer overflows and rebooting of the devices (Kim 2008).

Insecure neighbor discovery

The IoT deployment architecture requires each device to be identified uniquely on the network. The message communication taking place for identification must be secure to ensure that the data being transmitted to a device in the end-to-end communication reaches the specified destination. The neighbor discovery phase before the transmission of data performs different steps, including the router discovery and address resolution (Kim 2008). Using neighbor discovery packets without proper verification can have severe implications in addition to a denial of service.

Buffer reservation attack

As a receiving node requires a reservation of buffer space for the re-assembly of incoming packets, an attacker may exploit it by sending incomplete packets (Sinthan and Balamurugan 2013). This attack results in a denial of service as other fragment packets are discarded due to the space occupied by incomplete packets sent by the attacker.

RPL routing attack

The IPv6 RPL is vulnerable to several attacks triggered through compromised nodes existing in the network (Hummen et al. 2013). The attack may result in the depletion of resources and eavesdropping.

Sinkhole and wormhole attacks

In the case of sinkhole attacks, the attacker node responds to the routing requests, thereby making the packets route through the attacker node; it can then be used for malicious activities on the network (Dvir et al. 2011; Weekly and Pister 2012). The attacks on the network may further deteriorate the operations of 6LoWPAN due to wormhole attacks in which a tunnel is created between two nodes so that packets arriving at a node reach the other node immediately (Ahmed and Ko 2016). These attacks have severe implications, including eavesdropping, privacy violation and denial of service.

Sybil attacks on intermediate layers

Similar to the Sybil attacks on low-level layers, Sybil nodes can be used to degrade the network performance and even violate data privacy. Communication by Sybil nodes using fake identities in a network may result in spamming, the dissemination of malware or the launch of phishing attacks (Pirzada and McDonald 2005; Wang et al. 2008; Zhang et al. 2014; Wazid et al. 2016).

Authentication and secure communication

Devices and users in IoT need to be authenticated through key management systems. Any loophole in security at the network layer or large overhead of securing communication can expose the network to a large number of vulnerabilities (Granjal et al. 2010; Raza et al. 2011; Granjal et al. 2014). For example, due to limited resources, the overhead of Datagram Transport Level Security (DTLS) must be minimized, and the cryptographic mechanisms that ensure secure communication of data in IoT must take into account both the efficiency and the scarcity of other resources (Mahalle et al. 2013; Sinthan and Balamurugan 2013).

Transport level end-to-end security

Transport level end-to-end security aims to provide a secure mechanism so that the data from the sender node is reliably received by the desired destination node (Brachmann et al. 2011; Granjal et al. 2013). It requires comprehensive authentication mechanisms, which ensure secure message communication in an encrypted form without violating privacy while working with minimum overhead (Brachmann et al. 2011; Granjal et al. 2013).

Session establishment and resumption

An attacking node can impersonate the victim node to continue the session between two nodes. Communicating nodes may even require retransmission of messages by altering sequence numbers.

Privacy violation on cloud-based IoT

A malicious cloud service provider on which IoT deployment is based can access confidential information transmitted to a desired destination.

11.3.3. *High-level security threats*

High-level security threats are mainly concerned with the applications executing on IoT, as described below.

CoAP security with Internet

The Constrained Application Protocol (CoAP), which is a web transfer protocol for constrained devices, uses DTLS bindings with various security modes to provide end-to-end security. CoAP messages follow a specific format defined in RFC-7252 (Shelby et al. 2014), which must be encrypted for secure communication.

Insecure interfaces, software or firmware

Various vulnerabilities in IoT include those caused by insecure software/firmware (Conzon et al. 2012). The code with languages such as JSON, XML, SQLi and XSS must be tested carefully.

Middleware security

The IoT middleware designed to render communication among heterogeneous entities of the IoT paradigm must be secure enough for the provision of services. Different interfaces and environments using middleware must be incorporated to provide secure communication (Young and Boutaba 2011; Liu et al. 2014).

11.4. Security solutions for IoT

Security threats in IoT exploit vulnerabilities of various components such as applications/interfaces, network components, software, firmware and physical devices, existing at different levels. The users in an IoT paradigm interact with these components through protocols, which can also be dismantled of their security measures. The countermeasures for security threats address vulnerabilities of this interaction at different layers to achieve a specific security level. Diverse protocols supporting the deployment of components add to the complexity of these countermeasures.

11.4.1. *Low-level security solutions*

For wireless sensor networks, jamming attacks relate to interference resulting in message collisions or in flooding the channels. An approach for detecting jamming attacks was proposed by Young et al. (2011). The detection of attacks is made possible by measuring the signal strength, which is then used for extracting noise-like signals.

Another anti-jamming mechanism using cryptographic functions and error correcting codes was proposed by Noubir et al. (2003). The approach works by encoding packets through division into blocks and interleaving the encoded packet bits.

An approach of detecting Sybil attacks using signal strength measurements was given by Demirbas and Song (2006). Their approach works by deploying detector nodes to compute the sender location during message communication. Another message communication with the same sender location but different sender identity is implied as a Sybil attack. The assumptions of the proposed approach make it applicable to static networks.

11.4.2. *Intermediate-level security solutions*

Threats arising from replay attacks due to the fragmentation of packets in 6LoWPAN are addressed by adding timestamp and nonce options to the fragmented packets. These packets are added to the 6LoWPAN adaptation layer corresponding to the fragmented packets.

Similarly, a content-chaining strategy that ensures an in-order transmission of fragments of IPv6 packets in 6LoWPAN is proposed. For secure neighbor discovery, the elliptic curve cryptography (ECC) is used. ECC public key signatures are used to identify nodes in the neighbor discovery phase. The encrypted data is then communicated to ensure node-to-node security.

Through a buffer reservation attack, the reassembly buffer of a node can be blocked. This attack is mitigated through a split buffer approach (Sinthan and Balamurugan 2013), which increases the cost of launching an attack by requiring complete fragmented packets to be transmitted in short bursts. A mutual authentication scheme for secure session management using symmetric key-based encryption methods was given by Park et al. The proposed scheme initially selects a random number, performs encryption and generates a session key, which is subsequently used for the encryption of another random number.

Similarly, another method of encryption using hashes for resource-constrained devices supporting hash functions was also proposed. It works efficiently due to small overhead of computations.

Another scheme of mutual authentication for fog computing-based environments having resource-constrained devices was suggested. The proposed scheme, called Octopus, requires a long-lived secret key, which is then used to authenticate with one of the fog servers.

11.4.3. *High-level security solutions*

To secure the CoAP-based Low-power and Lossy Network (LLN) connected with the Internet, an approach incorporating TLS and DTLS was proposed by Brachmann et al. (2011). The proposed approach works for scenarios where the 6LoWPAN Border Router (6LBR) connects the LLN with the Internet in order to access devices remotely.

Another approach to secure messages for applications communicating through the Internet using various CoAP security options was suggested by Granjal et al. (2014). The new security options related to CoAP are SecurityOn, SecurityToken and SeurityEncap. The SecurityOn option relates to the protection of CoAP messages at the application level. The SecurityToken option facilitates identification and authorization for providing access to CoAP resources at the application level. The SecurityEncap option uses configuration of the SecurityOn option and mainly performs transmission of data required for authentication and protection against replays.

An AES/CCM-based security is incorporated for protecting the messages. Using the above options, the proposed approach is shown to perform well in terms of the packet payload space, energy consumption and the communication rate.

Similarly, for IoT based on IP networks, a security model with 6LBR used for message filtration in order to provide end-to-end security was suggested. The TLS–DTLS tunnel can be created while using 6LBR for mapping during the handshake. Similarly, when two hosts share a common key, it has also been proposed to perform message verification or replay detection on the CoAP device.

11.5. Blockchain-based IoT paradigm: security and privacy issues

Heterogeneous interconnected IoT devices through blockchain networks may be susceptible to security and privacy issues that must be addressed as they may affect the quality of services provided by the IoT systems. Some of the most important security and privacy issues are discussed below.

11.5.1. *Lack of IoT-centric agreement mechanisms*

Several aspects are required to be improved in blockchain consensus protocols to be integrated in IoT applications, such as increasing the fault tolerance, resistance to denial-of-service attack and low communication complexity. However, in IoT systems, there are many heterogeneous IoT devices that feed different formats of sensory data into the blockchain network. Consequently, other validation rules must be created to meet the heterogeneity of sensed data.

11.5.2. *IoT device incorporation*

The blockchain network is merely helpful in maintaining an immutable distributed ledger. The IoT device requires a third-party library web3.js to communicate sensor information with the blockchain network, which may be susceptible to numerous attacks such as SQL and XSS attacks.

11.5.3. *Software update*

Initiating firmware updates ensures that IoT devices remain updated and protected from ransomware attacks. Most IoT devices function without a software update, making them more susceptible to a number of attacks.

11.5.4. *Data scalability and organization*

Without proper security measures, the inhomogeneity of IoT devices can lead to compatibility problems, resulting in strict security problems, similar to backdoor attacks for malware injection attacks.

The speed of the blockchain network in terms of throughput tells us about the number of dealings that can be validated per unit time and size of each dedicated block in the blockchain network. IoT systems also require micropayments for financial dealings and use some consensus mechanism. Hence, authenticating dealings takes up a lot of time and energy.

11.5.5. *Interoperability with the varied IoT devices organized lying on blockchain network*

Interoperability is due to the lack of consistency among inhomogeneous IoT devices, and there is an important requirement to handle data, device and user information, etc. shared across inappropriate IoT devices.

11.5.6. *Perception layer*

The perception layer deals with devices with low storage ability, etc. Blockchain technology is able to undertake this issue via a disseminated ledger for preserving an exclusive ID for all IoT devices. A device can be added to the network provided the consent of the network minor is approved.

Therefore, the information provided by the linked IoT devices is encoded. A selected and private key is allotted and pushed to the blockchain network.

11.5.7. *Network layer*

When the IoT device is linked to the network, it will begin communicating encoded information via committing blocks. The disseminated ledger can address these necessities by maintaining the ledger on each participant system and allocating each object its own rights when linked to the network.

11.5.8. *Processing layer*

A mixture of private and public blockchain networks is recommended to achieve the storage of IoT schemes instead of storing information in a central cloud structure. The public blockchain is used to store transactions involved with the timestamp, thereby confirming the immutability, non-repudiation, data reliability and validity of information. Blockchain can be useful as a secure communication layer when a request is made to share a user's personal information with a reliable third party for analysis.

11.5.9. *Application layer*

This layer is accountable for information recovery and conception where information is expected to be true on recovery from storage or the processing layer. Information recovery requests are fulfilled by end-users to receive replies to their many kinds of queries. Information stored in the blockchain network can be securely retrieved for analysis and real-time responses.

11.6. IoT Messaging Protocols[2]

IoT Messaging Protocols or Instant Messaging Protocols (IM) – for example HTTP, MQTT, CoAP, XMPP and AMQP – are mostly planned for IoT functions. Properties of those protocols are message organization (lightweight overhead and small).

11.6.1. *Hyper Text Transfer Protocol (HTTP)*

Asim (2017) contrasted HTTP with various contemporary protocols used in IoT environments. HTTP is unsuitable for embedded procedures with little power. It uses a client–server approach and a request–response model for messaging. Methods such as GET, POST, PUT and DELETE are used to update, create, read and delete processes accordingly (Dizdarevic et al. 2018; Banks and Gupta 2014).

11.6.2. *Message Queue Telemetry Protocols (MQTT)*

The MQTT protocol is simple, reliable and appropriate for resource-controlled devices and other situations similar to high latency and low bandwidth (Dizdarevic et al. 2018). When compared with other reliable messaging protocols, it has a lighter header and requires less power. Unlike HTTP, the MQTT protocol uses a publish/subscribe pattern. It is a perfect lightweight messaging protocol designed for mobile-to-mobile (M2M) communication and remote telemetry applications.

MQTT includes four major components (Sonawala et al. 2017):

1) Broker: works as a server and used for data checking among distant devices and sensors.

2) Topic: facilitates sensors and devices for creating data based on some topics.

---

2 See: Rani and Gill (2019).

3) Publisher: clients are devices that can publish messages.

4) Subscriber (Dizdarevic et al. 2018): subscribers can receive messages or play the roles of both (Sonawala et al. 2017).

To receive an equivalent message, a client can subscribe to a definite topic. "Publish" means sending information to the broker, going to sleep mode, and "subscribe" means receiving information from the broker (Sonawala et al. 2017). Brokers must categorize this sensory information into topics and dispatch to the subscribers. It is thought to set up an embedded link among middleware and applications as well as communications and networks (Luzuriaga et al. 2014; Salman and Jain 2017).

11.6.3. *Secure MQTT (SMQTT)*

SMQTT (Luzuriaga et al. 2014; Salman and Jain 2017) is a safe addition of the MQTT protocol. It uses lightweight encryption characteristics. MQTT includes the following important stages:

– Setup: registration of publishers and subscribers are done with the broker and obtain a secret master key as per key generation algorithm selected by the developer.

– Encryption: performed after data is published to encrypt the data.

– Publish: information is published and sent to the subscriber.

– Decryption: to decrypt the information using a secret master key.

11.6.4. *Advanced Message Queuing Protocol (AMQP)*

The Advanced Message Queuing Protocol (AMQP) is a session layer open standard and messaging protocol, similar to MQTT and considered ideal for industry. It runs over TCP policy and tracks publisher/subscriber construction.

The interoperability characteristics of AMQP are significant as it supports various platforms and is executed in different languages to exchange messages. It offers trustworthy performance in various applications. Luzuriaga et al. (2015) also compared the competencies of AMQP and MQTT via suitable dimensions among wireless networks and also considered the evaluation shown in the outcomes. Naik (2017) presented the valuation of four known messaging protocols, namely MQTT, CoAP, AMQP and HTTP for IoT. RabbitMQ is a famous application of AMQP messages stored in queues on a center node server before being sent to the client

(Dobbelaere and Esmaili 2017). It is a standard protocol that can function straightforwardly with other AMQP-compliant executions (Keoh et al. 2014).

11.6.5. *Constrained Application Protocol (CoAP)*

CoAP is a request–response synchronous application layer protocol. It is used in tiny devices with little power, less computation and communication capabilities. It is a web transfer protocol like HTTP, and able to extend the architecture from Representational State Transfer (REST) to LoWPANs (Tukade and Banakar 2018). It is constructed over the UDP domain to eliminate TCP overhead, thereby diminishing the requisite of bandwidth, resulting in diminished trustworthiness. At this point, IETF has formed CoAP with the opportunity of running over TCP (Saint Andre 2004). CoAP consists of two sublayers:

– Messaging: messages are exchanged via the two layers. The messaging sublayer provides redundant detection and trusted transfer of messages based on stop-and-wait messaging communication.

– Request/response: liable for transmission and can employ synchronous and asynchronous replies.

CoAP has four transmission modes, namely confirmable, non-confirmable, piggyback and separate. Confirmable and non-confirmable modes allow trustworthy and untrustworthy communication. Piggyback provides direct transmission to client–server communication and is recognized. In HTTP, CoAP uses get, put, push and delete request methods to handle the URI identifier (Banks and Gupta 2014).

11.6.6. *Extensible Messaging and Presence Protocol (XMPP)*

XMPP is an open standard tool for instant messaging protocols devised by IETF (Saint Andre 2004) and based on XML that can execute publish–subscribe and client–server interactions. It creates topics and publishes data by generic extensions. The client–server transmission in XMPP is implemented via XML streams. XMPP descriptions track TLS and DTLS encoding techniques to safeguard data integrity and confidentiality (Keoh et al. 2014).

Certain important applications are video calling, teleconferencing and chatting. It is a secure protocol associated with CoAP requests/responses in the IoT environment, as well as HTTP get and post methods through communication with the server.

11.6.7. *Relative study of different messaging protocols of IoT environments*

Based on the study and survey of literature in the related area, the performance analysis of various messaging protocols has been carried out based on different scales, including header and message size, architecture, quality of service, reliability, security, standards, licensing and encoding scheme.

Criteria	MQTT	CoAP	AMQP	HTTP	XMPP
Year	1999	2010	2003	1997	1999
Architecture	Client/broker	Client/server or client/broker	Client/broker or client/server	Client/server	Client/server
Abstraction	Publish/subscribe	Request/response or publish/subscribe	Request/response or publish/subscribe	Request/response	Request/response or publish/subscribe
Header size	2 Bytes	4 Bytes	8 Bytes	Undefined	Undefined
Message size	Small and undefined (up to 256 MB maximum size)	Small and undefined (small to fit in a single IP datagram)	Negotiable and undefined	Large and undefined (depends on the web server or the programming technology)	Undefined
Semantics/methods	Connected, Disconnected, Publish, Subscribe, Unsubscribe, Close	Get, Post, Put, Delete	Consume, Deliver, Publish, Get, Select, Ack, Delete, Nack, Recover, Reject, Open, Close	Get, Post, Head, Put, Patch, Options, Connect, Delete	HTTP GET and POST methods, Defined tags <presence/>, <message/> and <iq/>
Cache and proxy support	Partial	Yes	Yes	Yes	Yes
Quality of service (QoS)/reliability	QoS 0 – at most once (Fire and Forget), QoS 1 – at least once, QoS 2 – exactly once	Confirmable message (similar to at most once) or non-confirmable message (similar to at least once)	Settle format (similar to at most once) or unsettle format (similar to at least once)	Limited (via transport control protocol – TCP)	No quality of service
Standards	OASIS, Eclipse Foundation	IETF, Eclipse Foundation	OASIS, Eclipse Foundation	IETF and W3C	IETF

Transport protocol	TCP (MQTT-SN can use the UDP)	UDF, SCTP	TCP, SCTP	TCP	TCP/IP
Security	TLS/SSL	DTLS, IPSec	TLS/SSL, IPSec, SASL	TLS/SSL	SASL and TLS
Default port	188/8883 (TLS/SSL)	5683 (UDP Port)/5684 (DTLS)	5671(TLS/SS), 5672	80/443 (TLS/SSL)	5222
Encoding format	Binary	Binary	Binary	Text	XML
Licensing model	Open source	Open source	Open source	Free	Open source
Applications/ supporting organizations	IBM, Facebook, Eurotech, Cisco, Software AG, Red Hat, Tibco, Amazon Web Services, M2Mi, InduSoft, Fiorano	LargeWeb Community Support, Cisco, Contiki, Erika, Iotivity	Microsoft, Bank of America, Barclays, JP Morgan, Goldman Sachs, Credit Suisse	Global Web Protocol Standard	Skype, O'Reilly

Table 11.1. *Comparisons between message protocols*

11.7. Advantages of edge computing

The edge computing model stores and processes data on edge devices without uploading it to a cloud computing platform.

Compared with conventional cloud computing, edge computing has benefits in terms of quick response and real time. Since it is closer to the data foundation, information storage and calculating tasks can be carried out in the edge computing node, reducing the in-between data broadcast process. It highlights closeness to users and provides users with improved smart facilities, thus refining data broadcast presentation, confirming real-time dispensation and shortening the interval time. Edge computing provides users with a variety of quick response services, particularly in the field of automatic smart development, video analysis and other site awareness; a quick response is important. Since edge computing is only responsible for the tasks that lie within its own capacity, the dispensation of data stands in the neighborhood. There is no need to upload data to the cloud to keep away from dangers caused by the network broadcast method, ensuring the security of data. When data is attacked, it only affects local data, not all data.

It reduces the amount of data transmitted on the network, reduces the broadcast price and network bandwidth strength, reduces the power consumption of neighboring tools and recovers calculating competence. Edge computing provides data storage space and computing power at the end of the network, providing nearby intelligent Internet services, extending support for the digital transformation of a variety of industries and meeting the data diversification prerequisites of diverse industries. It plays an important role in content delivery network, industrial Internet, energy and smart home transportation games, etc.

11.8. Conclusion

Some serious security and utility issues may arise when integrating blockchain with IoT technology. IoT safety constrains depend on its four-tier structure to detect potential security and privacy risks and alleviate such risks when using blockchain technology. This chapter highlighted new security challenges arising from the adoption of blockchain in IoT systems, which are the largest and require a driving force to focus on their solutions. The planned framework illustrates suggestions for a well-organized and secure integration of blockchain, IoT and edge computing to ensure the rise of their services. This chapter reviewed the literature on IoT messaging protocols.

Numerous lightweight and security protocols have been proposed in recent years. Some of the messaging protocols have been compared based on their performance.

11.9. References

Ahmed, F. and Ko, Y.-B. (2016). Mitigation of black hole attacks in routing protocol for low power and lossy networks. *Secur. Commun. Netw.*, 9(18), 5143–5154.

Alrawais, A., Alhothaily, A., Hu, C., Cheng, X. (2017). Fog computing for the Internet of Things: Security and privacy issues. *IEEE Internet Comput.*, 21(2), 34–42.

Arghire, I. (2019). Mirai-based botnet launches massive DDOS attack on streaming service. *Security Week* [Online]. Available at: https://www.securityweek.com/mirai-based-botnet-launches-massive-ddos-attack-streaming-service/ [Accessed September 2019].

Asim, M. (2017). A survey on application layer protocols for Internet of Things (IoT). *Int. J. Adv. Res. Comput. Scie.*, 8(3), 996–1000. https://doi.org/10.26483/ijarcs.v8i3.3143.

Banks, A. and Gupta, R. (eds) (2014). MQTT Version 3.1.1. OASIS standard.

Brachmann, M., Garcia-Morchon, O., Kirsche, M. (2011). Security for practical CoAP applications: Issues and solution approaches. *10th GI/ITG KuVS Fachgespräch Sensornetze (FGSN 2011)*, Paderborn.

Chae, S.H., Choi, W., Lee, J.H., Quek, T.Q.S. (2014). Enhanced secrecy in stochastic wireless networks: Artificial noise with secrecy protected zone. *Trans. Info. for Sec.*, 9(10), 1617–1628. http://dx.doi.org/10.1109/TIFS.2014.2341453.

Chen, Y., Trappe, W., Martin, R.P. (2017). Detecting and localizing wireless spoofing attacks. *2007 4th Annual IEEE Communications Society Conference on Sensor, Mesh and Ad Hoc Communications and Networks*, 193–202.

Christidis, K. and Devetsikiotis, M. (2016). Blockchains and smart contracts for the internet of things. *IEEE Access*, 4, 2292–2303.

Conzon, D., Bolognesi, T., Brizzi, P., Lotito, A., Tomasi, R., Spirito, M.A. (2012). The VIRTUS middleware: An XMPP based architecture for secure IoT communications. *2012 21st International Conference on Computer Communications and Networks, ICCCN*, 1–6. http://dx.doi.org/10.1109/ICCCN.2012.6289309.

Demirbas, M. and Song, Y. (2006). An RSSI-based scheme for Sybil attack detection in wireless sensor networks. *International Symposium on a World of Wireless, Mobile and Multimedia Networks (WoWMoM'06)*, Buffalo, Niagara Falls. doi: 10.1109/WOWMOM.2006.27.

Dizdarevic, J., Carpio, F., Jukan, A., Masip-Bruin, X. (2018). A survey of communication protocols for Internet-of-Things and related challenges of fog and cloud computing integration. *ACM Comput. Surveys*, 1(1), 1–27.

Dobbelaere, P. and Esmaili, K.S. (2017). Kafka versus RabbitMQ: A comparative study of two industry reference publish/subscribe implementations: Industry paper. *Proceedings of the 11th ACM International Conference on Distributed and Eventbased Systems*, ACM. https://doi.org/10.1145/3093742.3093908.

Dvir, A., Holczer, T., Buttyan, L. (2011). VeRA – Version number and rank authentication in RPL. *2011 IEEE Eighth International Conference on Mobile Ad-Hoc and Sensor Systems*, 709–714. http://dx.doi.org/10.1109/MASS.2011.76.

Gao, Y.Q., Bguan, H., Qi, Z.W. (2014). Service level agreement based energy-effifcient resource management in cloud data centers. *Comput. Elect. Eng.*, 40(5), 1621–1633. doi:10.1016/j.compeleceng.2013.11.001.

Granjal, J., Monteiro, E., Silva, J.S. (2010). Enabling network-layer security on IPv6 wireless sensor networks. *2010 IEEE Global Telecommunications Conference GLOBECOM 2010*, 1–6. http://dx.doi.org/10.1109/GLOCOM.

Granjal, J., Monteiro, E., Silva, J.S. (2013). End-to-end transport-layer security for internet-integrated sensing applications with mutual and delegated ECC public-key authentication. *2013 IFIP Networking Conference*, 1–9.

Granjal, J., Monteiro, E., Silva, J.S. (2014). Network-layer security for the Internet of Things using TinyOS and BLIP. *Int. J. Commun. Syst.*, 27(10), 1938–1963. http://dx.doi.org/10.1002/dac.2444.

Hong, Y.-W.P., Lan, P.-C., Kuo, C.-C.J. (2013). Enhancing physical-layer secrecy in multiantenna wireless systems: An overview of signal processing approaches. *IEEE Signal Process. Mag.*, 30(5), 29–40.

Hui, J.W. and Thubert, P. (2011). Compression format for IPv6 datagrams over IEEE 802.15.4-based networks [Online]. Available at: https://tools.ietf.org/html/rfc6282.

Hummen, R., Hiller, J., Wirtz, H., Henze, M., Shafagh, H., Wehrle, K. (2013). 6LoWPAN fragmentation attacks and mitigation mechanisms. *Proceedings of the Sixth ACM Conference on Security and Privacy in Wireless and Mobile Networks*, WiSec '13, ACM, New York, 55–66. http://dx.doi.org/10.1145/2462096.2462107.

IEEE (2012). IEEE standard for local and metropolitan networks – Part 15.4: LowRate Wireless Personal Area Networks (LR-WPANs) [Online]. Available at: https://standards. ieee.org/findstds/standard/802.15.4-2011.html.

Internet of Things World Forum (2014). The Internet of Things reference model. Internet of Things World Forum, C.S. Inc., Chicago.

Kang, J., Yu, R., Huang, X., Zhang, Y. (2018). Privacy-preserved pseudonym scheme for fog computing supported Internet of vehicles. *IEEE Trans. Intell. Transp. Syst.*, 19(8), 2627–2637.

Keoh, S.L., Kumar, S.S., Tschofenig, H. (2014). Securing the Internet of Things: A standardization perspective. *Internet Things J. IEEE*, 1(3), 265–275. https://doi.org/10. 1109/JIOT.2014.2323395.

Khan, M.A. and Salah, K. (2018). IoT security: Review, blockchain solutions, and open challenges. *Future Gen. Compu. Syst.*, 82, 395–411.

Kim, H. (2008). Protection against packet fragmentation attacks at 6LoWPAN adaptation layer. *2008 International Conference on Convergence and Hybrid Information Technology*, 796–801. http://dx.doi.org/10.1109/ICHIT.2008.261.

Kushner, D. (2013). The real story of stuxnet. *IEEE Spectrum* [Online]. Available at: https://spectrum.ieee.org/telecom/security/the-real-story-of-stuxnet [Accessed September 2019].

Liu, C.H., Yang, B., Liu, T. (2014). Efficient naming, addressing and profile services in Internet-of-Things sensory environments. *Ad Hoc Netw.*, 18(Suppl. C), 85–101. http://dx. doi.org/10.1016/j.adhoc.2013.02.008.

Luzuriaga, J.E., Perez, M., Boronat, P., Cano, J.C., Calafate, C., Manzoni, P. (2014). Testing AMQP protocol on unstable and mobile networks. *Internet and Distributed Computing Systems Conference Proceedings*, Fortino, G., Fatta, G., Li, W., Ochoa, S., Cuzzocrea, A., Pathan, M. (eds). Springer, Cham. https://doi.org/10.1007/978-3-319-11692-1_22.

Luzuriaga, J.E., Perez, M., Boronat, P., Cano, J.C., Calafate, C., Manzoni, P. (2015). A comparative evaluation of AMQP and MQTT protocols over unstable and mobile networks. *2015 12th Annual IEEE Consumer Communications and Networking Converence (CCNC)*, Las Vegas. doi: 10.1109/CCNC.2015.7158101.

Mahalle, P.N., Anggorojati, B., Prasad, N.R., Prasad, R. (2013). Identity authentication and capability based access control (IACAC) for the internet of things. *J. Cyber Secur. Mobility*, 1(4), 309–348.

Mouradian, C., Naboulsi, D., Yangui, S., Glitho, R.H., Morrow, M.J., Polakos, P.A. (2018). A comprehensive survey on fog computing: State-of-the-art and research challenges. *IEEE Commun. Surveys Tuts.*, 20(1), 416–464.

MQTT (2016). MQTT essentials Part 1 to 9: Detail study on MQTT. *Hive MQ* [Online]. Available at: http://www.hivemq.com/blog/mqtt-essentials-part-6-mqtt-quality-of-service-levels.

Naik, N. (2017). Choice of effective messaging protocols for IoT Systems: MQTT, CoAP, AMQP and HTTP. *IEEE International Systems Engineering Symposium (ISSE)*, 1–7, IEEE.

Noubir, G. and Lin, G. (2003). Low-power DoS attacks in data wireless LANs and countermeasures, SIGMOBILE Mob. *Comput. Commun. Rev.*, 7(3), 29–30.

Park, N., Kim, M., Bang, H.C. (2015). Symmetric key-based authentication and the session key agreement scheme in IoT environment. In *Computer Science and its Applications*, Park, J., Stojmenovic, I., Jeong, H., Yi, G. (eds). Springer, Berlin, Heidelberg.

Pirzada, A.A. and McDonald, C. (2005). Circumventing sinkholes and wormholes in wireless sensor networks. *International Workshop on Wireless Ad-Hoc Networks*, January.

Postel, J. (1980). User datagram protocol, 1980 [Online]. Available at: https://tools.ietf.org/html/rfc768.

Rani, D. and Gill, N.S. (2019). Review of various IoT standards and communication protocols. *Int. J. Eng. Res. Technol.*, 12, 647–657.

Raza, S., Duquennoy, S., Chung, T., Yazar, D., Voigt, T., Roedig, U. (2011). Securing communication in 6LoWPAN with compressed IPsec. *2011 International Conference on Distributed Computing in Sensor Systems and Workshops (DCOSS)*, 1–8. http://dx.doi.org/10.1109/DCOSS.2011.5982177.

Rouse, M. and Wigmore, I. (2016). Internet of Things. *TechTarget* [Online]. Available at: http://internetofthingsagenda.techtarget.com/definition/Internet-of-Things-IoT.

Saint Andre, P. (2004). Extensible messaging and presence protocol (XMPP): Core RFC 3920. RFC Editor.

Salman, T. and Jain, R. (2017). Networking protocols and standards for Internet of Things. In *Internet of Things and Data Analytics Handbook*, Geng, H. (ed.). John Wiley & Sons, New York.

Satyanarayanan, M. (2017). The emergence of edge computing. *Computer*, 50(1), 30 39.

Shailesh, S., Joshi, K., Purandare, K. (2018). Performanc analysis of RabbitMQ as a message bus. *Int. J. Innova. Res. Comput. Commun. Eng. (IJIRCCE)*, 6(1), 242–246.

Shelby, Z., Hartke, K., Bormann, C. (2014). The constrained application protocol (CoAP) [Online]. Available at: https://tools.ietf.org/html/rfc7252.

Sinthan, D.U. and Balamurugan, M.-S. (2013). Identity authentication and capability based access control (IACAC) for the Internet of Things. *J. Cyber Secur. Mob.*, 1(4), 309–348.

Sonawala, N.M., Tank, B., Patel, H. (2017). IoT protocol based environmental data monitoring. *IEEE Proceedings International Conference on Computing Methodologies and Communication*, 1041–1045.

Subramanian, H. (2018). Decentralized blockchain-based electronic marketplaces. *Commun. ACM*, 61(1), 78–84.

Sun, X. and Ansari, N. (2016). Edge IoT: Mobile edge computing for the Internet of Things. *IEEE Commun. Mag.*, 54(12), 22–29.

Tukade, T.M. and Banakar, R.M. (2018). Data transfer protocols in IoT – An overview. *International Journal of Pure and Applied Mathematics*, 118(16), 121–138 [Online]. Available at: http://www.ijpam.eu.

Turner, V., Gantz, J.F., Reinsel, D. (2018). The digital universe of opportunities: Rich data and the increasing value of the Internet of Things. *EMC*, November 26, 2018 [Online]. Available at: https://www.emc.com/leadership/digitaluniverse/2014iview/index.htm.

Wang, W., Kong, J., Bhargava, B., Gerla, M. (2008). Visualisation of wormholes in underwater sensor networks: A distributed approach. *Int. J. Secur. Netw.*, 3(1), 10–23.

Wang, G., Mohanlal, M., Wilson, C., Wang, X., Metzger, M., Zheng, H., Zhao, B.Y. (2013). Social Turing tests: Crowdsourcing Sybil detection. *Symposium on Network and Distributed System Security*, NDSS.

Wazid, M., Das, A.K., Kumari, S., Khan, M.K. (2016). Design of sinkhole node detection mechanism for hierarchical wireless sensor networks. *Sec. Commun. Netw.*, 9(17), 4596–4614. http://dx.doi.org/10.1002/sec.1652.

Weekly, K. and Pister, K. (2012). Evaluating sinkhole defense techniques in RPL networks. *Proceedings of the 2012 20th IEEE International Conference on Network Protocols (ICNP), ICNP '12, IEEE Computer Society*, Washington, DC, 1–6. http://dx.doi.org/10.1109/ICNP.2012.6459948.

Xu, W., Trappe, W., Zhang, Y., Wood, T. (2005). The feasibility of launching and detecting jamming attacks in wireless networks. *Proceedings of the 6th ACM International Symposium on Mobile Ad Hoc Networking and Computing, MobiHoc '05, ACM*, New York, 46–57. http://dx.doi.org/10.1145/1062689.1062697.

Young, M. and Boutaba, R. (2011). Overcoming adversaries in sensor networks: A survey of theoretical models and algorithmic approaches for tolerating malicious interference. *IEEE Commun. Surv. Tutor.*, 13(4), 617–641. http://dx.doi.org/10.1109/SURV.2011. 041311.00156.

Zha, Z.M., Liu, F., Cai, Z.P. (2018). Edge computing: Platforms, applications and challenges. *J. Comput. Res. Develop.*, 55(2), 327–337.

Zhang, K., Liang, X., Lu, R., Shen, X. (2014). Sybil attacks and their defenses in the internet of things. *IEEE Internet Things J.*, 1(5), 372–383. http://dx.doi.org/10.1109/JIOT.2014. 2344013.

List of Authors

Aheli ACHARYA
Department of Computer Science
and Engineering
Netaji Subhash Engineering College
Techno City
Garia
Kolkata
India

Kaveri BANERJEE
Department of Computer Application
Nopany Institute
of Management Studies
Kolkata
India

Trishit BANERJEE
Netaji Subhash Engineering College
Techno City
Garia
Kolkata
India

Dipankar BHATTACHARYA
Brainware University
Kolkata
India

Priyanka BHATTACHARYA
Department of Computer Science
and Engineering
Academy of Technology
Hooghly
India

Rajesh BOSE
Department of
Computational Science
Brainware University
Kolkata
India

Surajit BOSE
Department of Oral and Maxillofacial
Pathology and Microbiology
KSDJ Dental College & Hospital
Kolkata
India

Rajdeep CHAKRABORTY
Department of Computer Science
and Engineering
Chandigarh University
SAS Nagar
Punjab
India

Prasenjit CHATTERJEE
MCKV Institute of Engineering
Howrah
India

Ritam CHATTERJEE
Department of Computer and
Information Science
Raiganj University
West Bengal
India

Jayanta CHATTOPADHYAY
Department of Oral and Maxillofacial
Pathology and Microbiology
KSDJ Dental College & Hospital
Kolkata
India

Tanupriya CHOUDHURY
Department of Computer Science
and Engineering
Symbiosis Institute of Technology
Symbiosis International University
Pune
India

Arup DASGUPTA
Netaji Subhash Engineering College
Techno City
Garia
Kolkata
India

Anupam GHOSH
Department of Computer Science
and Engineering
Netaji Subhash Engineering College
Techno City
Garia
Kolkata
India

Debajyoti GUHA
Department of Computer Science
and Engineering
Siliguri Institute of Technology
Darjeeling
India

Amejul ISLAM
Department of Computer Science
and Engineering
Brainware University
Kolkata
India

Tauheed KHAN MOHD
Augustana College
Rock Island
Illinois
USA

Jyotsna KUMAR MANDAL
Department of Computer Science
and Engineering
University of Kalyani
India

Dipankar MAJUMDAR
Department of Computer Science
and Engineering
RCC Institute of Information
Technology
Kolkata
India

Surajit MANDAL
Department of ECE
B.P. Poddar Institute of
Management & Technology
Kolkata
India

Shillpi MISHRRA
Department of Computer Science
and Engineering
Techno India University
Kolkata
India

Shaon Kalyan MODAK
Department of Computer Science
and Engineering
Brainware University
Kolkata
India

Koushik MUKHOPADHYAY
Department of Computer Science
and Engineering
Brainware University
Kolkata
India

Debdutta PAL
Department of Computer Science
and Engineering
Brainware University
Kolkata
India

Debasmita PAUL
Department of Computer Science
and Engineering
Netaji Subhash Engineering College
Techno City
Garia
Kolkata
India

P.K. PAUL
Department of Computer and
Information Science
Raiganj University
West Bengal
India

Anabel PINEDA-BRISENO
National Technological
Institute of Mexico
Mexico City
Mexico

Vertika RAI
Department of Allied
Health Sciences
Brainware University
Kolkata
India

Shalini RAMANATHAN
National Institute of Technology
Tiruchirappalli
India

Mohan RAMASUNDARAM
National Institute of Technology
Tiruchirappalli
India

Sandip ROY
Department of
Computational Science
Brainware University
Kolkata
India

Soumen SANTRA
Department of MCA
Techno International New Town
Kolkata
India

Animesh UPADHYAYA
Department of Computer Science
and Engineering
Brainware University
Kolkata
India

Index

Other titles from

in

Computer Engineering

2023

CHOUDHURY Tanupriya, KHANNA Abhirup, CHATTERJEE Prasenjit,
UM Jung-Sup, BHATTACHARYA Abhishek
*Blockchain Applications in Healthcare: Innovations and Practices
(International Perspectives in Decision Analytics and Operations Research
Set – Volume 1)*

PAI G A Vijayalakshmi
*A Textbook of Data Structures and Algorithms 1: Mastering Linear Data
Structures
A Textbook of Data Structures and Algorithms 2: Mastering Nonlinear Data
Structures
A Textbook of Data Structures and Algorithms 3: Mastering Advanced Data
Structures and Algorithm Design Strategies*

2022

HOMÈS Bernard
*Advanced Testing of Systems-of-Systems 1: Theoretical Aspects
Advanced Testing of Systems-of-Systems 2: Practical Aspects*

2020

DARCHE Philippe
*Microprocessor 1: Prolegomena – Calculation and Storage Functions –
Models of Computation and Computer Architecture*
Microprocessor 2: Core Concepts – Communication in a Digital System
Microprocessor 3: Core Concepts – Hardware Aspects
Microprocessor 4: Core Concepts – Software Aspects
*Microprocessor 5: Software and Hardware Aspects of Development,
Debugging and Testing – The Microcomputer*

LAFFLY Dominique
*TORUS 1 – Toward an Open Resource Using Services: Cloud Computing
for Environmental Data*
*TORUS 2 – Toward an Open Resource Using Services: Cloud Computing
for Environmental Data*
*TORUS 3 – Toward an Open Resource Using Services: Cloud Computing
for Environmental Data*

LAURENT Anne, LAURENT Dominique, MADERA Cédrine
Data Lakes
(Databases and Big Data Set – Volume 2)

OULHADJ Hamouche, DAACHI Boubaker, MENASRI Riad
Metaheuristics for Robotics
(Optimization Heuristics Set – Volume 2)

SADIQUI Ali
Computer Network Security

VENTRE Daniel
Artificial Intelligence, Cybersecurity and Cyber Defense

2019

BESBES Walid, DHOUIB Diala, WASSAN Niaz, MARREKCHI Emna
Solving Transport Problems: Towards Green Logistics

CLERC Maurice
Iterative Optimizers: Difficulty Measures and Benchmarks

GHLALA Riadh
Analytic SQL in SQL Server 2014/2016

TOUNSI Wiem
*Cyber-Vigilance and Digital Trust: Cyber Security in the Era of Cloud
Computing and IoT*

2018

ANDRO Mathieu
*Digital Libraries and Crowdsourcing
(Digital Tools and Uses Set – Volume 5)*

ARNALDI Bruno, GUITTON Pascal, MOREAU Guillaume
Virtual Reality and Augmented Reality: Myths and Realities

BERTHIER Thierry, TEBOUL Bruno
From Digital Traces to Algorithmic Projections

CARDON Alain
*Beyond Artificial Intelligence: From Human Consciousness to Artificial
Consciousness*

HOMAYOUNI S. Mahdi, FONTES Dalila B.M.M.
*Metaheuristics for Maritime Operations
(Optimization Heuristics Set – Volume 1)*

JEANSOULIN Robert
JavaScript and Open Data

PIVERT Olivier
*NoSQL Data Models: Trends and Challenges
(Databases and Big Data Set – Volume 1)*

SEDKAOUI Soraya
Data Analytics and Big Data

SALEH Imad, AMMI Mehdi, SZONIECKY Samuel
*Challenges of the Internet of Things: Technology, Use, Ethics
(Digital Tools and Uses Set – Volume 7)*

Szoniecky Samuel
Ecosystems Knowledge: Modeling and Analysis Method for Information and Communication
(Digital Tools and Uses Set – Volume 6)

2017

Benmammar Badr
Concurrent, Real-Time and Distributed Programming in Java

Héliodore Frédéric, Nakib Amir, Ismail Boussaad, Ouchraa Salma, Schmitt Laurent
Metaheuristics for Intelligent Electrical Networks
(Metaheuristics Set – Volume 10)

Ma Haiping, Simon Dan
Evolutionary Computation with Biogeography-based Optimization
(Metaheuristics Set – Volume 8)

Pétrowski Alain, Ben-Hamida Sana
Evolutionary Algorithms
(Metaheuristics Set – Volume 9)

Pai G A Vijayalakshmi
Metaheuristics for Portfolio Optimization
(Metaheuristics Set – Volume 11)

2016

Blum Christian, Festa Paola
Metaheuristics for String Problems in Bio-informatics
(Metaheuristics Set – Volume 6)

Deroussi Laurent
Metaheuristics for Logistics
(Metaheuristics Set – Volume 4)

Dhaenens Clarisse and Jourdan Laetitia
Metaheuristics for Big Data
(Metaheuristics Set – Volume 5)

2014

BOULANGER Jean-Louis
Formal Methods Applied to Industrial Complex Systems

BOULANGER Jean-Louis
Formal Methods Applied to Complex Systems:Implementation of the B Method

GARDI Frédéric, BENOIST Thierry, DARLAY Julien, ESTELLON Bertrand, MEGEL Romain
Mathematical Programming Solver based on Local Search

KRICHEN Saoussen, CHAOUACHI Jouhaina
Graph-related Optimization and Decision Support Systems

LARRIEU Nicolas, VARET Antoine
Rapid Prototyping of Software for Avionics Systems: Model-oriented Approaches for Complex Systems Certification

OUSSALAH Mourad Chabane
Software Architecture 1
Software Architecture 2

PASCHOS Vangelis Th
Combinatorial Optimization – 3-volume series, 2nd Edition
Concepts of Combinatorial Optimization – Volume 1, 2nd Edition
Problems and New Approaches – Volume 2, 2nd Edition
Applications of Combinatorial Optimization – Volume 3, 2nd Edition

QUESNEL Flavien
Scheduling of Large-scale Virtualized Infrastructures: Toward Cooperative Management

RIGO Michel
Formal Languages, Automata and Numeration Systems 1: Introduction to Combinatorics on Words
Formal Languages, Automata and Numeration Systems 2: Applications to Recognizability and Decidability

SAINT-DIZIER Patrick
Musical Rhetoric: Foundations and Annotation Schemes

TOUATI Sid, DE DINECHIN Benoit
Advanced Backend Optimization

2013

ANDRÉ Etienne, SOULAT Romain
The Inverse Method: Parametric Verification of Real-time Embedded Systems

BOULANGER Jean-Louis
Safety Management for Software-based Equipment

DELAHAYE Daniel, PUECHMOREL Stéphane
Modeling and Optimization of Air Traffic

FRANCOPOULO Gil
LMF — Lexical Markup Framework

GHÉDIRA Khaled
Constraint Satisfaction Problems

ROCHANGE Christine, UHRIG Sascha, SAINRAT Pascal
Time-Predictable Architectures

WAHBI Mohamed
Algorithms and Ordering Heuristics for Distributed Constraint Satisfaction Problems

ZELM Martin *et al.*
Enterprise Interoperability

2012

ARBOLEDA Hugo, ROYER Jean-Claude
Model-Driven and Software Product Line Engineering

BLANCHET Gérard, DUPOUY Bertrand
Computer Architecture

BOULANGER Jean-Louis
Industrial Use of Formal Methods: Formal Verification

BOULANGER Jean-Louis
Formal Method: Industrial Use from Model to the Code

CALVARY Gaëlle, DELOT Thierry, SÈDES Florence, TIGLI Jean-Yves
Computer Science and Ambient Intelligence

MAHOUT Vincent
Assembly Language Programming: ARM Cortex-M3 2.0: Organization, Innovation and Territory

MARLET Renaud
Program Specialization

SOTO Maria, SEVAUX Marc, ROSSI André, LAURENT Johann
Memory Allocation Problems in Embedded Systems: Optimization Methods

2011

BICHOT Charles-Edmond, SIARRY Patrick
Graph Partitioning

BOULANGER Jean-Louis
Static Analysis of Software: The Abstract Interpretation

CAFERRA Ricardo
Logic for Computer Science and Artificial Intelligence

HOMÈS Bernard
Fundamentals of Software Testing

KORDON Fabrice, HADDAD Serge, PAUTET Laurent, PETRUCCI Laure
Distributed Systems: Design and Algorithms

KORDON Fabrice, HADDAD Serge, PAUTET Laurent, PETRUCCI Laure
Models and Analysis in Distributed Systems

LORCA Xavier
Tree-based Graph Partitioning Constraint

LECOUTRE Christophe
Constraint Networks / Targeting Simplicity for Techniques and Algorithms

2008

BANÂTRE Michel, MARRÓN Pedro José, OLLERO Hannibal, WOLITZ Adam
Cooperating Embedded Systems and Wireless Sensor Networks

MERZ Stephan, NAVET Nicolas
Modeling and Verification of Real-time Systems

PASCHOS Vangelis Th
Combinatorial Optimization and Theoretical Computer Science: Interfaces and Perspectives

WALDNER Jean-Baptiste
Nanocomputers and Swarm Intelligence

2007

BENHAMOU Frédéric, JUSSIEN Narendra, O'SULLIVAN Barry
Trends in Constraint Programming

JUSSIEN Narendra
A TO Z OF SUDOKU

2006

BABAU Jean-Philippe *et al.*
From MDD Concepts to Experiments and Illustrations – DRES 2006

HABRIAS Henri, FRAPPIER Marc
Software Specification Methods

MURAT Cecile, PASCHOS Vangelis Th
Probabilistic Combinatorial Optimization on Graphs

PANETTO Hervé, BOUDJLIDA Nacer
Interoperability for Enterprise Software and Applications 2006 / IFAC-IFIP I-ESA'2006

2005

GÉRARD Sébastien *et al.*
Model Driven Engineering for Distributed Real Time Embedded Systems

PANETTO Hervé
Interoperability of Enterprise Software and Applications 2005

Printed and bound by CPI Group (UK) Ltd, Croydon, CR0 4YY

27/10/2024

14580735-0004